COUNSELLING WOMEN
IN VIOLENT RELATIONSHIPS

Counselling Women
in Violent Relationships

PAUL LOCKLEY

FREE ASSOCIATION BOOKS / LONDON / NEW YORK

First Published in 1999 by
Free Association Books Limited
57 Warren Street, London W1P 5PA

ISBN 1 85343 451 5 (hbk); 1 85343 452 3 (pbk)

A CIP catalogue record for this book is available from
the British Library

Produced for Free Association Books Ltd by
Chase Production Services, Chadlington, OX7 3LN
Printed in the EC by T.J. International Ltd, Padstow

CONTENTS

Preface   vii

1   Defining and Definitions   1

2   Client Lives   17

3   Oppression Through Theory   36

4   Before Counselling in Violent Relationships   52

5   Work With Couples   72

6   Feelings, Risks and Consciousness-Raising   99

7   Communication and Boundaries   117

8   Work With Individuals   129

9   Separation and Leaving   155

10 Continuance, Love and Self-Identity   177

11 Counsellor Support   207

12 Conclusion   214

Bibliography   218

Index   247

PREFACE

This book is a product of working as a social worker, as a counsellor, and as a group worker over twenty years with people, many of whom have been subjected to personal violence by their partners. By knowing such people and their partners over many years, it has been possible to build up pictures of different lives and to see them in their social context.

Care has been taken to ensure a high degree of accuracy. Different accounts by those seen by myself have been compared with those of other relevant people. Also, the different accounts of incidents and situations given by the same person over time have been compared. These have been supplemented by my own observations of those involved and my interaction with them, in both formal and informal settings.

Special appreciation is due to Leigh, for her comments on one of the draft copies, her cooperation over ten years, and for the use of her diaries. In addition, quotes from different people have been used not only to give their perspectives and accounts, but also to put them across as individuals in their own right.

As ever, many thanks go to Dr Charles Anderson, Lecturer in Post-graduate Education, University of Edinburgh, for reading through a draft of this book and for his helpful comments.

1 DEFINING AND DEFINITIONS

Introduction

Imagine, if you will, sitting in the upper circle of a theatre, waiting for the curtain to go up. The play is *The Importance of Being Ernest* and there is a full house, at least a thousand theatre-goers. This means you are looking down on about five hundred women, all dressed in their finest. Statistically, at least a hundred of them will have been subjected to domestic violence. As the curtain has not moved, you while away the time by wondering exactly which women have been hit, punched, and worse. You look at the faces. Everyone seems quite happy. Obviously someone has got it wrong. Either the statistics are incorrect or partner violence happens to other people, not the sort who go to the theatre. Anyway, the play is starting, and you are here to enjoy yourself.

Bravo! Bravo! The play has ended and the audience is highly appreciative. Eventually, Ernest and Algey, Lady Bracknell and Miss Prism, and the rest of the characters disappear from view. A happy ending? Certainly, but for me reality insists on biting back. Making our way out of the theatre, a client's words come back to me.

Colette: 'You knew when he was going to explode as the vein in his temple would throb. You could see it. His face would change and then it was best to get out of the way. But that day I wasn't quick enough and he punched me, knocking me over the couch. I got up and ran but he jumped the couch and punched me again. Down I went and was now crawling about on my hands and knees so he could not punch me. But he boots me again and again, as if I was a dog. Eventually he just got tired and sat down and turned on the telly. "United at home." United at home? I was wondering what the fuck he was on about, but it was the football. God help me if they lose, I thought.'

What strikes me – and you understand by now that I am not the perfect theatre companion – is the prevalence of social blindness in respect to such violence. Child abuse now takes up the majority of the time and effort of Social Work Departments, but domestic violence itself is bypassed. Only recently have the police begun to take seriously assaults in the home, which if between strangers in the street would result in charges of aggravated assault or attempted murder.

This social blindness to the physical abuse of women is reflected in the work of counsellors. If a counsellor has twenty women on a caseload, then it is likely five of these will have been abused and the counsellor will be aware of probably one or possibly two cases as involving abuse (See Maynard, 1985). Even counsellors are not immune to a certain blindness to physical abuse, and this a result of not only technical difficulties in identifying abuse but also the attitudes and beliefs of counsellors who fail to react to what are often quite obvious signs of abuse.

Partner abuse in the United States is relatively common, occurring in up to a third of married couples (Koss, 1990), yet it is frequently missed by counsellors or therapists (Hansen et al., 1991), even when couples come for help with marital problems. One sample showed that of couples labelled as non-violent by their therapists, over a half of the 'non-violent' husbands had in fact been violent towards their wives (Holtzworth-Munroe et al., 1992). Among women who were repeated victims of violence requiring police intervention, 65 per cent have been counselled in the past – and usually did not return for a second time as a result of the counsellor not even asking about the violence (Goodstein and Page, 1981).

A definition of violence

There has been much argument about the precise prevalence of the physical abuse of women, and much of this arises from the differing definitions used. Indeed, there have been many terms used for this form of abuse, such as 'battering', 'domestic violence', 'intimate violence', 'partner violence' as well as 'physical abuse of women' (Hanmer et al., 1989). These different terms, reflecting slightly different perceptions, belief systems and values, do make the estimation of such violent behaviour more difficult than we might initially suspect.

The first definition that might be considered is a legal one, that it is violence against women and intended to inflict bodily harm on another person, against the wishes of that person (Walker, 1970). The difficulty is that violence is not defined in Law, only violent acts, as under Section 47 of the Offences Against the Person Act, 1861. However, the interesting aspect is that they involve actual bodily harm but this does not have to be severe. This tends to go against the common view that violence must be grievous harm, whereas it is any hurt or injury that is calculated to interfere with a person's health or comfort (R v. Miller, 1954: 2 QB 282). By Law, violent acts can even cover those which cause hysterical or nervous conditions, such as those caused by pestering (*Vaughan* v. *Vaughan*, 1973 3 ER 449).

New definitions of violence

The general perception of partner violence remained that of personal physical damage until Susan Griffin's analysis of rape. Then, what had previously been categorized as a sexual crime under the Law was viewed by her as an act of sex and violence, which was used to control women and perpetuate male dominance (Griffin, 1971:29). Although this was not universally accepted, it did become apparent that some of the previous certainties of the legal definition were not so steadfast. It also pointed out that legal definitions had their own context and so could vary, as noted in the following:

1. Legal terms such as rape varied between legal systems. For instance, the Law of Ireland includes penetration of the mouth and anus in its legal definition, while Canada has replaced the concept of rape altogether by that of sexual assault where penetration is a redundant criterion.

2. The concept of rape has also varied over time. Until the end of the sixteenth century, a woman was not considered to have been raped if she later became pregnant. Pregnancy implied she must have enjoyed the experience, otherwise her womb would not have opened; and if she enjoyed the experience then she must have consented to it.

3. The variable nature of rape may be seen in the fact that rape within marriage became a legal offence in Scotland in 1989, and in England and Wales in 1991. Thus there is no universal concept of rape, but concepts that are constantly changing. In the case of *State* v. *Stevens*, the Supreme Judicial Court of Maine upheld the conviction of a woman on the charge of raping a thirteen-year-old boy (510 A2d 1070, 64 ALR 4th 1123 1986). Though not called rape, there is a similar case in Scottish Law in the case of *Vaughan* v. *HM Advocate* (1979 SLT 49).

What the example of rape definition showed was that the Law was not necessarily the best or the only definer of human behaviour. Though rape and violence are separate under the Law, they are much closer behaviourally. Bearing this in mind, it comes as little surprise that up to a third of women who have been physically abused by their partners have also been sexually abused by them (Frieze, 1983; Russell, 1982).

Investigating sexual violence

Once the legal categories are ignored, then any new definitional process requires research to understand such behaviour as sexual violence. What research did show was that what previously had been taken as fact, was built on myths. For instance, rape was a common rather than an isolated act (Koss and Harvey, 1991), most victims did not dress provocatively (Rodabaugh and Austin, 1981), and rape was not usually perpetrated by strangers (London Rape Crisis Centre, 1982; Lloyd, 1991). In a study of college students, it was found that only a minority of rapists were sexually stimulated beforehand (Koss and Oros, 1982). It became apparent that although categorized as a sexual act, violence was the more important characteristic of rape.

Facts were thus brought to light, but also it was shown that several assumed facts were false. These myths were often used in legal cases, thus making the Law a poor source of definitions. Arguments based on perceived truths such as 'The woman can stop the sexual violator at any time', 'The woman really enjoys it', or 'The woman provokes the attack' have been identified as false through empirical research (Feild and Barnett, 1978).

Rape myths

Just as facts have to be explained, so does the existence of rape fallacies. In short, why did the Law appear to get things wrong? One indication is given by the finding that sexual myths are more likely to be held by sexual violators (Burt, 1982) compared with the general public, and they provide convenient support for those wanting to force sex on others. This view is reinforced not only by the prevalence of male sexual aggression against women correlating with such rape myths (Malamuth, 1983), but also by those myths being believed to an equal extent by other violent offenders (Hall et al., 1986). This suggests a degree of similarity between sexual and other violent offenders. Indeed, the acceptance of interpersonal violence by men is positively associated with their self-reported likelihood of committing rape (Check and Malamuth, 1983).

Thus the role of such misinformation about rape may be seen as a way of sexualizing the use of force, making it easier to see the rapist as an extreme individual rather than what statistics show; namely, that rapists are common in society and associated with male gender dominant beliefs. Moreover, rapists are likely to have a macho personality, endorse callous sex attitudes towards women, and see violence as manly (Murnen, 1988).

Redefining rape

The judicial system is made up of members of society and so is likely to reflect commonly held myths. However there is a further factor. Legally, violence was seen very much from the violator's stance. Indeed, this was the main interest of the judicial system. But using a violator's slant on the definition of rape is dangerous. What takes place might not be seen as rape or violence from the perpetrator's perspective (Brownmiller, 1975). The alternative is to use a definition of rape based on the victim's perception of what has taken place (MacKinnon, 1987:87). The drawback to this definition is that it makes the legal definition of rape less clear (Estrich, 1987), as every woman is allowed her own definition.

Nevertheless, if we do pay attention to the experience of victims then we find not only that rape is associated with violence, but also that the experience can be gender-perceived. If rape is not the act of a sex-driven individual against a stranger but a relatively common act, usually between people who know each other, then by looking at such experiences we can get a glimpse of what really happens.

Annmarie: 'What was the most sickening thing that used to turn my stomach was he would knock the fuck out of you and then expect you to go to bed with him. That used to turn my gut but you had to, or you were accused of being with somebody.'

Whether the above is sexual or violent, acceptable or not, depends on the person subjected to this behaviour, to their interpretation of it, provided the behaviour was intended by the man. It becomes irrelevant how the man sees the behaviour if the result is unwanted.

Leigh: 'Jimmy would jump on top of me and have sex. Wham, bam! There was no consideration for me, no tenderness. A few minutes and then it would be over. Then he would say, 'That's what I call making love.'

It may be noted that the argument has shifted from what is the definition of rape to who legitimately should define rape. But this rests on a hidden assumption; that women should define rape as they are its victims. And we can extend this process to saying, if women define the concept of violence then it is assumed they are the victims.

Violence in reality

The most obvious fact about relationship violence is that it is meted out by men on women in almost all cases. Certainly this is my experience, and rests not only on accounts of violence, but also on evidence such as bruising, blood and medical reports. This informal knowledge is supplemented from official sources. A survey over three months in 1992 in the West Midlands, England, gave a figure of 97 per cent for cases of violence involving men against women, while an analysis of Scottish police records gave a figure of 99 per cent (Dobash and Dobash, 1977/78). Admittedly, these figures refer to cases brought to official notice. However, other researchers have also found that women are the victims of partner violence (Lystad, 1975). This is borne out by analysis of victim surveys (Gaquin, 1977/78; McLeod, 1980). These results are mirrored in the United States Crime Survey covering partners' assaults during the years 1973–77. It showed that 95 per cent of all assaults were by men on their female partners or ex-partners.

Counter-evidence about relationship violence

It is surprising in view of the previous findings that Gelles (1974) claimed that wives are as violent as husbands. Straus and Gelles (1986) found that the amount of violence by wives was slightly greater than that of their partners, and that husbands are more likely to be the victims and are more likely to be severely hurt (Straus and Gelles, 1990). Furthermore, it has been said that wives are more likely to initiate violence (Straus, 1980) and more likely to use weapons (Shupe et al., 1987). This surprising set of results has been strengthened by the further claim that battered men are unlikely to come forward to complain of their situation (Shupe et al., 1987). If all this is true, then women have no greater claim to forward their gendered view of relationship violence than men. This in turn means a gender-neutral definition of relationship violence is to be preferred.

As the results of Straus and Gelles go against my own experience, this leads me to question why I might have been misled. However, the methodology of the two researchers was attacked by the Dobashes and others (1992) for failing to attend to consequences of violence; in particular, the fact that far more women were seriously injured compared to men and tended to cause damage only in retaliation to violence inflicted on them. Furthermore, research suggests that it is men who are more likely to report partner violence than women (Rouse et al., 1987). Another difficulty concerning Straus and Gelles' research is that they used a definition of violence which covered actions such as slapping and pushing. This raises the question as to whether they should be covered by a term such as violence (Pan et al., 1994).

Leigh: 'I had been looking forward to seeing how they would show that lassie being battered in Coronation Street, but it was nothing, a mere slap. They should have shown what it's like to get your head really kicked in so you can hardly see and you're left with concussion. They made battering to be nothing, and I was mad.'

So if we look to a victim's experience of violence, then minor force may not be seen as violence. This has implications, as those most likely to use severe force are men. However, if we include minor reactions within our definition of violence, then women are suddenly labelled as equally violent as men.

Physical aspects

Any understanding of partner violence comes in part from looking at the severity of force employed, and this is largely determined by the physical sizes of those involved. We may note that in almost all cases of violence, the man is bigger, heavier and stronger than the woman. In several cases known to me, the weight of the man was double that of the woman. This means that violence by women against men is rarely the same as that by men against women (Sierra et al., 1991). Women tend to use violence in retaliation, but often we discover women will not fight back because of the strength differential. This view is reinforced when we observe that there is more fighting back in situations where partners are close in physique, such as in many abusive lesbian relationships (Walker, 1986). In fact, the whole question of retaliation by women is affected by their lesser physique and a need to take the man by surprise and avoid further retaliation.

Tracy: 'He's started hitting us, he's hit me on the nose. He's hitting us once or twice a week or heading us. He kens I can't fight him back.'

However, this does not mean women do not want to fight back. They are merely restricted by their physical abilities.

Leigh: 'I wish I knew how to stick the nut on him and to karate chop him on both ears. I would do that, and then run away and lock the kitchen door before he came to.'

This means that in order to physically overcome her male partner, a woman either has to take him by surprise, when he is incapacitated, or use a weapon. In the United States one survey showed that 61 per cent of the victims of female homicides were either very drunk or asleep (Ward et al., 1969). However, if the male partner is then seriously hurt or worse, the plea of mitigation, using force which is equal and opposite, may be closed (Scutt, 1981). Women are faced with difficulties under the Law which equates men and women, though physically this is usually a nonsense.

Feminist definitions

Not surprisingly, a refusal to accept the legal view of partner violence is common to feminists. By looking at what they see as the reality of partner violence, feminists are able to criticize legal views as failing to take the following on board.

1. Partner violence is generally characterized by a pattern of ongoing violence, and this is more than a series of separate acts. This pattern of violence constitutes a means of domination and control.

2. Legal definitions amount to a male perception of harm and what is dangerous (Stanko, 1985). This is determined by the fact that society is patriarchal, dominated by male institutions and organizations, backed by male knowledge, rules and norms. Not only is the Law itself a male product, but so are decisions as to relevance to a particular case, the analysis of a case and the application of the rules of precedent (Mossman, 1986).

Furthermore, the feminine perception of violence is that which includes the whole experience, not just the physical aspects.

Leigh: 'The worse thing was the way he constantly brought me down. I found that worse than being punched and kicked.'

So violence is seen to include verbal aggression, as this is a relevant part of women's experience.

Making new definitions of violence

The new feminist definitions of violence include the distress suffered by the victim. Legally, the use of a knife as a threat when committing rape is no more than threatened violence; it is not actual violence. But the distress is such that it should really be considered as violence. This not only seems common sense, but also links up with the appreciation that threats of violence can be more damaging than physical violence.

For instance, if women are coerced verbally into unwanted sex, this creates greater self-blame (Murnen et al., 1989) and greater consequent adjustment problems (Mynatt and Allgeier, 1990) than being physically forced. However, such distress is ignored because victims of violence are largely ignored by the legal process (Wright, 1991).

Forms of the new definitions

The different forms of violence are linked through Kelly's concept of the continuum of violence, ranging from murder at one extreme to forms of sexual harassment, such as staring, at the other; all are forms of violence, products of men's control and domination of women. One advantage of this revised view was that it drew attention to areas of behaviour that had been overlooked, such as flashing, which is highly distressing to women (McNeill, 1987) even though there is no physical contact or overt threats. The victims of this behaviour were very upset and so subjected to a form of violence.

However intuitively incorrect it may seem to call flashing a form of violence, flashing is a form of male behaviour which is intrusive and controlling. It could be likened to rape, which has violence as a major aspect. In fact, intrusive sexual contact is only too typical of male behaviour. Kelly and her co-workers (1991) found that 60 per cent of girls up to the age of sixteen were the recipients of unwanted and intrusive sexual contact. What may seem to be merely intrusive is in practice controlling. American research showed adult harassment was experienced by 40 per cent of women federal government workers and only 15 per cent of men over a two-year period, and the harassers were almost always men (US Merit Systems Protection Board, 1988).

Feminine perceptions regarding violence

There is a danger in extrapolating from a few examples a general view about violence. In particular, we have to question the feminist perception of reality as much as the legal view. Women are seen as living in fear of crime and assault (Baken, 1979). Yet such fear seems misplaced. In fact, young men are the most likely to be assaulted and one in three women assaulted are assaulted by women (Widom and Maxfield, 1984). In the United States it is young men who are most likely to be murdered (Roth, 1994). However, dangers lurk in mere statistics. Men are more likely to be assaulted in the street and by a stranger. This often happens in places and situations known to be dangerous, such as pubs at closing time, the post-match wearing of football colours at away games, visiting certain areas at night. So men can avoid potential danger (Gottfredson, 1984). Even when confronted with danger in a public place, it should be noted that there is an escalation of tension and aggressive behaviour, and men can defuse, ignore or escape this process (Berkowitz, 1978). However, women are most likely to be assaulted by someone they know, often their partner and in their home. It is very difficult for them to avoid danger. In addition, they have a real fear of rape. This sexual fear hardly touches the behaviour of men.

Difficulties with feminist definitions

Feminist perspectives support the idea of violence, including partner violence, being a form of male control. However, just as legal definitions are the product of a certain section of society, so the same applies to feminist definitions and the idea of a continuum of violence. Just as there are reasons to support such definitions, so there are also objections.

Physical damage is qualitatively different from emotional damage, as even feminists will admit (Kelly, 1994:42). Couples may threaten to damage each other, and parents will do the same to their children, but there is a world of difference between threats and action. Arguments between couples may be bilateral with mutual threats and putdowns, but actual physical violence is very much unilateral, with women fighting usually only in retaliation, if at all.

Yet another difficulty about using very wide definitions based on the concept of a continuum of violence is that they can be misleading. In their investigation of children aged eleven to twelve who bully and are bullied, Lagerspetz and others (1988) used a threefold approach; looking at physical aggression, verbal aggression, and indirect aggression – the latter covering behaviour such as malicious gossip, trying to get others to dislike someone, and becoming friends with another person as revenge. The outcome was that boys indulged in the most physical aggression, verbal aggression was about equal, and girls carried out the most indirect aggression. On a narrow definition of violence, boys indulge in it most. However, with an extended definition, girls are equally violent. Admittedly, this was not an investigation of adult partners, but it is suggestive. This relates only to children, not adults, but it is of potential relevance if we see violence as a product of socialization.

Development of violence

My preference is provisionally to see violence as intended actual physical harm against another person. The wider definitions of violence are less helpful and are better designated by using different terms. It is true that by taking violence to be constructed and defined as merely intended physical harm, we might be seen to be downgrading behaviour such as harassment and intimidation. In fact, these are important aspects and they are referred to when they accompany violence, but they are not taken as part of violence. By linking violence and aggression too closely, we can diminish violence, treat it as something extraordinary, whereas it is not so unusual an occurrence. For instance, 28 per cent of Canadian women will be battered by their partners sometime in their life (Statistics, Canada), and in the United States, 27 per cent of women will be sexually assaulted in their life-time by someone they know (Rogers, 1994). In Britain, a random survey of households in Islington, London, showed that a third of women had experienced some form of violence in their lives (Mooney, 1993) and a national survey of lone parents indicated that violence was a reason for separating in 20 per cent of the cases and the main reason in 13 per cent (Bradshaw and Millar, 1991). The number of women subjected to violence in Britain is huge. The Citizens' Advice Bureaux alone have estimated they have dealt with 25,000 cases annually (Binney et al., 1981).

So violence is physical harm which underpins the sexual, intimidatory, verbal, emotional and isolating aspects of physical abuse, and violence itself is a form of control. This model mirrors that used by the Domestic Abuse Intervention Project in Duluth, Minnesota.

Definitions and politics

What should be appreciated is that definitions in the human sciences are part of a political process. Feminist writings in particular have seen a widening of definitions (Kelly and Radford, 1987:243) but it has been in dictated directions and certain areas are ignored or minimized. Abusive lesbian relationships (Lobel, 1986), elder abuse, bullying in schools (Olweus, 1991) and in prisons (Woolf and Tumim, 1990), racial violence by white women (Mama, 1989) and child abuse by women, are often played down. This perpetuates the stereotype of girls and women being totally passive and caring. However, if we turn our attention to children who are violent at some time towards their brothers or sisters, then figures of 83 per cent for boys and 74 per cent for girls have been given (Straus, 1980). An investigation into the behaviour of schoolgirls showed that all of them had witnessed a fight and 89 per cent had been in at least one fight themselves (Berkowitz, 1982). We have to beware of taking a stereotypical view of the behaviour of men and women, and always try to stay grounded in reality.

The differential expression of aggression

One way of clarifying violence is to see it as proceeding from aggression, the threat or attempt to be violent. Aggression is a product of the body's fight-or-flight response and is thus linked with biological constitution and functioning. It is a predispositional but not a necessary state for violence (Sabourin et al., 1993).

The expression of aggression lies in gender socialization, a process which starts from birth, when male and female infants are equally capable of showing distress through crying and exhibiting temper tantrums (Goodenough, 1931). But at the age of three weeks male infants are treated differently by their mothers, being held longer. By the age of three months, girls and boys are being given different gender-specific toys to play with (Goldberg and Lewis, 1969). Interestingly, it is men, as the patriarchal leaders, who are more concerned with reinforcing gender differences (Hoffman, 1977) and seeing that their sons, especially, should have 'proper' toys (Fagot, 1978).

Boys are also given greater autonomy, whereas girls are subjected to greater maternal control (Oakley, 1972). By the age of eight months, boys begin to have the edge on girls, to be more dominant, though this may be no more than a reflection of differing physical strengths (Strayer and Trudel, 1984). They are also more adventurous and more likely to move away from their mothers by the time they are a year old (Ban and Lewis, 1974).

By the second year, aggression is used to gain possessions, such as toys, and at this age boys are beginning to win out. This may reflect differences in socialization, in particular the greater role of the father in raising sons (Morgan et al., 1988). By the third year aggression is being used for dominance (Weisfeld and Linkey, 1985). By the age of four, boys want to be 'tough', a macho stage which is characterized by a preference for boys as friends, and girls are usually seen as 'sissy'. There are arguments about group leadership in play and who 'is best'. Girls tend to play in small groups with their best friends, with the emphasis on relational closeness (Lever, 1978; Harris and Gross, 1988).

Dominance

With male aggression comes the formation of dominance hierarchies, starting at the age of four and largely in place by the age of six. Dominance is achieved mainly by verbal means and social skills (Savin-Williams, 1987); those less proficient will tend to use physical force. Girls also form hierarchies, but these are rarely determined by physical means (Humphreys and Smith, 1984). Young boys are encouraged or are less likely to be stopped from games of rough-and-tumble (Humphreys and Smith, 1987). Boys are prepared both for aggression and even violence, but they also learn how to control themselves. However some are less good at understanding or keeping to the rules and can be unduly aggressive or violent (Pellegrini, 1988).

The formation of hierarchies leads to a decline in physical aggression (Hartup, 1974). This does not mean that control disappears, only that there is less need to be physical, partly because children learn to control their behaviour and present a face different from the way they feel (Harris and Gross, 1988). Also, being dominant has a range of benefits for boys, such as attracting attention (Hold-Cavell, 1985), having the right to lead the group at play (Savin-Williams, 1987) and being allowed to mediate in conflicts (Ginsburg and Miller, 1981). The overall result tends to be popularity with one's peers (Weisfeld et al., 1987). These hierarchies tend to remain stable for up to ten years (Weisfeld et al., 1987), while single-sex groups tend to reinforce and widen the different gender behaviours. The macho male stage, to be seen in many cultures, lasts until pre-adolescent boys begin to get interested in girls (Omark et al., 1975).

With an interest in the opposite sex comes a modification in male behaviour, with an increase in teasing, which can be seen in part as an exercise in power (Shapiro et al., 1991), but also as a means of entering into opposite-sex interactions without risking the expression of interest in the other person (Sluckin, 1981). Play for adolescent boys can become more vigorous and there can be a definite edge to the behaviour, a desire to win. This can be transferred to play with girls, becoming more pronounced in eighteen- to twenty-year-olds indulging in horse-play, during which there is a greater likelihood of violence.

Bullying

One way of connecting aggression with violence is through bullying. Rough-and-tumble continues until one person gains the upper hand and the other submits, either by running away or by making it obvious that he or she wants to end the play by using a formal signal, such as saying 'Pax!'. However, sometimes the other child will not stop and then what was play degenerates into bullying. Boys bully three times as much as girls, but they tend to bully other boys rather than girls (Roland, 1980) and boys that are younger (Rigby and Slee, 1991). Bullying for girls tends to consist of teasing and exclusion, whereas for boys it is teasing and the use of physical force (Roland, 1987). Interestingly, 20 per cent of the child victims of bullying themselves were bullies, though this was against children other than those who bullied them (Roland, 1980). In Norwegian high schools, 9 per cent of pupils are victims, 7 per cent are bullies, and about 2 per cent are both (Olweus, 1991), and similar figures apply to other countries such as Britain (Smith, 1989) and the United States (Perry et al., 1988). Such violence can last for several years (Olweus, 1977) and is not confined to other pupils but can extend to teachers, parents and siblings

(Olweus, 1984). It seems that much of the nature of partner violence is actually laid down earlier in life, as is the reaction to it. Moreover, there is no neutrality in the reaction to bullying. Those schools that do not fight it, allow it to be institutionalized (Askew, 1989).

Leigh: 'I was bullied at school because I used to speak differently from the rest of them. I stood up to this one girl but it did no good. In the end I moved to another school. It wasn't just me who was bullied. It happened to others, even to some of the teachers.'

In fact, in the United States it was found that high school violence, usually between boys, resembles that of both college students and married persons (Makepeace, 1981). Girls tend to avoid overt conflict (Tannen, 1990) in order to preserve relationships (Oliker, 1989).

In relation to partner violence, it may be indicative that bullying has been perceived as a product of different physical sizes (Greenbaum, 1982), a sense of failure when unable to exert other forms of control (Mendler, 1992), and underlying fears of inadequacy (Roberts, 1988).

Violence and gender interactions

Despite the interesting pointers provided by the behaviour of children, we should also appreciate its complexity. The more indirect and subtle approaches to personal interactions of girls may be changed when they find that such approaches are often ineffective with boys (Maccoby, 1990). For instance, we find that the expression of anger is more direct in opposite as opposed to same-sex relationships (Allen and Haccoun, 1976). Yet, paradoxically, it seems that although boys express anger towards girls, they do not like doing so (Blier and Blier-Wilson, 1989). This fact suggests that boys find a greater difficulty than girls in the expression of anger, which may be released as male violence (Dutton and Strachan, 1987). Certainly, the expression of anger and failing to acknowledge problems in relating are more likely to characterize men than women (Jacobson et al., 1994). Indeed, one of the problems in marital conflict is that so many men tend to smooth over matters rather than face a possibly emotional discussion (Schaap et al., 1987).

The complexity of children's behaviour might also indicate that we tend to simplify and stereotype gendered behaviour. The view of women as not exerting power and their language being indecisive is almost certainly owing to a male lack of appreciation of the use of indirect as opposed to overt forms of power (Tannen, 1991). Adolescent boys see relationships in a more adversarial light and are less likely to take responsibility for what happens in the relationship (Pleck et al., 1993). As parents become less important in forming adolescent behaviour, so other influences take their place to some extent. American research shows that the media, particularly television and videos, reinforce crude sexual stereotyping, and this includes the portrayal (Malamuth and Briere, 1986) and acceptance of male violence (Comstock and Paik, 1994). This is not to say that the media is the direct cause of violence, but it should be noted that not all readers, listeners and viewers are able to resist media messages (Milavsky et al., 1982).

Group life and violence

Violence is not just behaviour that pertains to individuals; it can be a group phenomenon as well. It can arise from within groups, and the family is usually the most important group influence on growing children. Violence, particularly that of boys and young men, is usually seen in peer groups. What happens is subject to informal rules and violence falls within those rules. Breaking of those rules by individual gang members upsets the system and leaves those who appear out of control as objects of dislike by the rest of the gang (Patrick, 1973).

Definitions: aggression, violence and growing up

Human violence has been differentiated from aggression; the latter consisting of threats, either attacking or defensive. Aggression is biologically based, whereas violence is socially learned behaviour which develops from the earliest age. Thus violence is not behaviour that springs just from partner relationships but behaviour that characterizes social relationships in general. As learned behaviour, it is not a simple reaction but sets of behaviour patterns that grow more complex as the child grows into an adult, and as adults grow older and understand more of their social world. Violence being social behaviour reflects society in general, and this includes power relations such as patriarchy. However, there is no one form of violence. People learn different things in their social world, interact with it, and so there are variations in forms of violence.

Violence is almost always a means to an end. Children soon discover they can control and dominate through violence, and use it for that purpose. However they also discover that aggression rather than violence is in general an even more efficient way of achieving these ends. This learning continues through life.

Outcome

Counsellors have the choice of more than one definition of partner violence. It is apparent that there is no single correct one. This is no drawback, provided any use of a definition is made transparent. For those counselling clients in violent relationships, the benefit of working through definitions springs from the process of working through relevant information and concepts rather than coming to a conclusion. Being familiar with different definitions and perspectives is also helpful as it allows counsellors to see situations in a broad perspective, and avoid ignoring, minimizing or rationalizing what is taking (or had taken) place.

2   CLIENT LIVES

Introduction

Discussions about definitions of partner violence are important for counsellors in order that they may establish their baseline and their own views and values. This is necessary for any counsellor, and should have been addressed in training. It is especially important in any form of family or couples work, as all of us have been part of a family and are quite likely to be in some form of partner relationship. As a result, we all tend to have our own personal views which can affect our counselling. In particular, some counsellors find it difficult to fully take on the person-centred core values and may be judgemental about male batterers and sympathetic rather than empathic with women who are subjected to violence. This does not mean that counsellors have to take a neutral stance; indeed, much of the later work will be about dealing with the power imbalance in client relationships.

Looking to client lives

Counselling relies on counsellors being able to understand those whom they help and this rests on the assumption that people act rationally and can be understood. Even those judged clinically insane act rationally, though they may base their actions or behaviour on false feelings, thinking or perceptions of the world. We assume everyone can understand us and we can understand everyone, otherwise social interaction would be impossible. However, any approach which rests on immediate comprehension is likely to be determined by surface behaviour, and this can be misleading because deeper reasons for behaviour are not appreciated. Behaviour that is not understood is subject to moral interpretation, such as praise, criticism and blame. The more feelings the situations of clients evoke, the more likely is such an interpretation. From my experience, those very close to partner violence may need help to work through attendant feelings, and avoid the imposition of past feelings onto clients. Finally, past direct or indirect experiences of violence can lead to violence becoming a personal agenda with the result that aspects can either be diminished or over-emphasized.

Agendas and violence

Those moving into counselling women in violent relationships often get caught up with the idea of violence. This may mean that other aspects of the client's situation tend to get overlooked. Violence is just one part of the client's situation, which can include the client feeling trapped, the responses of others, and the continuing risk. This is illustrated in evidence given to a Parliamentary Select Committee.

Respondent: 'I have had ten stitches, three stitches, five stitches, seven stitches, where he has cut me. I have had a knife stuck through my stomach; I had a poker put through my face. I have no teeth where he has knocked them all out. I have been burnt with red hot pokers. I have had red hot coals thrown over me. I have been sprayed with petrol and stood there while he has flicked lighted matches at me.'

Questioner: 'What finally drove you out of the marital home?'

Respondent: 'My children asked if they could leave. They were being beaten. I stuck it as I never got a chance to get out. I went to the Welfare three times but they were just interested in keeping the family together. And if you have children you have to go to them.'

Questioner: 'Did you ever consider going to the police?'

Respondent: 'I nicked my husband. He gave me ten stitches and they held him in the nick over the weekend and he came back Monday. He was bound over to keep the peace, that was all. On Tuesday he gave me the hiding of my life.' (Report to the Select Committee on Violence in Marriage, 1975:16, 19, 21)

Most people concentrate on the violence and fail to see that it is reinforced and even amplified by what subsequently happens. Feminist writings and research have been useful in taking a wider view of the situation and giving an overall picture of what happens. Even in cases of extreme violence, as in the previous and the following example, other aspects have to be considered.

Respondent No. 2: 'I was in the house and he came in and did not have any money. I refused point blank to give him any money, so he started smashing my ornaments. He was holding my throat trying to strangle me and beating my head on the wall because I still would not give him any money. Then he took wee Andrew and kicked him across the sitting-room – and that was when I called the police. The police came down and said it was just a domestic quarrel and there was nothing they could do about it, but they would phone the doctor to get him to give me a tranquilliser. I was taken into the hospital with a nervous breakdown. Then the psychiatrist took in my husband and spoke to him, but they could find nothing wrong with him because he was a split personality.' (Report to the Select Committee on Violence in Marriage, 1975:255)

As counsellors, we too have to see the whole picture and deal with client situations where violence is just one factor, albeit an important one.

Development of violence and the relationship

This wider perspective begins with how people get on together. Indeed, some clients' problems start even before the violent relationship has begun. Unrealistic expectations and ungrounded beliefs about the relationship are themselves good predictors of the likely degree of distress within such relationships (Epstein and Eidelson, 1981), though not necessarily of violence. Perceptions are important, especially if both partners tend to see negatives in the relationship, and attribute them to the other person or to themselves rather than to attendant situations or circumstances (Jacobson et al., 1985). Equally unhelpful is the discrediting of positive actions by the partner (Fincham et al., 1987). Some clients' problems are thus part of an overall difficulty with relationships in general. It is worthwhile remembering that unrealistic expectations of relationships might also be applied to the counsellor. It is also easy for counsellors at times to go along with these optimistic expectations as they boost self-esteem.

Variation in partner violence

Male use of physical force starts from an early age and can be part of the inventory of a person's possible behaviour. This means violence can occur at any stage in partner relationships, as when couples first date, but is more common after potential partners have become serious or have had sex together (Cate et al., 1982). Violence can continue when couples settle down and live together. Even the elderly can be abused, usually by their spouses (Bourland, 1990). In short, violence can attend any relationship at any time. There is no way of determining beforehand who may be a batterer or battered. We have to avoid misleading stereotypes and see violence as being possible in any intimate relationship.

However, what can be said is that violence by men to their partners is vastly more common compared with violence by women (Cate et al., 1982; Deal and Wampler, 1986). Getting married does not decrease the likelihood of violence – in fact, the opposite seems the case. Key points in the relationship such as marriage and pregnancy make the woman more liable to violence (Home Office 1995:38). It should be said that one study did question whether pregnancy did increase the risk of being physically abused and suggested a negative answer (Gelles, 1988), but this has not been the general consensus. Pregnancy does stoke up the fires of jealousy and my experience has been that it can be a dangerous time for some women.

Debbie: 'He dragged me off the couch and kicked me in the stomach and severed the baby's umbilical cord. The baby died. I was five months pregnant at the time. It was a baby boy I lost.'

Counsellors find that violence can start at critical life-stages such as marriage or pregnancy. This can arise through the male partner no longer feeling in control as a result of role changes, new expectations and responsibilities.

Ben: 'It was OK until I had to take responsibility, then I would get into a flap. Hitting was a relief valve.'

Counsellors are very unlikely to deal with initial violence but are more likely to work with couples having problems associated with relationship and role changes. There has to be an awareness that violence is a possibility. However, initially most partner relationships display no violence, at least for a matter of a few weeks or months. Then the violence starts. Of those subjected to violence, half were assaulted within the first year of marriage or cohabitation, but fewer cases emerged after three years (Dobash and Dobash, 1970). Once violence has begun, it is likely to escalate in frequency and intensity over time (Carlson, 1977).

Ben: 'It started more as fun to begin with – a slap on the shoulder. But then it went to a punch on the shoulder, to a slap in the mouth, then a punch in the mouth.'

Moreover, women can be subjected to violence over many years (Pahl, 1985). One of the first cases I worked with, twenty years ago, was that of a mother who had been subjected to violence over seventeen years. Half the women who have experienced violence do so within ten years of being married and half of the couples where there has been violence had children under five. In fact very few of the women subjected to violence were childless (Borkowski et al., 1983).

Violence is almost always accompanied by verbal aggression, usually the culmination of a build-up of arguments, angry silences, sarcastic comments, and a raised level of tension. What is difficult to convey is the intensity of such aggression. The following example arose out of the blue and was conducted at shouting level, which suggests some of the difficulty associated with counselling couples.

Greg: 'You, shut your puss!'

Rosann: 'You, shut *your* fucking puss!'

Greg: 'I'm about to speak to the man!'

Rosann: 'Don't you ever speak to me like that. Who the fuck do you think you are?'

Greg: 'I'll speak as I fucking want! Don't give me cheek.'

Me: 'Can all of us ...'

Rosann: 'You're fucking ignorant ...'

Me: 'Right! That's enough ...'

Greg: 'Bastard!'

Some counsellors find it difficult to take such outbursts, especially as they are quite likely to be dragged into the argument if not careful. No matter how often couples are told not to behave in such a manner and however controlling the counsellor tries to be, such shouting matches are likely to occur at some time.

Foretelling violence

Acceptance of clients is not easy when confronted with those *in extremis*, who appear not to be acting rationally. This may be extended from the violator to his victim. We begin to have difficulty in accepting women who associate with men who are violent. Yet the woman client does not choose the violence, she chooses the man. Women clients have little or no expectation of being involved in violence (Drake, 1984), especially if they have had no experience of it in the past. This can apply even when the women is aware of her partner's violence before deciding to live with him.

Diane: 'I knew he could be violent before we stayed together, but I was young at the time, thought I was in love with him, and always thought it was someone else's fault, not his. Even when he hit me I made excuses for him and blamed myself.'

In other cases we find abusers will not be known as violent, but start for no apparent reason and it comes as a complete surprise.

Annmarie: 'I remember him coming home from the ice-hockey practice and he was injured. He turned round and thumped me. I asked him, "What was that for?" and he said, "I didna' ken. I'm sorry."'

Me: 'Did it ever become apparent why he hit you that time.'

Annmarie: 'No. No.'

Sometimes sudden violence would be associated with drinking, but this is still insufficient as an explanation.

Elaine: 'Sometimes he would come back after he had been drinking and would hit me and I never knew why. There would be no reason for it.'

Faced with what seems to be inexplicable behaviour, female partners try to understand. However, even with explanations, women may feel no better about what has happened.

Leigh: 'On one occasion I was watching TV with his brother and sister-in-law and Jimmy came in drunk and went punch, punch, slap across the face – for no reason at all. His brother said, "That's a bit flaming off, isn't it?" "I never touched her, I never touched her!" Another time he asked for his lighter so I tossed it to him. He jumped up and punched me in the midriff. Afterwards he said he was sorry, but it was too late by then. Often he would sober up and then jump on top of me, violently, for sex and then roll off. I reckon he really must have hated me and got a kick out of what he did.'

However, we should not imagine that intimate violence is a matter of occasional isolated occurrences that come out of the blue. Often women can sense when they are liable to be attacked (Walker, 1979). In turn, they react and behave to try and prevent any attacks. The whole episode can then become almost a ritualistic set piece of behaviour, the two partners manoeuvring before the man becomes violent. For instance, Stephanie could tell by her partner's expression if he was about to hit her, and anything she said would cause Jack to start. But if she kept silent, Jack would then upbraid her for refusing to talk. If she then tried to argue the point, she would be hit. If she refused to talk she would also be hit. All of this is not just about Jack inflicting harm on his partner; it is all about control. In addition, the significance of the attacks being unexpected is twofold. They point to the violence being very much unilateral, coming from the man and not being a direct product of the couple's interaction. In addition, the form of attack is such as to prevent any negotiation or form of reasoning and subsequent action. The jump to crisis is a way of avoiding a solution to whatever the man's problem might be.

Signs and control

Sometimes a woman will imagine that she can help her male partner and so end his violence. From my experience this is not likely to be successful. The man has to want to stop, rather than his partner wanting him to stop. The same applies to counselling. Counsellors cannot simply stop partner violence. All they can do is to show clients a path to non-violence, along which the client may or may not decide to walk. This in turn leads to implications for counsellors, who should be able to read warning signs and push the safety aspect – whatever the feelings of female clients.

Leigh: 'Jimmy at one point tried to deny my very existence, ripping up my photo, birth certificate and marriage lines. He wanted to destroy me; I thought he was going to top me. I know other lassies whose men did the same and were in real danger.'

It might also be noted that intimidation may be felt not just by the female partner, but also by all those around. In this way, Jimmy was able at times to control not only Leigh but everyone around him. Counsellors will then have to consider their own position and their role with regard to particular clients. This in turn can only be sensed through a knowledge of possible client situations, as they will not always tell the counsellor.

Annmarie: 'He would go to the pub and come in at 4 or 5 o'clock in the morning. You had to sit up and wait on him. You had to, or you would get a hiding from him for not being up. You used to lie on the couch, absolutely exhausted, and as soon as you heard the door, you would jump up as I was petrified of him, but then I loved him. And you weren't allowed to ask questions or you got hammered for that.'

Often counsellors find the real difficulty is being able to withstand client control rather than actual violence. Part of the reason is that physical violence rarely takes place in counselling, but control by male clients does occur. Thus abuser control rarely comes from violence but usually from the anxiety that it might occur. Another method is for threats to come out of the blue, for no apparent reason, so that no one is sure what is happening. Men almost plan their abusive behaviour. They may brood over situations, stoke up their resentments, and let themselves be violent.

Doing the right thing

Part of the trouble for women in violent relationships is that they cannot do the right thing. Whatever they do is wrong – according to their partner. This is a necessary aspect of abusive control. Violence can then erupt and female partners are left with the choice of either accepting it or trying to fight back. And, again, this is likely to be a no-win situation.

Me: 'Was there anything that would mollify him or prevent you from being hit?'

Annmarie: 'There was nothing you could do about it. I used to hit back, but not at first. To begin with I took it and then at the end thought, "To fuck with this!" and I hit him back. But I got it worse. If you hit him back you were a street-fighter, you were this, you were that, and he actually used to spit in my face. I was scum. He used to get my head down on the floor and his foot on my head and rubbed my face into the carpet. I had carpet burns on my face, the lot.'

It is not easy for counsellors to remain unaffected when hearing of such treatment, but the assumption that the answer is to tell women clients to leave such situations may be more for the benefit of the counsellor than the client. Part of the difficulty is for counsellors to accept, if temporarily, that women will not move out of abusive relationships.

Tracy: 'Now he hits me three or four times a week. And he treats me like a man. He watches me to see if I'm looking and then heads me. I would leave him, but no one would have me.'

The alternative of advising a woman that she can best escape violence by doing everything her partner demands is not necessarily helpful. The more the woman tries to do the 'right' thing, the more her partner might criticize. Control is exerted by this means. Women will speak of 'constantly being on edge', 'walking on eggshells', 'living on my nerves', and in such acute anxiety they are more biddable. Women find that whatever they do is not enough, not right and not appreciated, so they try harder and harder to do what they think the partner requires, failing to understand that there never will be any way of satisfying him.

Annmarie: 'The funny thing is the lassie Jamie is with now is mucking about, yet I never mucked him about. I did everything for him and she lives in a shit-hole. In fact her house is like a red-light area and she mucks around left, right and centre. She's had him up to his eyes in debt; he was never in debt when I was with him, and yet he seems quite happy. What I could never ever come to terms with is that he had everything with me and he blew the whole lot. I used to sit and say, "If I did this, if I did that" but he would not have changed.'

The difficulty is that any change for violent men means that, in their estimation, they are losing control. They have to deal with not only violence but also a loss of control and having to find other ways of interacting.

Jealousy

Control is seen in violence, but more commonly in the twin aspects of male jealousy and possessiveness. Client jealousy is of practical importance in counselling as the counsellor can become the object of jealousy (Allan, 1989). In addition, jealousy can greatly affect the male partner's perception of situations and relationships, so that he may appear to act in a totally unreasonable manner.

Debbie: 'He would not let me talk to anyone. When I spoke to a teacher at the school, he said she was a dyke and we were having an affair. If I spoke to anyone, then he could not understand I was being friendly – I was flirting. If I was going out and putting on make-up then he would ask me who I was putting it on for. I would say I was just tidying myself up, but he would say, "For whom?" and I would say, "For myself. OK?" He said, "No, it's not OK. I'll go out with you." I could not make him understand that I wanted a break. I did not want him with me twenty-four hours a day.'

Jealousy acts so that no amount of proof will satisfy the man, and any incident can provide evidence that his partner is acting against him, being unfaithful in sexual and other matters. After a time the woman may begin to learn what will give rise to jealousy. This is not easy, as a jealous man can see sexual significance is almost any form of behaviour and men tend to be jealous as a consequence of their patriarchal role (Wiederman and Allgeier, 1993). In fact, jealousy may have nothing to do with the female partner at all, but be solely the man's concern.

Annmarie: 'When we were married, there were times he would hit me and accuse me of having an affair, but it was him who was mucking about. He was just sticking his blame onto me. Once I went out with two other girls for a drink and I was the last one out of the taxi. He then accused me of having an affair with the taxi-driver, his current girlfriend having left the house sometime earlier.'

Male jealousy, and it is usually sexual jealousy, can lead to unprovoked partner violence, yet it can be a product of the man's imagining and have little connection with reality. This argues against the idea that the violence must result from the couple's mutual interactions and the woman feeling that she must take some responsibility or blame for what is happening (Berk et al., 1983).

Trying to cope with the abusive situation, the abused woman might further re-interpret her partner's jealous actions to maintain her own self-esteem.

Leigh: 'I realized that he was jealous. That's a good thing isn't it? Shows that he cares.'

This can affect helpers such as counsellors, who may see the client as very naive, rather than understanding that she is trying to bear the almost unbearable.

However, we have to be careful of seeing men or violent men as simply jealous. This is a feeling that can occur in anyone; it is not a male characteristic. An investigation of schoolgirl violence showed that jealousy, along with the maintenance of self-respect and social status, was one of the principal reasons given for fighting (Campbell, 1982). What is different is that some men will allow jealousy to become a principal trait, and then find they cannot escape the world that they have constructed.

Male possessiveness

Male possessiveness – in part another product of patriarchy – is usually accompanied by sexual jealousy. The male idea that the woman belongs to her male partner is reinforced by practical steps to ensure that this is indeed the fact. Steps can include isolation of the woman by discouraging visitors, cutting connections with the woman's family, not going out together, and the woman being timed if she goes out on her own.

Annmarie: 'My pals weren't allowed to come to the house. And every pal that I had was a whore, and I wasn't allowed to go out on my own. If I went down the street, I was to do my shopping in half an hour, and be up the road.'

Me: 'And did he time you?'

Annmarie: 'Oh aye. Aye, he timed me. "Who were you talking to? What shops were you in?" It was unreal.'

Often male control is done indirectly, so the woman would be allowed out but this becomes such a performance that she finds it preferable not to do so.

Leigh: 'When I came back there would be this interrogation. "Where have you been? What did you go out for? Who did you see? Why did it take so long? Who saw you? Who did you meet?" In the end, you felt guilty whatever you did.'

Also, possessiveness and jealousy can be such that all men are regarded by the male partner as being attracted to 'his' woman and consequently likely to take her away. Thus any scenario can be seen as a possible example of unfaithfulness.

Annmarie: 'With the coal fires and the smoke, the walls were getting yellow, so I decided to wash them one night, just to get the smoke off them. I will never forget that. He came up the road and accused me of having someone else in the house. You could not get it through to him it was all rubbish.'

This is merely the first act in the scenario, as the woman in turn is aware of the man's attitude and likely behaviour, so she must take precautions.

Annmarie: 'Aye, he was jealous, possessive. I used to sit in the pub with my head down and not look at anybody because I didn't want to get accused of anything.'

Then there are the man's actions against the woman's perceived attempts to be herself, such as getting a job or going to evening classes. Being herself would be seen as being independent and so preparing to leave. As a result, the man might then take further precautions by making the woman unattractive to other men. For example, he might restrict her money so that she could not buy clothes for herself. Another tactic involves violence against the woman resulting in disfigurement, either temporarily or permanently.

Collette: 'He used to punch me so my face was swollen, and said that now no one would want me. He said if he wasn't to have me then no one else would.'

There can also be difficulties where there are children from a previous marriage or relationship to the woman. The man identifies the children closely with the woman and this can mean they too may be subjected to violence.

Debbie: 'At first Rod insisted the children call him Dad, then he tried to pass them off as his. Then he hit them. Finally, he wanted them in care, so there would be just the two of us.'

The men involved, on the other hand, rarely realize that they are jealous, but see themselves as acting normally at the time. Again, inexperienced counsellors may accuse such men of being jealous and then end up in arguments about this. But the argument is not about jealousy alone, but about control, in this case between counsellor and client. Rather than arguing, the aim must be to bring understanding to the situation.

Ben: 'I thought I was in love, but it was over-love, it was suffocating. I was smothering my wife.'

Only in retrospect are such men able to see their behaviour as unusual. And this requires firm input from others. The distortions in perception can be so ingrained that neither being nice and reasonable, nor being directive and overpowering, is likely to be best. Counsellors have to be firm, not in their views but in getting male clients to look to their behaviour and themselves, to understand their own behaviour.

Ben: 'I was very jealous. I was in bed with my wife and she moved in bed, though fast asleep. I thought she was sneaking out to go with my mate who was sleeping next door. So I hit her, and she woke up and said, "What's going on?"'

For both men and women there can be confusion as to the nature of the feelings they have for their partners. Love, jealousy, dependency and caring may be difficult to disentangle. This might be in part a product of the person's past history but can also be the result of being in a relationship where a person's perception is strongly influenced by those of his or her partner. But this may not be the end of the matter. If a woman is repeatedly accused of doing something, then sometimes she decides she might as well do it, as there is nothing to lose. If discovered, this confirms the man's suspicions.

Work for counsellors

What should be understood is that women may be wanted as male possessions, not for their sake. The male sense of himself is then bound up with the ownership of his female partner, so any attempt by her to leave is not merely a loss but an attack on his identity. A man may even go so far as to kill his partner rather than let her go, the often unspoken fear being that she is leaving for another man. This is an extreme case, but counsellors have to be aware of the role they play and how it might be perceived. Most clients who are batterers or battered are in relationships, so counselling is likely to be seen as a disturbance of the status quo. Counsellors have to deal with the feelings that their presence evokes, feelings that are often evidenced only indirectly.

One decision that counsellors have to make is whether they want to work with abusive men, either individually or as part of a couple, or just with abused women. Whatever the nature of that decision, it seems to me that there has to be knowledge of male abusers and understanding. There is always the danger that trying to understand male violence is seen as in some way minimizing it, excusing it, or even condoning it. This is a dangerous fallacy. To be able to counteract violence we have to understand it. Also, to understand women who have been abused we have to understand male behaviour. After all, that is what abused women try to do. By attending merely to their situation and feelings, we risk seeing women as victims and underestimating their ability and power to change their circumstances. It is important to know what has happened and does happen, before seeing the situation through the lens of theory.

The following is just one man's account so should not be taken as typical, but it does point to several different possible sources of violence.

Me: 'You were the eldest boy in the family; did that make a difference to you? Did you have to look after the others?'

Jimmy: 'Oh aye! All my brothers, if they got a battering at school then I would have to do some battering or I would get battered myself.'

Me: 'Who would batter you?'

Jimmy: 'My old man. My old man was a bit of a fighter in his day.'

For Jimmy, violence was not just an individual but a family characteristic. With other boys the local gang might be the more important group, but for Jimmy to be part of a family was to defend it or perhaps the myth of the family, as life at home was hard.

Jimmy: 'Since the age of fourteen, any chance of a go at the bizzies [police], we would have a go at them. We used to smash their cars and that. Really, there was a war between our family and the police.'

Once this habit of fighting against forces that appeared to threaten the family was established, it continued. What happened in a person's early years can be important but is not determining. But, like many a habit, the violence was difficult to disown and stop.

Jimmy: 'I did nine months for police assault, and then joined the army, but this did not last long – fifteen months. They slung me out for decking a sergeant-major.'

The attacks were now interpreted as being less against the family and more against himself. Though Jimmy might at times seem to be bound by family ties, we should not ignore the fact that violence by now did have some attractions.

Jimmy: 'I had just turned twenty-one and we were at a dance one night. My younger brother Matt got into a fight with four guys. I ran down to help him. Two of them landed in hospital, one with a fractured skull and a broken jaw. Me and my brother were charged with attempted murder. My younger brother was coming up sixteen, so I took the rap for him. He walked, and I got two years for it.'

What we see is a family and its members with a certain set of beliefs and values, and also an acceptance of them. Violence against the person in particular situations was quite normal, but this does not mean there was a belief in violence for its own sake.

Jimmy: 'Now they are attacking old ladies but we didn't do that. Nowadays they will just hit anything. Some of them want locking up for life, I'm fucking sure of that.'

Adhering to certain family and subcultural rules of behaviour normalizes actions, and the fact that Jimmy did show restraint under certain circumstances went towards legitimizing his role. But the rules also provided shackles for him. Adherence to the rules over a long time meant that they were not second nature to him; they were his nature. He could change, but he had to institute that change, otherwise he is locked in a pattern of behaviour.

Me: 'So then you got involved in assault and robbery. How did this come about?'

Jimmy: 'It was just a case of money, Paul. Skint, always having to depend on a giro. Fighting, getting put in jail, why not put it to good use? And that's how I got into robbery again. When I did the first one, that was the hardest. But once the first is over and you see how easy it is, you're like this – "Oh, this is barry!"'

Me: 'Did you get any sort of buzz from doing it?'

Jimmy: 'Oh yes! Definitely! It's a challenge because you are like that – "Oh no, how am I going to take that?" But if you are determined to take that, you will take it.'

Not only does violence become a functional part of a life-style, but it is a pattern difficult to undo. Jimmy appears to have become trapped by his own violence, but in fact he was trapped by his own rules and his perceptions.

Me: 'Do you think you get a sort of status through what you've done, assault and robbery as opposed to, say, shoplifting?'

Jimmy: 'Aye, aye! You get a name – "Oh, he's a game lad, he's done this, he's done that." So you get a name among the crew like, of being all right.'

Me: 'Do you feel frightened of yourself, that you might go over the limit?'

Jimmy: 'Aye, definitely! I mean you never get a rest, Paul, you are always on edge. Anyone like myself or Gav, anyone who has a reputation has got to watch not just the police but everyone else.'

What work with abusers does is to take the counsellor beyond the stereotype of them being bad, of their behaviour being pathological. Abusers are people in their own right, though liable to behaviour that is unacceptable. They have to be helped to understand their own behaviour and its effects, which means a service should be provided for them. Counsellors have to be aware that there is likely to be much rationalizing, minimizing or denial. This leads to the situation where counsellors should not accept at face value what is said, and this in turn can affect the working relationship.

Some counsellors may have difficulty in accepting that a client might simply be lying to them. If clients are seen on their own, there is a natural tendency to believe and even side with them. This has been reinforced by the idea that those helping and counselling abused women should not be neutral, as neutrality applied to a power-biased relationship merely reinforces the imbalance and the position of the controlling abuser. While this is true, it fails to address the fact that counsellors have to know the reality of the situation. This reality includes power-biased relationships and their effects on client behaviour and possible counsellor feelings, perspectives and intervention. Thus a balance has to be kept between the apparently pleasant Jimmy, and the reality for Leigh, his partner.

Leigh: 'Jimmy was nuts about me – until he got drunk. And then he used to use weapons on me. Once he stood over me – I was on all fours – and he landed me with a piece of wood. Wallop! wallop! wallop! There was blood splattered up the flaming fridge, blood up the cooker, a pool of blood on the floor.'

The danger of stressing non-neutrality is that it so easily leads to blaming. Instead, the counsellor should avoid this moral position and move towards the job of investigating risks to clients and how best they may be avoided. These risks are to women but also indirectly to their male partners.

Leigh: 'I wanted to get rid of him; the feeling kept building up till I couldn't take any more. Then I thought of killing him. That gave me such a fright as I was serious, completely calm. It was a relief when I had decided to kill him with a sharpened screwdriver. I never thought I had it in me, but things kept coming at me, coming at me, coming at me, and it seemed the only way. He would not go away. In the end I had to run away from my flat. Why should we take years of regular beatings?'

Counsellors discover that some men will hit their partners and yet never do the same to the children. This illustrates that even men who are violent are capable of self-control. They can be responsible for their actions, which is not the case if they are demonized, which denies their responsibility and also fails to appreciate the frightening nature of abusers who are in control.

Ben: 'When you hit you always hold a wee bit back, otherwise you would knock them doolally [senseless].'

By looking at what actually happens – where on the body a woman is hit, the refusal to stop the violence, the apparent lack of reason for the assaults – we can begin to gain an idea of what happened.

The police

The hardest tasks of the counsellor include those of being empathic and yet non-judgemental, understanding and yet not condemning, to see the imbalance in relationships but not take sides. Understanding client situations is only part of our role, as we also have to know how to use that understanding in a way that helps clients. But even understanding couples is not enough. We also have to understand those who do not understand, and these can include families but also other helpers or agents of society.

Understanding and the police

Understanding violent abusers and the abused is still not enough to ensure good counselling. Account has to be taken of how all relevant others will react to the abuse and the role that they might play. The counsellor's reaction to the role of outsiders will also be part of the overall equation.

Previous reference has been made to the Report to the Select Committee on Violence in Marriage (1975) and descriptions of two cases of battering. What may also be of interest was that another witness to the Committee, a Chief Superintendent, said that action would be considered only if the assault was deemed serious – say, a limb was broken. Damage such as black eyes was not serious. Furthermore, even in serious cases, charges would not be raised unless the woman pressed them. The severity assessment resembles to some extent the American stitch rule used by the police in Washington DC, where unless a woman received a certain number of stitches to the wounds inflicted, the case was adjudged not serious (Field and Field, 1973).

The British explanation of police procedure was that many witnesses, usually the abused women, would withdraw charges before or at Court, though as most men plead guilty to assault the argument is hardly convincing. Feminist complaints about police procedure rested in part on differential justice being afforded to women but also, indirectly, on the American finding that arresting the batterer was the most effective course of action, halving the percentage of repeat violence cases (Sherman and Berk, 1984). Prosecution also lessened the chance of abusive men being re-arrested on the same charge and the amount of violence used in any subsequent offence (Jaffe et al., 1986). In Britain, it was also suggested that arrest rates were far too low (Bell, 1981), a fact rationalized by the idea that prosecution may be bad for the family (Lerman, 1986).

Police attitudes

Attention may be drawn to recent developments in police practice. Improvements were seen as being required, and in 1990 the Home Office issued Circular 60\1990 which states, 'a violent assault in a domestic setting should be treated as seriously as a violent assault by a stranger'. However, a Home Office Research Study (1995) showed that two thirds of officers saw policing domestic violence as a different job from that of policing other violent crimes. Also, any charges brought tend to be Breach of the Peace, a minor infraction compared with assault charges. The study also pointed out that the police get annoyed when women retract charges against their partners (p. 22). The police annoyance is to some degree understandable as withdrawn cases can leave the police and solicitors open to criticism from the Court (Borkowski et al., 1983, pp. 117–18). Also, in England and Wales, the police have to second guess whether the Crown Prosecution Service is likely to proceed and whether a prosecution would be in the public interest (Buchan and Edwards, 1991). In Canada there is a no-drop policy, so that women cannot drop charges against their abusive partner. However, this is not totally effective. If women do change their minds then they may actively hinder prosecution (McGillivary, 1987). Incidently, we should not forget that policemen themselves might be violent in the home and so do not take a neutral stance when they are called to exercise discretion in their job. In fairness, it should be noted that the police may well be sympathetic; they are not totally insensitive to violence, especially when they have to deal with it themselves.

    Leigh: 'Jimmy would always do it when there were no witnesses, so I knew it was no use charging him. One of the police, I think he was a sergeant, said he couldn't do anything, but he would write to the Council to help me get a house if I wanted.'

It has been my experience that police policy and practice have changed for the better over the last ten years, but this is not yet universal. Moreover, some women have low expectations of the police and so will not bother to involve them.

Judicial system

If abused women have difficulties with the police at times, the same applies to the judicial system. Let us continue the case of Leigh, with the follow-up to the police intervention.

Leigh: 'There weren't any witnesses that time also. So I took the hair he had pulled out and put it on the counter in Leith police station, and asked if that would do. In Court, the first thing they said was, "Were you drunk?" Battered, you are completely on your own. You feel you have to deal with it all yourself. They even suggested I must enjoy it or I would leave.'

Difficulties increase if the abused woman is a mother. Even after the parents have separated, the father is likely to have visiting rights, which can put the mother at risk (Johnston, 1992). This risk has increased with the implementation of the 1989 Children's Act (Hague and Malos, 1993:152), with its stress on the importance of the family and fathers being allowed access. Furthermore, the Child Support Act of 1991 deems that women have to cooperate in tracing separated fathers. It recognizes only as an exceptional circumstance allowing a woman not to cooperate with pursuit of the ex-partner for maintenance. This is when there is a risk of harm or undue distress, which the woman has to prove. In addition, often when an ex-partner does contribute to the Child Support Agency, then he expects that contribution to give him rights, such as visiting the children (Clarke et al., 1993). Even worse, fathers might try to get the children to stay in order to lessen their liability to pay maintenance (NACAB, 1994).

If the assistance rendered by the Law and judicial system is open to criticism, then the same can be said of Housing Authorities (Bull, 1991) and social work (Maynard, 1985).

Counsellors and other agencies

Abused women may need help from a variety of sources: medical, financial, legal, housing, and educational if children are involved. To facilitate contact with outside agencies and maximize resultant consideration, counsellors should give clients an understanding of their remit and working. This is dependent on having a realistic and well-grounded relationship with agencies, a requirement more difficult in practice than might first appear. Part of the difficulty arises from counsellors themselves, who can have attitudes about such agencies ranging from indifference, to being patronizing, resistant, to outright mentally confrontational. Whatever the rights or wrongs of the situation, counsellors have to do the best for their clients and this includes cooperating with those they might prefer to see as the enemy.

Counsellors have attitudes resulting from their own backgrounds, experiences and also from their views of what is right. This can come in part from their beliefs, both moral and theoretical; the latter coming in part from past training.

3   OPPRESSION THROUGH THEORY

Introduction

Explanations, hypotheses and theories of partner violence are sometimes seen as neutral pictures of what happens rather than perceptions, moulded by time, place, experience, and the history of ideas. There is no neutrality in explanations of human behaviour. Indeed, every theory of human behaviour can also be seen as a social and political statement, reflecting the social context of the times and of the theoreticians who construct them. This applies to theories of partner violence, which are influenced in content by patriarchy. It is very difficult to rid theories of such influence. Any testing process used for the confirmation of particular theories can itself be patriarchally biased, resting on patriarchal definitions, methods and the modes of drawing of conclusions.

There are many theories applicable to violent relationships and it is helpful if counsellors are familiar with them. These theories may be assumed to be correct by counsellors, but also by other counsellors, other helpers or by clients. Sometimes theoretical concepts are not even questioned but taken as facts.

Biological theories

The most patriarchal of theories are those which rest on a strictly biological basis. They rely for their explanatory power on the concept that men and women are biologically different, and it is this difference that explains not only male and female behaviours but also the fact that basically they cannot be changed. This leads to the concept of what is natural – male behaviour for men, female behaviour for women. The corollary is that there is unnatural behaviour.

These theories relevant to partner violence include those based on ideas of genetically-based aggression. Some genetic abnormalities produce aggressive and violent behaviour as in Lesch-Nyhn's disease (Palmour, 1983). However, arguing from such a small sample of genetic abnormalities to the behaviour of those with normal genetic make-up is dubious. Also, there is no evidence for inherited aggression or violence. Few attempts have been made to relate biological factors directly to violence. One example of this approach was to see the XYY chromosome in men as productive of violence, its presence explaining male violence. The difficulty is that there is no evidence that this chromosome in fact causes violence (Schiavi et al., 1984). Another model is based on aggression being a product of the fight-or-flight response and subject to changes in the levels of the neurotransmitters serotonin and norepinephrine (Brodie and Shore, 1957), and low serotonin metabolism is linked with violence (van Praag, 1991). However, neurotransmitter levels vary naturally in the individual (Mazur and Lamb, 1980). Sex hormones, which differentiate between men and women, have been linked directly to partner violence. Unfortunately, there is little evidence that raised levels of testosterone or other androgens affect aggression (Dixson, 1980). Again, the assumption that hormonal levels are static for any individual is unfounded.

Naive psychological theories

There is a continuum of theories which move from those centred on the body, the biological, to those of the mind, the psychological and the psychiatric, all of which reflect differing degrees of patriarchy.

There are psychological theories which are strongly biologically based and view aggression and violence as an instinct or drive, which helps the survival of the individual and the species. Such theories, based on the behaviour of animals, fail to point out that partner violence as opposed to aggression is characteristic only of humans.

Some theories which actually attended to human behaviour centred on variations in parent–child bonding: the absence of fathers in childhood leading men to become wife-beaters (Campbell, 1985); inadequacies in the mother–child bonding (Galenson, 1986) or through the psychopathology of the mother (Osofosky, 1988). Not only is there no good evidence for such theories, but they put the responsibility for partner violence on external or internal factors, not on the people involved – men in particular.

Personality trait theories

A more sophisticated view seeks to connect partner violence with its participants, and also to explain why some men are more violent than others through personality traits (Ball, 1977; Elbow, 1977). There are two main problems with this approach. First, it is insufficient as relational and situational factors are being ignored, so partner violence cannot be adequately explained (Gelles and Cornell, 1985:71). Second, the approach taken was grounded in psychiatric thought. Women who were abused were seen as suffering from psychological disorders, though research showed women who had experienced violence were no different from other women (Star et al., 1981; Okun, 1986; Gondolf, 1988). Despite such weaknesses, clinical intervention and treatment did not reject the concepts (Davis, 1987), as they fitted in well with existing modes of helping and intervention. So these forms of help contributed to women seeing partner violence as their fault (Ferraro and Johnson, 1982).

Learned helplessness and love addiction

A less deterministic theory was that of learned helplessness, developed from Seligman's experiments with animals. These were confined in dangerous, high-stress situations from which they could not escape. As a result, they eventually lapsed into passive, helpless behaviour (Walker, 1978/79). This behaviour, learned helplessness, was forwarded as an explanation of why women did not leave their violent partners.

The cause of violence was seen as being in the victim and her upbringing; rigid sex-role socialization and being treated as a pretty doll rather than a growing girl. The seeds of helplessness, once planted in childhood, spread into the women's relationships with men. They see men as all-powerful and incapable of being stopped in their behaviour. The cumulative exposure to violence produced behaviour that was given the label 'battered woman syndrome'. Walker saw the batterer as producing a cycle within the woman of tension build-up, followed by an explosion when tension was released, followed by a stage of loving contrition when the perpetrator promises not to repeat the behaviour. Repeated behaviour results in a depressive syndrome characterized by low self-esteem, self-blame, fatalism, passivity and a reluctance to seek or accept help. This condition is healed through therapy, which breaks dependency, the learning of communication skills and empowering themselves to become more assertive.

This model ignores the fact that women are not helpless but seek help from numerous sources (Pahl, 1978; Dobash and Dobash, 1979; Dobash et al., 1985), and my experience confirms that the picture of helplessness is simply untrue. What may seem to be helplessness is shock, from which the woman soon recovers, or lack of relative risk-free options. But the real problem with this explanation is the cause being seen to be within the woman. Women are seen as suffering from depressive behaviour which explains their illogical conduct. What was not considered is that their behaviour was quite normal and any problems are to be found in their assailants, and the fact that the violence is inflicted by men.

Another victim-centred approach has been that of Norwood (1985) who sees women who end up in bad relationships as being addicted to such relationships because they love too much. She sees women who suffer persistent violence as seeking out dangerous men and situations. However, there is little evidence for such a simplistic idea, and I have not found that women choose danger rather than what they see as a happy life. Some women have good relationships before ending up in a violent one, but in no way do I see that as a search for a bad relationship.

However, the idea that women are in some way the cause of violence inflicted upon them is surely so extraordinary that it requires an explanation in itself.

Female masochism and partner violence

The idea that women in some way enjoy the violence inflicted on them rests on the idea of masochism. In 1886, Krafft-Ebing, in his book *Psychopathia sexualis*, drew attention to forms of sexual behaviour including sadism and masochism. These he took as the extremes of male and female behaviour (Hauser, 1994). Such behaviours were then pathologized, and applied to the general population by Freud, who said: 'Women need to be overpowered by men to experience sexual pleasure in their vagina' (Freud, 1956). Similar views were expressed by other psychoanalysts, even if they were women such as Deutsch (1944) and Bonaparte (1963), both of whom described intercourse as a masochistic act for women.

Apart from the lack of testing and the methodological weaknesses in such arguments, we have to appreciate that Freud's thought reflected the social climate of the time (Brown, J., 1964) and its patriarchal and sexist view of women (Millett, 1972:179). Apologists have proclaimed that his work is not a product of patriarchy but an analysis of it (Mitchell, 1975). This runs counter to my reading of it. Freud also misunderstood masochism, which is intended to stimulate the use of imagery. The pain produced releases endorphins, morphine-like chemicals in the brain, which give a feeling of exhilaration. This effect may be used by either men or women (Weinberg et al., 1985). Codewords are used by masochists to ensure stimulation does not become unendurable (Omerod, 1994). All of this may be contrasted with the situation of abused women who have little possibility of stopping or escaping the unwanted violence.

Nevertheless, psychoanalysts have viewed women's decisions to stay in an abusive relationship as examples of female masochism (Snell et al., 1964). Also, self-punishment, submission and suffering are taken as female characteristics (Shainess, 1984), which trigger or exacerbate crimes against them (Shainess, 1986). The sexist aspect of female masochism may be seen partly by the fact that though it is emphasized, little is said about the possibility of male sadism. Perhaps the final irony is that truly consensual sado-masochism is not viewed as violent or abusive by most commentators. However, the legacy of the highly patriarchal theories of Freud is that women have been blamed for violence. Psychoanalysis has been most powerful in the United States where its theorizing is a major factor affecting conviction rates for sexual offences (LeGrand, 1973). It has even led to the idea of victim-precipitated rape, where the victim is seen as the cause of the crime (Amir, 1971), by allowing some form of sexual intimacy or not resisting strongly enough. The idea, unsurprisingly, has been much criticized (Weis and Borges, 1973).

The nature of sado-masochism is decided by experts, not by those involved in such behaviour (Weinberg et al., 1985). But this psycho-analytic concept may be recycled into the public domain, affecting subjects' views of themselves. It even lives on in psychiatry. Although the term has been taken out of the *Diagnostic and Statistical Manual of Mental Disorders* (American Psychiatric Association, 1987), the definitive reference book of the American Psychiatric Association, it has reappeared under the guise of 'self-defeating personality disorder' (Caplan, 1987).

Psychiatrizing violence

The role of experts stating the normal nature of human behaviour is most strong in psychiatry, where violence has been taken as symptomatic of a clinical condition (Schlesinger et al., 1982:148). The terms 'battered spouse' and 'battered woman' were added to the International Classification of Diseases in 1979, as personal interactions were progressively psychiatrized.

The extreme psychiatric view was that women who were battered suffered from serious emotional and mental illnesses and should be institutionalized for long-term therapy (Bowder, 1979). A rather less extreme view is that of explaining women's reactions to violence, through the Stockholm Syndrome, where enforced proximity increases a woman's attachment to her abuser, an idea taken from the experience of those taken hostage (Dutton, 1992). Unfortunately, there is no evidence that abused women do not experience greater attachment through being abused. My experience points to the opposite.

What is actually happening is that psychiatrists are treating women who have been abused as abnormal, paying little attention to the abuser. When they do, abusers are labelled as having anti-social personality disorders (Grossman, 1991), which is largely meaningless and is little more than a reason not to treat them.

Family therapy and systems

Partner violence may be seen as purely individual, as an interaction between a couple, or as involving a group if there are children or others in the home. It has been pointed out that what happens in a relatively closed system such as a family is that one action leads to a reaction, which in turn produces further reactions. The final outcome is a complex series of actions and reactions, of feedback and feedforward loops. Such complexity makes it impossible to identify just one person who caused any specific piece of behaviour in the family. This means there is no linear causality in the functioning of families, but rather, a more complex circular causality. Another outcome is that it is impossible to say that any one person has total power in such a system (Bateson, 1972).

The difficulty is that the concept of circular as opposed to linear causality fails to take into account personal power (Dell, 1989) and the preponderance of male to female violence. Also, putting the responsibility of the violence on the family functioning rather than the violator seemed unsatisfactory. The neutral stance of the therapist as a concept was attacked by feminist workers who saw that marriage and the family are central elements of a patriarchal society (Bersoni and Chen, 1988), and there is no neutrality in the family. Personal relationships are immersed in both societal and interpersonal sexist practices that saturate and constitute women's experiences (Yllo, 1984). This means that a neutral stance is not acceptable as it reinforces the existing inequality in the family or between a couple (Willbach, 1989).

Second-order theories

These objections were taken on board and there emerged second-order theories. These were largely begun by Bateson, who was reluctant to intervene in people's lives. It was suggested that family workers had to rid themselves of theories as they entered each therapy session, as Bion had advocated (1970), and it was not necessary to produce any change (Hoffman, 1985:395). Clients are expected to orientate themselves so they will be content, whether the situation changes or not (Atkinson and Heath, 1990). Clearly, this is little use to clients who are being abused. In fact, the actual methods used for second-order therapy substitute one form of therapist control for another (Golann, 1988), however actions of the therapist are described, such as giving the family system a 'bump', (Hoffman, 1985:388), or a 'nudge' (Tomm, 1987).

The other difficulty was the disavowal of power in human situations, which led to the idea that there is no given reality, so all accounts or stories are equally valid. This flight from realism (Parry, 1991) fails as it allows an invented account, or a lie is given as much weight as any other account. A compromise position was then forwarded that some client accounts could be better than others (Pocock, 1995), but this led to the difficulty of giving preference criteria, other than falling back on some concept of a given reality. However, post-modernists argue that therapists do not need to know the truth; their job is to know how to help others (Goolishian and Anderson, 1992). But this also requires power. This results in the curious idea that therapists do have power but simply do not use it (Cantwell and Holmes, 1994).

The problem for me of post-modernist thought, whether constructivist, phenomenological or deconstructionist, is the rejection of an objective reality. This is based on the idea that what we actually know of the world is in the form of concepts. But everyone has their own concepts so everyone has different realities. But no one could function with separate realities; we must be able to communicate and interact with others. Thus the world is what we agree it is, through the sharing of meanings. There is no ultimate truth and no objective reality. However, this fails to distinguish adequately between reality, a representation of reality, and a description of that representation of reality. The confusion of these, which is a confusion of categories, leads to absurdities or the misuse of language. For example, the use of deconstructionism was started in order to analyse historical texts; it is an analysis of language. Thus it is not applicable to real life or even to scientific statements that are capable of refutation. Similarly, meanings are not about things, about reality, but about the use of language. They change over time, and it is research and investigation, often by science, that tend to change them as more is known about reality. The danger of idealism in theories is that such liberalism – that anyone's idea and so anyone's reality is as good as anyone else's – leads to moral relativism and the inability to assign responsibility for actions on to anyone. And this is precisely the course used by abusers.

Theories and abuse by counsellors

Those subjected to partner violence find that their suffering does not end with the physical abuse. It is compounded by the actions of others, whose attitudes and beliefs are related to theories of personal violence. If these people hold positions of power, whether political, judicial, professional or academic, then they are likely to further oppress the abused.

The theories alluded to, and only a few have been mentioned, all tend to have three principal weaknesses. They are unproved and at times even unprovable. They are very much products of particular social conditions, and tell us more about those conditions and the theoreticians than about human behaviour (Pastore, 1949; Sherwood and Nataupsky, 1968). Finally, so much emphasis is given to the theoretical model that facts may be re-interpreted to fit them (Shields, 1975). The outcome is that some counsellors have taken views of relationship violence far removed from reality. Linked with counselling practice, the result has been the possibility of further abuse of women by counsellors.

Helping and the nature of partner violence

Although many theories about violence against women run counter to common sense, yet they appear to get backing from the fact that they may be used as guides to successful helping and counselling. This apparent confirmation is open to several objections.

Counsellors, as has been noted earlier, tend to miss or ignore cases of violence in relationships. Thus how useful helping is when so much is not done is open to question. In addition, it is assumed that helping is effective and so supports the theories employed. Indeed, some researchers are convinced of its effectiveness (Luborsky et al., 1975; Parloff, 1978; Smith et al., 1980; Lambert et al., 1986) yet the research methodology of such studies was weak (Shapiro and Shapiro, 1982; Strube and Hartmann, 1982; Prioleau et al., 1983), lacking tight randomized selectioning process and controls, and failing to take account of the placebo effect by not using blind trials. Caution had also been expressed about the effectiveness of marital and family therapy (Gurman and Kniskern, 1977; Wells and Dezen, 1978; Bagarozzi and Rauen, 1981). Doubts about the effectiveness of psychotherapy and counselling rest largely on a lack of scientific evidence (Epstein, 1995). Post-modernist researchers have tried to escape the rigours of scientific testing by employing less demanding methodologies such as single-subject designs (Kratchowill, 1978), case formulation approaches (Persons, 1991) and the heuristic paradigm (Heineman Pieper, 1989). These may be seen as acceptable methods of scientific enquiry (Silverman, 1991), but give only the weakest degree of confirmation of effectiveness.

The fact that it is trained professionals who are counselling or helping is seen to be a guarantee of effectiveness. However, the usefulness of training has to be questioned, though there is little convincing research on this subject. In family therapy one study has shown that training produced gains during the first year but this was counteracted by a further year's work (Stolk and Perlesz, 1990). Another perspective is to look at the work of helpers who have not been trained, the paraprofessionals. Surprisingly, it was discovered that the paraprofessionals had slightly better client outcomes on the whole (Durlak, 1979). This brought a strong response from Nietzel and Fisher (1981), who were, however, unable to dismiss the result. A more sophisticated study by Hattie, Sharpley and Rogers (1984) again showed that the outcome results favoured paraprofessionals. Thus professional training is not known to be effective, though it is assumed to be so.

The role of couples counselling

The criticism of effectiveness of helping may itself be criticized in that helping should be directed not to individuals but to the couple. Individual helping fails to take account of the fact that any help given could be undone by the partner (Hafner, 1977), so it was suggested that all couples should be treated together (Martin, 1977), thus eliminating the feelings of rejection, jealousy and hostility by the excluded partner. This became doctrine, especially for those counsellors wedded to a systems approach (Haley, 1967), even though this approach is not always successful (Keeney, 1979). In cases of partner violence, many women are reluctant to talk about it unless the counsellor raises the topic. However, if the partner or spouse is present, then women clients may never mention it at all. Disclosure of violence in the presence of the male partner increases the risk of retaliatory violence (Giles-Sim, 1983; Pressman, 1989), but even fear of disclosure can result in battering. As a result, it is best if couples are seen separately at first until it is discovered whether there is violence involved (Goldner, 1993).

Seeing couples together might seem to be the more effective method of helping, but this risks actually exacerbating the violence. For this reason, feminists tend to advocate the use of battering groups for men and support groups for battered women (Bograd, 1984: Pressman, 1989) as preferred forms of helping. In fact, any helping can be for good, or for ill; it can bring about a deterioration of the client's situation if care is not taken (Lambert et al., 1977). Abused women run special risks as counselling clients, as being helped can increase the likelihood of violence.

Further thoughts about helping

Battered women may be offered help and, feeling vulnerable, they are likely to accept. Such help may turn out to be useful, ineffective, or oppressive. Helpers almost always want to be of use and not worsen the plight of women in or from violent partnerships, but this does not mean they will not end up being oppressive. Good intentions are simply not enough. Help given may be of debatable usefulness and such help may also rest on an unsubstantiated theoretical basis.

The question now arises as to why this state of affairs continues. In part it arises through helpers being given training to work in an approved manner, but seldom investigating the effectiveness of what they are doing (Masson, 1992). Trainers are equally unlikely to suggest that helping may be ineffective or counter-productive.Training uses certain theories which are assumed to be correct or partially correct. These theories can determine their own forms of assessment and so can become self-verifying. The fact that work with clients can meet with apparent success seems to justify the training and its theoretical assumptions. Helping practices become almost immune to attack once the practitioners are professionalized. Helpers are then in a position to forward and employ highly dubious theories (Ofshe and Watters, 1995) and forms of therapy (Masson, 1990). This reflects the fact that social helping has become an industry (Halmos, 1978) which continues to grow (Pedder, 1991), and not only offers help but increasingly, as in the United States, markets and creates a market for it (Zilbergeld, 1983).

Using theories in counselling

Much of counselling today is eclectic, with counsellors borrowing theories either because they favour them or because they judge them to be appropriate for specific clients and their situations. I also believe that many theoretical concepts, such as masochism, have entered the general consciousness and so we tend to employ them without really considering their nature and applicability. When counselling women in violent relationships, apart from being aware of the theory we might be using or misusing, there are specific areas to watch.

1. By adhering to a simple medical model we pathologize relational violence and move it to the sphere of abnormality. This gives the impression that it is uncommon and so counsellors rarely consider it, whereas it happens in a great number of couples. Thus violence is missed or the signs ignored because of its apparent infrequency.

2. Some theories follow the medical model and see violence as applicable purely to individuals and not to society as a whole. They then imagine that counselling will be sufficient, rather than seeing it as merely one aspect of what should be an overall interagency helping. There can be a sidelining of practical issues such as risk, security, accommodation and finance which can be major impediments to some form of resolution of abused women's difficulties. In addition, counsellors have failed to recognize the need for social

measures, such as changes in legislation and anti-discriminatory measures. Admittedly, these are not within the remit of counselling but do indicate that more than counselling is required.

3. The medical model also makes it more likely that the woman is seen as contributing to the violence. Apart from theoretical views that allow this to be possible, we also have to accept that it is women rather than their partners who come for help. If helpers are to do anything then it is with the person in front of them, and seeing them as pathological does legitimize intervention.

We should beware of assuming that social theories are similar to physical theories, neutral descriptions of the world. In fact, social theories are influenced by the prevailing social conditions and the nature of the relevant theorists. In particular, many theories of violence can be seen as being essentially male and promoted, albeit not consciously, as instruments to maintain control.

Feminist helping

One theoretical approach has attempted to take on board some of the difficulties and present a more acceptable and non-abusive form of helping. It springs from the general feminist perspective that women's problems arise from their oppression and sex-role socialization. These result both in internal barriers, such as low self-esteem and powerlessness, and external barriers, such as hierarchies being erected and subordinate roles being allocated to them. Such barriers make life problems more likely for women, though they might not realize the fact nor relate their problems to patriarchy in society. Feminist help rests partly on a client-centred perspective, with an emphasis on client choice and empowerment. However, there is also a movement away from the purely individualistic outlook to linking up with other women who shared similar difficulties (Greenspan, 1983).

Support for this perspective rests on the fact that the great majority of adult abuse cases are of women being battered. Male power characterizes society as a whole and is also to be found in the family. Power variations in the partnership, such as where there is status inconsistency and couples are of two different statuses (Hornung et al., 1981), or where there is domination by one partner, especially if that partner is the woman (Coleman and Straus, 1980), render violence more likely.

The outcome has been an approach to battered women which includes the following:

1. The provision of practical help, such as Women's Aid hostels. These provide sanctuary and also help with the practical process of

leaving a partner. The best course is to help the client devise safety plans for herself and her children, if any, (Fleming, 1979) and also to rehearse such plans (Neidig and Friedman, 1984). There should be a step-by-step overall plan. This short-term plan for personal safety should be distinguished from the long-term one of separation and independence. It can be unhelpful to press women towards premature separation before they have begun to deal with some of their feelings (Walker, 1979), as this can turn the helping process into a power struggle between the abused and the helper (Stulberg, 1989).

2. Help is given by voluntary helpers, often those who have them-selves been abused in the past. There is some distrust of profes-sional experts because of their abuse by theory, and reliance is placed on peer-helping instead. Helping organizations are aimed to be non-hierarchical. There is a promotion of ideas of support as opposed to therapy, as the latter continues the concept of patriar-chal expertise and imbalanced power relationships.

3. Empowerment and self-determination are aided by consciousness raising, where members come to understand their situation based on a feminist analysis. This can be extended by the use of advocacy and the promotion of women's rights and causes in society in general.

Counselling and approaches to helping women subjected to partner violence

By noting the patriarachal views and practices in society, feminists have highlighted an important factor. Only by taking account of that factor when counselling can we really hope to be of use, but the following are some aspects of feminist practice that require modification.

1. The idea that the abusers and abused should attend groups fails to attend to client choice and the fact that many people prefer not to join groups. Also, groupworking is not necessarily helpful (Lockley, 1996), and hierarchies in groups cannot be eliminated entirely (Freeman, 1972).

2. Some of the suspicions of professionalization are well merited (Kelly, 1989), especially if they include rule by experts, and the promotion of neutrality and depoliticization. Unfortunately, anti-professionalism can also lead to a lack of critical self-monitoring and universally high-quality service.

Summary and partner violence in context

Partner violence is one of many forms of overall human violence. There is always the danger that by restricting any investigation to just one chosen area, this can itself act as a source of bias. Although patriarchy is a major overall factor in intimate relationships, it is not the only factor. These other factors occur to a greater degree in other forms of violence, but also apply to partner violence, and they include the following.

1. The greater the approval of legitimized violence, the greater the rate of infant homicide (Baron and Straus, 1988). Similarly, a high support for killing in war is associated with a high murder rate (Archer and Gartner, 1984), child abuse (Shwed and Straus, 1979) and rape.

   Social legitimization may be said to permit a culture of violence. On the other hand, the passing of specific laws, as was done in Denver, along with the giving of information and raising of public awareness of the issues, helped to decrease the rate of child abuse, as measured by the rate of hospitalization, to 5 per cent of the initial figure for the period 1960–75 (Kempe and Kempe, 1978).

2. Public violence in Western countries is mainly an arena of young men pitted against other young men. The extreme example is the United States where not only are adolescent youths involved in violence, but they also have a worryingly high probability of being killed (Children's Safety Network, 1991). The risks are seven times greater for black youths (Roth, 1994). Interestingly, a recent trend has been the increase in the amount of girls involved in gang violence (Hausman et al., 1994). In Britain public violence is also most commonly found among young men, but we should bear in mind that of all reported physical assaults on women, a third of the assailants were women (Widom and Maxfield, 1984).

3. Abuse towards the elderly is comparatively little researched, but data from the United States shows the abuse originates more from spouses than adult care-giving children or relatives (Pillemer and Suitor, 1989), and can be a continuing form of abuse begun early in the marriage (Sengstock, 1991). The majority of abusers are men (Tatara, 1990), the ratio being given as 3:1. This is a lower figure than the ratio of younger men:women abusers and might be explained by differing strengths and powers in the relationship (Sengstock, 1991).

4. If we look at physical child abuse then we see that much of it revolves around the question of child control and discipline. Force

may be used to try to control children (Oldershaw et al., 1986; Trickett and Kuczynski, 1986), and this often includes physical means such as slapping or spanking (Herzeberger et al., 1981). The reason given for physical disciplining is that children are misbehaving and need to be kept in line. This was often in response to either crying or screaming in very young children or for 'being naughty' (Kadushin and Martin, 1981). But what is naughty is very much up to the interpretion of parents (Brandon, 1976). This interpretation can vary, especially if the parents are under the influence of high emotion, as when arguing. Parents might then interpret almost any child action as needing physical intervention and so be physically abusive (Reid et al., 1981). When children are physically abused it is usually the result of perceived disciplining by one or both parents (Schindler and Arkowitz, 1986). In the United States, of all officially reported cases the assailants were estimated to be male in 40 per cent (Bersherov, 1978) to 55 per cent (American Humane Society, 1978) of cases. Information from a British shelter showed 54 per cent of abusive husbands and 37 per cent of abused wives had abused their children (Gayford, 1975).

5. Although it has been argued that partnership violence between lesbians is not the same as heterosexual battering, it is important to see the process as being virtually identical. From a reading of Kerry Lobel's book (1986) on the subject, the similarities covered include a difficulty in accepting the idea of such violence generally, that the violence increases in severity and frequency over time, and that the batterer can have battered previous partners. Also, the lesbian batterer is often jealous and possessive, does not accept responsibility for her actions, and may apologize but still not stop the pattern of abuse. Victims can have pent-up anger and thoughts of killing their partner, discover that resistance to the violence can make matters worse, and after leaving the relationship may be tempted to return and are usually pressurized to do so.

Like violence between heterosexual couples, lesbian violence is common and has been given an estimated incidence of 40 per cent among couples (Bologna et al., 1987). In fact, it is easier to see lesbian battering as a product of intimacy and note its association with jealousy, possessiveness and other male battering characteristics.

Result of comparing forms of violence

Violence, as may have been noted, is not simply gender-based but is founded on power inequality. This is an important observation, as some writers have emphasized gender alone, rather than gender as a form of insititutionalized power imbalance. Applied to counselling, we find that has to be modified in order to take account of such imbalances. Furthermore, we see that other forms of violence are not totally separate but are other aspects of power imbalances.

Women who are pathologized

If women's behaviour is explained in a way different from the way those women view it, then there have to be very good reasons indeed for adhering to such a different view. Nor is simply referring to expertise sufficient, as expert views are often no more than the pathologizing of abused women in accordance with the patriarchal values endemic in society. Nevertheless, three possible situations appear to support the experts' perspective that simple explanations are not enough.

1. Women who are abused are often reluctant to end the relationship. This might suggest masochism but a more commonsense view comes from women who find leaving difficult due to financial and housing reasons, the upset to the children, and threats by their partner if they did leave. They might also have positive feelings for their partner, or be misled by his excuses, apologies and promises not to repeat the action.

2. Similarly, some women who leave their abusive partners later return to them. On the other hand, 90 per cent of such women were still away from their partners after eighteen months. More-over, many of the returnees would leave again if given the opportunity (Binney et al., 1981). They usually return because the difficulties in (1) above have not been solved.

Strings of abusive relationships

The third situation, clients who go from one abusive relationship to another, requires a more detailed explanation. A woman subjected to violence by one partner might be seen as having bad luck, but when the woman has a run of four or five abusive relationships then we might well conclude that this woman must in some way be bringing about the abuse. However, there are more commonplace explanations of strings of abusive relationships. First, if the likelihood of bad relationships is relatively high, then it is statistically probable that a substantial number of women will have strings of bad relationships. Second, abusive relationships are more likely than non-abusive ones to break up, and after ending there will be a greater proportion of abusive men in those available. Third, it has been noted that abusive relationships may not be abusive at the very start, so women can move into further relationships without an inkling of how they will turn out. Also, some women who have left very bad relationships may move to others which seem preferable – even if abusive.

Leigh: 'Jimmy caught me when I was vulnerable. There were folk after me, and I thought he would protect me. Well, he did do that, no one bothered me, but in time I discovered he too would hit me.'

In addition, if women have care of children, which is often the case, there may seem to be fewer options available to them.

Annmarie: 'I thought it would be good for the kids to have a father and there aren't many men who will take on a whole family. He was prepared to do it.'

The irony is that the significance of these strings of abusive relationships is related to women, not men. Patriarchy results in men being seen as superior and so they are not pathologized, though there is more reason to do so.

Pearl: 'He hit the lassie before me, and since we've split up, Josh has been with two lassies permanent I know of, and he has battered the both of them.'

As with the female masochism debate, the role of men tends to be ignored. In addition, there is a tendency to take too cognitive a view. The seriousness of the abused woman's situation might be no more important than the fear, anger or anxiety she feels. But these feelings diminish, especially in the absence of the male abuser. So another relationship, even if there are risks attached, does not seem so bad after a while, and probably better than the idea of living on one's own.

Summary of abused lives

When discussing partnership violence, there is a tendency to concentrate on the physical risks and dangers. However, there is plainly much more to abused lives. They can be happy on occasions, but the pattern of abuse shapes the relationships. There is fear, anxiety, jealousy, possessiveness, blame and self-blame, attempts at coping and retaliation to an extent that is hard to comprehend to those unaccustomed to violence. When mention is made of leaving a partner and escaping the violence, we have to realize that there are many matters to be considered. What is involved is not simply changing abusive behaviour or being abused: the whole of a person's life may be involved.

4   BEFORE COUNSELLING IN
VIOLENT RELATIONSHIPS

Introduction

Counselling in violent relationships can result in considerable benefits for the women involved. Alternatively, it can make matters worse, even to the point of endangering those being helped. Good intentions simply are not enough. Any help given has to be effective and take on board the fact that poor work can have serious consequences. In addition, the intervention arrival of a third party, a counsellor, into the life of a couple in a violent relationship brings its own risks. In one case, I saw a client, with her husband's agreement, on a regular basis. Later, I discovered that client was battered every time she returned home from seeing me. Thus it is essential that even experienced counsellors should review their practice when working with women in violent relationships to minimize dangers to clients.

Counselling and power

The review of practice has to be fundamental and concentrate on the concept of power, in particular the imbalance of power between counsellor and client. This reflects a similar imbalance of power within the clients' relationships. Counsellors should work on themselves and look to their own experiences with power and relationships. This is an ongoing process whereby counsellors discuss their past, especially those involving power imbalance and violence. The former are very common and include parental, school and work relationships. Such discussions examine what happened in the past but also bring the past into the present, integrating the past into present beliefs and attitudes. This can be done by counsellors reflecting on the past and tracing out how it has affected them over the years. There is no simple cause and effect, rather a gradual synthesis of many different events from the past which may influence later personal development. The same can be done with violence from the past, and often the nature of violence has to be illustrated as counsellors can take a limited approach, and see violence as not impinging on their past. Smacks from parents, beatings at school, fights in the school playground, violence in sport, are to be added to fights in the home, both as children and as adults.

All of this may be connected by counsellors to their attitudes and beliefs around power and violence. It is essential that counsellors are able to get in touch with their feelings and allow themselves to honestly investigate their views of personal relationships. This should also include ideas about arguments, oppression, conflict and resolution. These can be linked with discussions about gender roles, attitudes, and boundaries.

Conflict

One important aspect of counsellors' self-analysis is the review of their abilities to cope with expressed feelings and conflict. Clients under stress are likely to be very forthright, and some counsellors can feel very uncomfortable with the sheer intensity of the emotions expressed, and this can even be to the point where they are disenabled by that intensity. Some counsellors do have difficulties with clients in conflict and this requires attention. Counselling can help clients to seek paths to a degree of freedom from relational dependency, but this can lead to increased conflict.

Thus counsellors have to be prepared for arguments and see them not as precursors to violence but as a way clients can learn to pre-empt violence (Infante, 1987). In fact, counsellors have to assist clients to confront conflictual issues, as avoidance is unhelpful in the long term (Gottman and Krokoff, 1989). Some people see satisfaction in a relationship as related to the lack of conflict, whereas a more realistic view is that it is more likely to be linked to how conflict is handled (Noller et al, 1994). So for work on self, it is useful if counsellors pay attention to how they have dealt, and do deal, with conflict.

Counsellor gender

Client self-expression may seem to be affected by the counsellor's gender. Male counsellors can be seen as bearers of patriarchal values and reinforcers of male power in relationships. This theoretical concern should be tested against empirical evidence. What my clients have told me – and it should be said they are not a representative sample of abused women – is that what they wanted was someone they could talk to and with whom they could feel at ease. To my surprise, this was unrelated to gender, as one client explained:

Chantel: 'I just wanted someone to speak to, someone I could speak to. When you are like that, man or woman doesn't matter. It never really registered that you were a man. Of course, if you had started shouting or whatever, then it would have come up in lights – "Man". I suppose it was when I was about to tell you and said, "I don't know if I can trust you." Most people say, "Of course you can, blah, blah, blah", but you said, "That's right, you don't know whether I should be trusted. You can trust me, but perhaps other people have said that to you ..." Too fucking right I thought, and I just started talking. I didn't decide you were OK or ... could be ... I just went ahead. Yap, yap, yap, yap, yap.'

This seems to apply even when clients have strong feelings about gender and related issues. This is because if there is a good relationship then the client scarcely notices counsellors as people.

Leigh: 'See, all men are bastards. There's not one who's worth a shit. Bastards. Oh, I don't mean you, Paul, by the way. I don't think of you as a man. Oh, no! I don't mean that either!'

The subject is of some importance as writers on working with abused women do not often ask them what clients want and how they see the situation. They also tend to underestimate the ability of clients to appreciate the interactive nature of counselling and other forms of help.

Joyce: 'At first I didn't care who it was, man, woman, or chimpanzee. Once we got talking then sex was the last thing on my mind. In time, you find you use different people in different ways. So I found it useful to speak to women.'

Me: 'Would it have helped if you changed to a woman counsellor?'

Joyce: 'No. As I said, it was good to have both men and women. You noticed me as a woman and that was important, made me feel normal. When you feel like shit it gives you a wee boost. Mind, the last thing I would have wanted was any man trying something on or making remarks.'

Core values

Power relationships affect not merely consellors as persons but also their counselling. If we look at the person-centred approach then the core values still apply, but account has to be taken of the effect of power. Thus in imbalanced counselling relationships when working with women clients subjected to violence, empathy can degenerate into sympathy, and positive regard changes into clients being seen solely as victims. Acceptance of the client can drift into condescension. When dealing with male abusers, empathy, positive regard and acceptance can prove difficult. All of this should not happen if we treat clients as people in their own right. Yet to be a counsellor is to take up a role, and there is the temptation to see clients in their role as clients rather than people placed into a role.

The situation is even more difficult in practice, as people are aware of how others regard them or might regard them. Thus abused women can concentrate on their suffering and ignore the positive aspects of the relationship or fail to mention it in order to be seen as a victim. They may also want to present an acceptable face to counsellors and so will agree and make promises for the sake of the counsellor rather than themselves. In a similar vein, male abusers can seem very reasonable and cooperative. Such possible client behaviour can reinforce the tendency of counsellors to drift away from the Rogerian core values.

Truth and untruth

One of the difficulties that counsellors experience in relation to core values in practice is the fact that clients do not always tell the truth. In violent relationships where there is a power imbalance, there is likely to be a lot of covering up, defensiveness and misdirection. Often couples have got into the habit of interacting in a basically dishonest way and may continue to do so in counselling, even when it is in their best interests to be honest. Seeing clients individually decreases defensiveness but there is an increasing temptation for the counsellor to accept everything that has been said. The difficulty comes when the counsellor discovers what has been said is not true and known to be such by the client.

Counselling skills

Counsellors also have to consider extending their counselling skills to take account of power imbalances between themselves and clients, and between client partners. Importance has to be given to differing skills, and when they should be employed.

1. Listening is a very important skill, but, in the context of long-term counselling can be an exercise in power, the expert interacting with a client. No matter how sharing and empowering counsellors think they might be, their role still puts them in power. However, there are ways of lessening the imbalance, such as restricting the amount of counsellor listening. This may be surprising as listening is thought to be the major counselling skill. However, this is not necessarily the case. By not talking, the counsellor reinforces a professional role and sets up a power imbalance. Furthermore, any counsellor remark carries a great deal of weight simply because such interventions are rare and is also a way of directly influencing the client.

2. Thus counsellors talk and contribute more when working with individuals or couples in violent relationships, but this has to be

done in a particular manner. Counsellors should talk and take power in the counselling situation. This is required as in individual work with abused women, they are often traumatized or come with such low self-esteem they are unable to control themselves or their life. When working with couples, the abusive man will have control and this has to be changed to achieve progress. Once the counsellor has power, then it must be handed back slowly to ensure the woman, whether by herself or as part of a couple, is able to gradually take control of her life. Taking control is relatively easy as the role of counsellor – of helper, professional and expert – allows access to power from the very start. Returning power to women clients is not so simple and requires long-term work. It rests on various actions by the counsellor.

3. When working with couples, counsellors by active intervention have to ensure both clients keep to a useful agenda and not simply use the session to continue their habitual arguments or use it simply as an occasion to express feelings and no more. The counsellor has to show women clients that they are being listened to, that they are important as people in their own right, and yet the counsellor is not taking sides against their partners. Though most apparent when working with couples, the same applies when counselling individual abused women.

4. Positive reinforcement is a useful method of restoring power to women clients, but it must be used carefully. If over-used it can seem unrealistic to clients, and they then interpret the actions of the counsellor as being patronizing. This can be counter-productive. It makes women clients feel even more inadequate and their situation seemingly more hopeless. What counsellors should bear in mind is that these clients are usually unused to positives things being said about them or their feelings, thoughts or actions. Thus they have to be introduced slowly to positivity, to the idea that they are normal, effective people entitled to respect. The main counselling problem is that the self-esteem of abused women clients can be so low that they can see almost any positive remark about them as unrealistic, patronizing or mere superficial politeness. For this reason, positive reinforcement has to be more than a simple remark; it has to be part of a process and requiring considerable work. Finally, when working with couples, positive reinforcement should not be directed solely at the women clients but equally at their partners. This reflects the fact that abusers can also be suffering from low self-esteem and need help to feel good about themselves and so feel good

about others. Furthermore, if the male abuser thinks the counsellor is taking his partner's side, this can lead to a reaction against the partner outside the counselling arena.

5. A common result of low self-esteem in women clients is a lack of self-confidence and their need to know that how they feel is normal, what they think is not the product of some form of madness, and what they do is of validity. Affirmation works on two levels. In individual counselling, women clients will often describe what they intend to do and then ask, 'What do you think?' One response is simply to put the question back to the client and ask what she thinks. The drawback is that this fails to respond to the affective aspect of the question, that the client is asking a question of *you*. You are part of a relationship and the situation requires more than a purely cognitive reaction when working with those having low self-esteem. Another option is that of answering the question as honestly as possible, which at least shows the client that she is being taken seriously. The third option is that of not only reviewing what the client has said, but also relating it to her. Thus even if what she has said appears quite unrealistic and the action is not affirmed, yet the person is affirmed. Supportive observations include, 'It is good to see you are really thinking about what to do and taking the initiative. You said in an earlier session you never knew what to do, but it seems to me that you are not giving yourself credit for what you can do. Would I be right?'

6. Another practice that may require modification in the light of power imbalance is that of the counsellor asking questions. Most clients expect questions and are happy to respond. However, abused clients can view any questioning as being imposed upon, reminiscent of interactions with their partners. This can happen no matter how gentle and tactful the probing. Also, the lack of any client observable reaction should not be taken as acceptance of what is taking place. It may be helpful to bear in mind the following points.

(i) Asking a lot of questions is likely to be unhelpful. I find it best to encourage clients to speak and to avoid questions by using remarks such as, 'Tell me about it ... .' or the use of statements like, 'So the two of you argued ... .'

(ii) Circular questioning, such as asking how one partner views the behaviour of the other should be very sparingly used with both present. Too often this merely gives opportunities for partners to criticize each other and for old and empty arguments to be started.

(iii) There may be times when it is important to know the answer to a question, such as whether the client has been hit recently. The direct approach may elict a negative reply: after all, if the client has not mentioned any violence, then she may have inhibitions about admitting the fact. For the counsellor to persist in questioning may be viewed by the client as harassment. A change in tactics is required and this calls for the asking of indirect questions, such as: 'Do you ever find that when you argue, things get out of hand?'; asking about behaviour that might lead to violence, such as: 'Do you drink in the house or go to the pub?'; asking about behaviour that often accompanies partner violence, such as possessiveness: 'Do you go out together or have friends visit?'; or asking clients how they see their behaviour or situation, such as: 'Do you see yourself as being hard done by?'

Trainees sometimes ask whether it is best simpy to allow clients to tell their own story and for counsellors to avoid questioning, probing, or pushing clients on certain matters. This objection ignores the need for structure to be introduced into any counselling and also the need for specification. Much of the discussions or arguments between couples take on either a vague or even vacuous content. Communication can descend into little more than providing triggers for the release of feelings. The following is a slightly adapted version of two clients talking together.

'Must you always do that?'

'What?'

'You know!'

'What? *What?* ... I'm not doing anything.'

'You are so, and you know it.'

'Are you trying to pick an argument?'

'Trust you to say that!'

To the outsider there has been no factual information passed and even the two people concerned may have little idea precisely what the discussion is about. It may, for example, be a leftover from a previous argument or a ritualized entering into a new argument. So what is required is specification, both parties knowing exactly what they and their partner are talking about. This applies equally to individual clients, who can express general anxiety which is diminished in part by them particularizing as to their precise concerns, fears and apprehensions.

Leo: 'Does my head in.'

Me: 'OK. So it can be annoying. And you don't like her drinking too much ... Who buys her the drinks, by the way? Does Carrie buy her own?'

Carrie: 'Ha!! As if I have any money! He buys the drinks.'

Leo: 'I let her have some money for a drink if she asks.'

Carrie: 'Yes, bloody beg in front of your mates.'

Me: 'So Carrie might go over the score, drinkwise, but you are paying for her drinks.'

Leo: 'Just to shut her up.'

Carrie: 'Oh yes, you're good at shutting me up. Boot. Not in front of his mates. He should have married one of them.'

Leo: 'You wonder why I shut her up? You behave and then I'll take you out.'

Clearly, this is just the start to a much longer investigation, yet it does reveal several underlying themes which are in the end related to violence. The nature of counselling is that of a process, and counsellors can help clients to delve deeper and deeper into what they, the clients, really feel and think.

Delabelling

An important way of acting against power imbalances is through delabelling, the operation of helping clients to shed derogatory or diminishing labels which others have attached to them. These labels become internalized so that clients believe what others say about them. In the case of partners, labelling can arise through the constant use of descriptors such as 'liar', 'unstable', 'manipulative', 'slut', whore', 'stupid'. However, these are often less powerfully attached than the terms used by professionals and those in positions of power. The descriptors can be 'hysterical', 'uncooperative', 'masochistic', 'poor coper', and their use in reports can ensure their longevity. Yet as long as clients are stereotyped, reduced to generalized categories, and not seen as themselves, they will have no faith in themselves and will be unable to exert power for themselves.

The situation will not be righted by the counsellor just telling clients that they are not hysterical, or whatever label may have been imposed. Instead, delabelling should be seen as a process which can be divided into different stages.

- Identifying the labels that clients may be carrying. This comes from clients, as their behaviour is affected only by those labels that are known to them. However there can be a problem in that abused clients can imagine that they have been labelled in certain ways, that people are calling them names or implying certain stereotypical qualities about them when this is not the case. These should not be rejected but should enter into the delabelling process as they still represent how clients imagine others see them.

- Using the labels, the counsellor and client can work through the extent to which they are applicable and non-applicable. It is important that clients are helped to describe, for example, when they are hysterical or might be thought to be hysterical. Simply pressing the view that the client is not hysterical is insufficient in that this is not what the client believes. So the counsellor discusses the idea of 'being hysterical' or expressing very strong feelings. This is contrasted with not expressing such feelings. What may be emphasized is the rationality of the client's behaviour from the client's perspective. The counsellor then moves the idea of abnormality not residing in the client but in the client's situation. The final stage is getting the client to explain to myself, as counsellor, why she should not be termed 'hysterical' and how others should view her.

  This model can be more complicated with abused clients. What we might see as a derogatory label, such clients with low self-esteem may judge to be a quite positive tag. Being labelled can appear to clients to be helpful. For instance, seeing herself as a victim can give some sense of meaning to a client and it also allows her to identify and associate with others so labelled. However, with the label can come connotations of passivity and resentment which can put a break on positive action. It should be noted that any label applied to abused women, such as 'victim' or 'survivor', carries implications and connotations which can prove positive or negative.

Modified counselling and the here-and-now

Other aspects of counselling that require a degree of modification include the concept of the here-and-now, how clients now feel about past events. We find that past incidents concerned with battering affect clients in complex ways.

1. Strong feelings from the past can intrude on those of the present, causing clients to be unsure about how they now feel. This applies particularly when abused women are asked how they feel about

their partners and their feelings are confused between feelings of how things were and feelings of the present, and the difficulty in distinguishing the two.

2. Present feelings can be distorted through client interpretation and re-interpretation of what took place. Part of this arises from defence mechanisms, which are used by clients to deny, minimize, rationalize or blame others with regard to the situation. After a time it becomes difficult to disentangle reality from what has been constructed.

3. The third difficulty can be that of post-traumatic stress, when the past can come to dominate the present, and abused clients are unable to say how they feel at present except through the past.

Rather than the counsellor trying to work out what might be a client's real feelings – which even the client may not know – it is better to discuss how what has happened might have affected present memories, explanations and feelings. Clients are the best people to identify such changes. But, perhaps more importantly, the process of trying to identify such changes helps clients to understand themselves to a greater degree.

Incidently, the effect of violence trauma on women clients is much less than I initially expected. This is mostly the result of clients not coming to counselling until the pattern of violence has been established, except in exceptional cases. Abused women have had time to come to terms with the effects of trauma, both physical and mental to a large degree. Also, the ability of women to fight back, even if it is not physical but purely mental, such as planning revenge, diminishes some of the feelings of helplessness.

Goal-setting

For people who see themselves caught in situations from which they cannot escape or with problems they cannot solve, the achievement of set goals is important not only for allowing them to escape their predicament but also for allowing them to regain confidence in themselves and their own abilities. Goal-setting is an essential means to bringing improvement to the client's life, but a lack of success can worsen matters. With abused clients, there can be pressure put on those involved to act quickly and come to a satisfactory solution. Counsellors are expected to come up with the required answers and so can get caught up in everyone's expectations. The outcome can be that they deal with situations little better than clients. Counsellors themselves have to goal-set as much as any client to be able to deliver real help to clients. With many abuse affected couples, crises are a way of life. It is easy to become submerged in these short-term situations, and sometimes crises arise for this very reason – to divert attention from any long-term objectives, such as separation or large-scale behaviour change. The easy task is to get clients to involve themselves in crisis work; the difficult task is that of getting clients to attend to long-term objectives.

Whatever the nature of the difficulties, it is worth discussing goals and goal-setting with clients. There are three factors that should be remembered when talking with clients.

1. Goals have to be for the clients or client, and not for anyone else. Clients might want things better for the children, want change because of a Court order, or decide they must do what their counsellor wants them to do. This is insufficient. Goals have to be for clients. Abused women have to be brought to appreciate their own worth, understand that they can exert power, and do things for themselves rather than others.

2. If goals can only be achieved by their initiators, then this has to be built into goal-setting. The difficulty is that many abused women see themselves as incapable of any constructive action and leave others to take action. This reinforces the woman's powerlessness and feelings of hopelessness. So counsellors should avoid doing too much, even if this is what clients say they want.

3. Clients can carry out their own goals, provided such goals are realistic. To determine what is realistic usually requires the assistance of counsellors, as clients can be unrealistic. Counsellors can help clients identify why they might be taking an unrealistic view of what they can achieve. Abused clients in counselling can be affected by the atmosphere of acceptance and cooperation, so are eager in turn to appear to be helpful and equally cooperative. They may set goals not for themselves but for what they think the counsellor wants. Alternatively, they can set goals which they believe their partner wants. Their lack of belief in themselves makes abused clients very open to such behaviour, as living with an abuser has forced them to react to another's expectations.

4. Another aspect counsellors have to watch is the tendency of clients to choose goals that are global in their nature. Feelings of desperation about their situation can engender an all-or-nothing approach which is most unlikely to be successful. It has to be remembered that the smallest goal achieved has more worth than a large goal which proves unattainable. The opposite scenario is

when clients feel unable to do anything at all about their situation. Such feelings might not be acknowledged but counsellors find clients apathetic, seeing only obstacles, and not really believing in their chosen goals. A positive attitude is required of the counsellor, who is then able to help clients look at what they have achieved, however seemingly insignificant, before looking at what they can achieve.

Setting the rules

There is a paradox about counselling those in violent relationships in that counselling tends to be non-directive and power is shared equally between counsellor and client, yet the client situation and subject of counselling is characterized by power imbalance. Such imbalance can be at least contained by the use of rules in the client relationship, but this is rarely the case with abusive relationships. In both individual and couple counselling, the rules should be identified and this is not always so simple. The rules are not obvious, consisting of a matrix of shared understandings, agreements and promises. The next difficulty is the specification of the rules, and partners or individual clients are often unaware that there are such rules that apply to them. Part of the reason for this is that the rules are so straightforward that they are overlooked. For this reason counsellors might find it easier to suggest possible rules, as this illustrates possibilities and helps clients to determine what rules apply or should apply to their relationships. Possible rules include:

- partners should be faithful to each other and not play around;

- no violence to be used against each other, whatever the circumstances;

- both partners should be allowed to express their opinions;

- both partners should allow and respect each other's privacy.

The immediate practical difficulty in counselling is getting clients to state what the rules are – whether or not one or both parties adhere to them. This is another reason for the counselling suggesting possible rules, as they can be linked to expectations and understandings. Rules can then be linked with the rules that exist in the counselling session, such as no one should use violence against another person (in the case of couples) and everyone is allowed to express their opinion. The underlying thought behind this process is that if clients can keep to the rules within the counselling session, then they should be able to do so on the outside as well. Another useful aspect when working with couples is that there are behavioural rules in the counselling session, so this makes it more difficult to reject the whole idea of rules, which some abusive partners will attempt.

For abusive men, adhering to rules is a loss of control. This means that in couples work there is likely to be resistance, so it is worth taking time to get couples to discuss cooperation and its mutual advantages. But the big task for counsellors is getting clients to adhere to their personal agreed rules. Here the model can be taken from the counselling session itself. Counsellors should intervene when rules are broken and this should be from the very start. It is very easy to relax at the start of counselling, or think that counselling starts at a given time rather than from the moment clients walk into the counselling room, and allow clients to break rules. Once the pattern has been set it is very hard to change it. It should be remembered that many of the difficulties about violent relationships come from a breaking of understood rules – usually by men – and counsellors must underline the fact in practice that they are important, using the counselling session for this purpose.

We can use counselling to show how to react to the infringement of rules. For instance, the first time this happens a very mild intervention can be used. In the following example we see that Leigh's intervention was treated by being ignored.

Me: 'Were there times, Jimmy, when you felt Leigh did not understand how you felt? ... Anything that strikes you?'

Jimmy: 'Well, a typical example is when Leigh disappeared.'

Leigh: 'I used to disappear when I thought you were going to start. I could tell as you would go all quiet. I would nash [run away], and you would smash the flat up.'

Jimmy: 'I'm not thinking about that, I'm talking of other times.'

Me: 'So, you felt that when Leigh disappeared she did not understand how you felt.'

The point is that heavier interventions might be more effective, but what is being constructed is a learning experience. Clients have to appreciate what happens when they do or do not react to mild intervention. Often clients do not react to mild measures and this is itself worth investigating with them, how they fail to notice what is happening with their partner and themselves, how they react only to strong interventions. This ultimately leads up to the belief that violence is the only intervention that will have any effect, as the intensity of client intervention escalates. In the counselling itself, we find that stronger measures are required as couples fall into old behaviour patterns.

Me: 'I'm stopping the two of you right there. We have a rule about allowing the other person to finish what they are saying. Now even I have had to break that rule simply because I completely lost track of what was being said. I signalled to both of you to ...'

Lucy: 'He interrupted me ...'

Jim: 'My arse!'

Me: 'And you are about to do it again. Tell me, is this a common occurrence, the two of you talking to each other and not really listening?'

What is important is that rule enforcement is not a matter of counsellors taking control, but ensuring that clients realize what is happening and what they are doing. This will allow them to take control.

Intervening as a measure of control rather than as a method of learning is likely to be unsuccessful. What has to be realized is that counselling sessions with couples can get very heated, and counsellors can still show clients what can be done in a situation that is beginning to get out of hand.

Me: 'OK, the two of you have had a bit of a go at each other. I want to call a halt now, and I suggest we have a break in five minutes for a cup of coffee. I'll see what biscuits we have. Is that OK by both of you?' [Grunt of assent from Roy] 'I'm taking that as a "Yes".'

From an instructional point of view, continually intervening is governed by the law of diminishing returns and becomes increasingly ineffective. One way of countering this effect is to choose to intervene with regard to different rules. Other rules might encompass starting and ending times, confidentiality, and being non-judgemental. It is not necessary to have many counselling rules and we have to be realistic. Some clients will react poorly to the imposition of any rules and such patterns of behaviour are not quickly or easily changed.

Counselling contracts

Rules are initiated from the very start, being incorporated into counselling contracts. These are agreements, but they do not cover the roles of the participants, or the goals, strategies and techniques to be used, as suggested by some commentators (Maluccio and Marlow, 1974). They are simple agreements covering frequency and length of counselling, arrangements to ending, and failure to attend or postponements by either party. They are bilateral, so clients can bring counsellors to task, and so contracts are not an instrument of power. Counsellors sometimes use contracts as they are seen – by them – as the correct way of doing a professional job. However, they should also take into account what they might mean to the clients. The whole counselling experience does not start when problems are discussed but from the moment of contact.

Further modifications to the working practice

The result of conflict and violence to women in relationships is to affect both partners both affectively and cognitively. The first aspect can be seen by the fact that there is often a need for clients to ventilate, to express their feelings. However, this might not be obvious initially, as abused women learn to be circumspect in their behaviour and will not react unless a supportive working relationship, rather than just a working relationship, has been established. Furthermore, the extent to which clients can ventilate is largely determined by counsellors and how much raw emotion they can take. This is particularly the case with couples work, where the woman may take advantage of the protective presence of the counsellor and take the opportunity to unload on her partner.

Ventilation can be seen as short term and long term. Short-term ventilation is required for clients to let go their feelings, in order for them to be able to work cognitively, to be able to listen properly and analyse their own behaviour usefully. However, there is also long-term work to be done on the release of deeper client feelings, and with women these are often linked with guilt and kept hidden by coping mechanisms. Such work requires a degree of cognitive restructuring and this can often be realized in the following ways:

- Helping the client to identify the fact that she is ambivalent in her feelings.

- Encouraging the client to discuss how she sees and feels about this ambivalence. The client must be able to link with her ambivalence before being able to work on it.

- The client discusses with her counsellor the various conflicting feelings that contribute to her ambivalence. What can be helpful is asking the client to distance herself and then describe her situation to herself, but asking her to imagine that this does not refer to her but to Mrs Peters. What would she want to say to this mythical Mrs Peters?

- It should be noted that coming to any conclusion with the client is less important than allowing the client to work through issues for herself. The process can be more important than a simple 'answer'.

Once feelings have been put into place by the client, she will be better able to use reason and see situations clearly, to plan, and to draw conclusions. In fact, advances in affective and cognitive understanding go hand in hand, and the client slowly comes to understand what has been happening.

Leigh: 'I gave the impression that nothing was wrong with us, and others were to blame. At the time I really believed this and Jimmy would agree, so the two of us would blame outsiders for what was happening. I would say, "Wait till I get hold of so-and-so. I'll make her regret for trying to split us up." It was only as my feelings began to dwindle that I saw things different, saw them through someone else's eyes. Now I look back and wonder how I could have been so stupid – but I had feelings for him then.'

Strong feelings can form a barrier to those wanting to help as they affect the way people think. Such feelings may not be obvious, they may be well hidden. Counsellors and others may thus imagine that clients are fully in control of themselves and open to reason, whereas the reality is more complicated. Clients can construct their own world and set of meanings, and react in order to maintain this world.

Me: 'Did you get advice from anyone?'

Annmarie: 'Yes, but you never listen, you never listen to anyone at all. My pals used to say this or that to me, but none of it made any difference.'

While we note clients' difficulties, we should also remember that they apply in a different form to counsellors as well. The frequent failure of counsellors to identify and engage with the topic of relationship violence in their work points to clients having merely different problems.

Check points

The following points apply to counselling in general, but I have included them as they can be of special importance when working with abused women. They are also, from my experience, aspects that novitiate counsellors sometimes overlook.

1. Is the counsellor checking out with the client how she feels, whether she understands, and does she agree?

2. Has the counsellor checked out the client's views fully, rather than assuming they are obvious?

3. Has the counsellor considered the pace of counselling, and whether the client is being given time to reflect and internalize what has taken place in the counselling?

4. Working with abused women can take a long time, so structuring in the long term is important. It is easy for counsellors to get sucked into the short term, the immediate crises, and lose track of the overall direction and plan.

5. The degree of directiveness is related to structuring and should be monitored, decreasing as control is taken by the counsellor and then given back to the clients. Thus there is a link to ultimate client empowerment.

6. The counselling should, within the counselling trust and security, be challenging. Counselling has a degree of risk-taking, and this is required for any client change but also to ensure that dependency on the counsellor does not become a problem.

7. Account has to be taken of the counsellor/client boundaries, looking for both under- and over-involvement.

8. Perhaps the most common omission by new counsellors is that of discussing the working relationship with clients, including how they feel about it and whether they can ascribe trust, honesty, reliability, ease and support to it. The first task is not that of taking relationship problems to a supervisor but to the client.

Neutrality in work

There is one aspect which can confuse counsellors and that is the idea that they have to be neutral in an imbalanced relationship. Certainly, it is not their place to tell clients what they should want or do. However, there has to be a recognition that the advent of the counsellor does affect clients and their behaviour. If this was not the case then counselling would have no point. The client partnerships are enlarged, at least for a time, by a third party who has a remit, aims and objectives, and a certain belief system. If counsellors fail to uphold the rights of women and women partners then they are reinforcing the status quo and are taking a certain view and action about the abusive relationship. The idea that counsellors should not take sides between couples assumes that this is possible when there is an imbalanced relationship – and it is not possible.

What should be realized is that counsellors have to be very firm and positive in their work. They may judge behaviour but not clients. They should make their own views known, put forward as their own opinions. Sometimes counsellors imagine that being professional requires 'neutrality', and so fail to intervene appropriately or act supportively.

Summary

Counsellors should not imagine that counselling clients in violent relationships is simply another addition to the range of such helping. It requires some modification as a result of the power imbalance that characterizes such relationships. Counsellors should also realize that they are intervening, coming into a personal situation that has its own history. The resultant work might well be extensive and accompanied by a degree of resistance from clients. With women this is a good sign as it denotes they are exerting their own autonomy (Dowd and Seibel, 1990). The difficulties encountered do not arise just from the clients. Counsellors also import problems, as they react to client difficulties while trying to maintain their professional identity (Gottsegan and Gottsegan, 1979).

5 WORK WITH COUPLES

Orientation

The first step for counselling those in violent relationships must be to orientate themselves to the work, to work on themselves so they do not muddy the counselling with their own agendas and are able to cope with the intensity of the work. In particular, it is helpful for counsellors to think how they would deal with the abuser if he appeared. Counsellors do not have to work with abusive men, but contact with them is important in order to be able to understand more about the female partner's feelings and behaviour. Abused women can find their partner's behaviour difficult not because it is always abusive, but because the abuse can be varied with periods of pleasantness. Counsellors who do see the situation in terms of good and bad fail to understand the full picture. Much of the counsellor's self-work has been described in the previous chapter, but it is essential that counsellors continue to take stock of themselves and look at their own attitudes and beliefs, their own practice, their behaviour outside the counselling arena and their past history of relationships.

The final stage for the counsellor is to get beyond the simplification of bad abuser/victimized client. Rather, counsellors have to listen with an open mind and understand what is happening in a total sense. We should be able to take a professional view of what is happening, see it from a variety of perspectives, without sinking into ethical relativism and declaring that no one is responsible for what is happening. On the contrary, everyone – and this includes the counsellor – must be accountable for their actions and behaviour.

Identifying violence in a relationship

Women rarely come to counsellors and say they want help as they are being physically abused. If this were the case, then nationwide there would be millions of women being counselled for partner violence. This is not the case. Even those women who do come to the helping services are reluctant to obtain help with regard to their violent relationship. Thus the prime task for any helper or counsellor is the identification of personal violence. If you ask, What can be done? then I would suggest the following.

1. The counsellor builds up a caring relationship with the client but is ignorant of any abuse. Some clients will then want to tell the counsellor what is going on, but find difficulty in this, partly because they think they have deceived the counsellor to this point, partly because they are embarrassed to admit what is happening, and partly because their partner might have threatened them with violence if they do speak the truth. The counsellor always has to keep in mind violence as a possibility and to be sensitive to indirect messages from the client. Clients are unsure how counsellors will react and so test the water, seeing how the counsellor reacts to indirect suggestions. For instance, women clients have mentioned violent cases which have featured in the local paper, specific programmes on television, or something that has happened to a neighbour. All of these may have appeared completely offhand, but how the counsellor reacts is important. Dismissing them as irrelevant or being unworthy of comment can be a grave mistake. Of course, some clients may be simply gossiping, but part of the art of counselling is to be able to recognize the potentially important, what really does concern the client.

2. One aspect which I have found helpful has been to make known my own beliefs. When working with a great variety of clients, I have always said that the two things I found insupportable were violence against children and women. This has to be set against the context of stealing, illegal drug use, prostitution, and many other forms of behaviour which I would not condone, but see as belonging primarily to the client. Violence I see differently. However one may judge this stand, yet a stand and the open expression of that stand is important.

3. Clients may be helped for various difficulties in their life and yet still not disclose the fact that such difficulties may be related, at least in part, to an abusive relationship. As long as the client can be helped, then this can lay the basis for further work. Some clients want help, often quite practical help, before trusting outside helpers. Although counselling is portrayed as being separate from such practical helping, it is frequently useful if counsellors are also capable of delivering it.

4. If counsellors suspect a client has been abused then the suspicion can be checked out by possible signs. For instance, appointments cancelled or the client not turning up, the client turning up wearing heavy make-up, or the counselling atmosphere changing when the topic of violence is raised.

5. The simplest method of discovering if there is relationship violence would seem to be that of asking the client. This is often successful, but has to be carefully considered. It can place the client in a difficult position: either to admit the violence has taken place or to deny it. This gives room for manoeuvre, for the client to decide to reveal such information only after more work has been done.

6. Finally, the nature of a client's problems or accompanying information can lead counsellors to suspect possible violence. The signs may be many, such as male partners coming to counselling with women in a minding capacity, clients having problems with their children, the frequent use of alcohol by clients, regular visits to the doctor or the hospital. None of these signs is definitive, but they can combine with other indications to make us suspect violence.

Identification in practice

Some of these aspects came with an early case. June turned up at the Social Work Department where I was then working, and asked for an appointment. I noted that she was obviously pregnant and was shouting at the receptionist for what seemed to be no real reason. I felt something was not quite right, so I approached her and asked if she wanted any baby clothes. She declined in no uncertain language, yet returned next week just the same. We spoke only about the forthcoming birth. To my surprise, she asked to see me five days later, and described how her partner had attacked her, kicking her to the extent that she feared for her baby's life. This illustration might be more convincing if she had then attended for regular counselling, but she had told an outsider what was going on and that was important to her. She did not want anyone to contact her. I heard later that the baby was born perfectly normal and June had left her partner.

I mention this case as it does show the reality and also a little of the indefinable nature and uncertainty of personal helping. Having 'a feeling that something is not quite right' is seemingly a poor basis for contemplating intervention. If the pregnant mother was in danger should I have taken stronger measures? Was it pure luck that things worked out for the best? These questions are also applicable to counselling itself. One aspect of counselling difficult cases that is seldom highlighted is the counsellors' doubts as to whether they are really benefiting their clients. And if counsellors do not have such doubts, then they need to stop and review their practice. An essential part of counselling is knowing its limitations.

Alternative referrals

Once partner violence has been confirmed, then the counsellor has to consider what is best for the specific client, and this includes going beyond mere counselling. Counselling clients for problems such as stress can be done without reference to outside people or organizations. Counselling for severe alcohol problems may be assisted by outside connections such as the client's doctor and self-help groups. With partner violence, women who are counselled are likely to require from time to time the assistance of many agencies. It is quite possible for counsellors to see their remit as being completely separate and believe that it is the client's responsibility to contact the necessary agencies. However, when clients have been traumatised, lack all self-esteem and confidence, and are very much under the control of their partner, leaving clients to make their own arrangements is unrealistic and can be positively unhelpful.

What is helpful is the counsellor knowing about the various agencies that might be called upon and having links with them. These agencies can include:

Lawyers
Doctors
The Police
Local Authority Housing Departments and Housing Agencies
The Department of Social Security
Women's Aid
Local Social Work (or Social Services) Department

With experience, counsellors discover who are the most helpful lawyers (often women), how specific doctors are likely to react to partner violence, whether the local police will respond usefully, whether leaving local authority housing will be treated as making oneself intentionally homeless and so lose any right to being rehoused, whether the local Woman's Aid hostel is likely to have any places and what can they offer as regards help, and whether social workers will intervene (with the risk of the children being taken into care). In my experience, agencies will have certain stated policies, but it is essential to know the reality, especially where there is danger to life and limb.

Interagency work

It is interesting to note that connecting or working with those from other agencies presents certain problems. These are not the product of different personalities – though this is the explanation often forwarded. Interagency work can be difficult as the counsellor might be in contact with people who through their training and demands of the job, have different perspectives on helping and different remits. There are also other aspects, such as the differences in power, so one agency may be seen as 'unprofessional' and the other as 'uncaring'. Furthermore, organizations are often in competition, and this may ultimately be about the funding and continuing existence of those organizations. Finally, organizations can have their own internal pressures and stresses, and one way for them to cope is by being over-regarding of their own agency and downgrading of all others. All of this indicates that counsellors have to know other agencies well and have some understanding of their difficulties, views and remits. It is also at times necessary to identify and break down the stereotypes that exist between those in different lines of work.

If there are to be referrals to other agencies for part-work, then it is important that wherever possible there is some form of written agreement whereby the respective areas of work and agency remit are made known to all concerned, including the client. Another aspect that has to be hammered out is that of confidentiality. Helping organizations also have their own ideas and rules about confidentiality, and all of them tend to differ. It is essential that counsellors and clients are well informed about such differences.

Overall aims of counselling

The most important first step in counselling is to be sure of the aims of the contracted work and that the clients understand and agree to them. Counsellors often have a general idea of working with clients to make things better, but this is so vague that a more specific aim, such as reducing violence, may be preferred. Clients can want and even expect counsellors, from my experience, to make their partner relationship better, to end the relationship, to ensure the violence stops, to reduce the number of arguments, to improve sexual relations, or to make the children better behaved. Counsellors may belong to agencies and agencies can have their own aims, which in turn may be modified by referring agencies such as the police, social workers or Courts. The latter are themselves backed by the Law, in particular that which relates to violence in varying forms from assault to murder, and to child welfare legislation. What is not made transparent is what counsellors can actually deliver.

The first point is that counsellors can deliver none of the above. All they can do is to give clients the opportunity to carry out their own aims and objectives. Counsellors may try to influence clients, whether through giving information and explanations, promoting self-awareness, giving encouragement, modelling behaviour, reinforcing certain client behaviours or aiding communication and the expression of feelings, but in the end only clients can change themselves. This point has to be understood by counsellors, clients and all other related agencies or organizations. Counsellors are responsible for giving a professional and ethical service, but they are not totally responsible for the outcome of counselling. However, this is more complicated than it might seem, as to work in a professional capacity with clients in violent relationships does demand that their welfare is taken into account.

Clients from the very beginning have to take responsibility for the outcome of counselling, just as they have to take responsibility for their acts and behaviour. With this overall view, clients have to decide what they want out of counselling. This can actually take considerable time in counselling, as some clients do not know what they want or they are very ambivalent. Working with couples makes client aims even more complex as they frequently differ, and this can be at the centre of the relationship difficulties. Also, the aims may be deliberately concealed.

Individual or couples work?

Once relationship violence has been identified and other agencies have been informed as agreed with the client, counsellors are left with the question of whether counselling should be individual or include client partners. Individual work can give an incomplete picture, whereas couples counselling may well be controlled by the male abusers. In addition, the counsellor has to decide which would be the safer option for the woman client and which alternative the woman prefers. The difficulty is that abused women can be so used to making decisions for the benefit of others that they have difficulty in knowing what is best for them.

To help counsellors, it may be useful to put the whole situation in context. The percentage of battered women who receive help with regard to battering, other than medical, is difficult to estimate but is probably about 10 per cent. The percentage of men who receive help with regard to their partner's assaultive behaviour must be less than 1 per cent. As a result, help is provided for a minority of cases only, and this means there can be a selection of clients and this is done by imposing selection criteria on them. This need not be an obvious transaction, but it is a common way of rationing assistance given by the helping services. I first encountered such behaviour when referring a willing woman with severe alcohol problems to a local hospital. She was turned down as she 'had a poor prognosis'. Thus we should question accepted practice, that there should be no counselling if violence is still ongoing, as in the case of the Duluth Domestic Abuse Intervention Project which demands that there be no violence for at least three months if partners are to be seen together for counselling. Though the project's ruling seems eminently sensible, yet it might mean that some clients will lose out and will not receive help, if their male partners insist on being present and individual counselling is not considered an option by their abused partners.

This does highlight a problem, that those who are not helped tend to be excluded from counsellors' consideration of battering intervention programmes. As long as some clients are helped, we tend to forget the majority who are not helped and those who are excluded. It might also be that those who are helped are those with a good prognosis, either because the male partner has shown some flexibility or the woman has managed to leave her partner. This means that poor prognosis cases simply are not seen, and these might be the very cases which carry the greatest risk of injury or death to women.

Reconsidering the rules of intervention

Of course, the Duluth rule is a good general guide, but working with women in violent relationships, like much of personal helping, often turns out to be messier and more complex than it might initially appear. For the practising counsellor, the following may have to be taken on board.

- The making of rules is also an exercise in power, and women are thus being told what to do by helping agencies. For those who have been controlled by their partners, control by agencies might not be welcome.

- Agencies say that their rules are for the benefit of women, but abused women might have heard this before. Their partners will sometimes explain that the control they exert is for their benefit.

- Much of the helping of women is allegedly empowering for them, so it is paradoxical that the very first action of counsellors is to exclude them from any decision-making about the form of counselling, whether individual or couples. Empowerment comes not just from protective rules but also from being able to compose one's own rules to suit a person's particular wishes and circumstances.

- Many of my clients, coming from the lower social classes, have a suspicion – sometimes well placed – of helping agencies and of counselling. Rules may be seen not simply as rules but also as barriers to be circumvented. They are seen as barriers erected for the defence of those in power, not for them.

- The idea that an abuser will have changed sufficiently after three months of non-violence to allow couples counselling may be misleading. Patterns of behaviour can differ. Violence need not be frequent and continuous but there can be gaps, and then it is set off again by particular situations.

- Most helpers would prefer that abused women leave their partners or are helped so to do, and then receive counselling and support. However, many abused women still love their partners and do not want to leave them, even if they still remain at risk. All they want is for the violence to end. However, if they decide to stay with their partners then they may be denied help.

- Counselling women on their own is assumed to be safe, unlike counselling both partners. It is certainly safer, but I know of cases where women have still been abused by their partners, and part of the reason was that they were seeing a counsellor or helper.

What may be apparent is that there are no simple answers when it comes to personal helping. Each client is an individual and should be treated as such. Rules are useful as they do provide general reminders to counsellors, but in time and with experience we come to know when rules should be used flexibly. This may incur some risks for the client, but there are risks to any client. Counsellors have to estimate the course that is safest for clients and the one which will allow them to receive help. Overall, the question has to be asked, for whose benefit do the rules operate: the clients, the counsellors, or the agency?

The use of rules

My concern is not about the use of rules but their blind use. Usually, little explanation is given of the thinking behind them and little opportunity given for clients to work through them and so make their minds up about them. Sometimes there seems to be a reluctance to trust clients, which with abused women is a definite fault. If partners are to come for counselling, then it is required that there should be no violence in the sessions. But it is important that two clients recognize the reasons for this, and that counselling is about change and not a continuing of a troubled relationship. Admittedly, in the initial stages there may be limited time to work on all the aspects of the need for rules but it is important that counsellors open up two areas of work from the beginning.

From the very start, clients should appreciate that counselling is both participative and a reasoned process. By actively taking part in that process, clients are better able to transfer such behaviour outside counselling into their everyday lives. They also understand that there is no miracle solution, but they have to work through issues for themselves. This now makes greater sense of the rule of no violence during the counselling session, a rule which cannot simply be extended to cover what happens outside the session as there is no sure way of counsellors knowing or acting upon such external violence. But the no-violence rule acts as a signal to what is expected and the non-violence should be made transferable outside the session.

The rule of Law

It might be noted that there already exist rules about violence, and these are incorporated into the Law. This raises the question of how counsellors should use the Law and what should be said to clients on their referral for counselling. The first point is that no one is legally bound to inform on illegal activities, though it may be seen as a civic duty to do so. We might also note that legal proceedings are a good way of diminishing personal violence. So there seem to be good reasons for invoking the Law if a client continues to be violent. Indeed, counsellors who say they will invoke the Law if there is violence and then fail to do so, not only fail the woman and side with the abuser, but may also put the abuser's partner in greater danger.

The counter-argument is that woman clients may not want the involvement of the Law and have come for counselling for this very reason. Alternatively, they want such involvement but hope that the counsellor will take action rather than themselves. The counsellor has to work out what might be the most effective way of stopping the violence, bearing in mind the associated risks. For high-risk behaviour the Law might have to be invoked, but counsellors should remember that this should be with the agreement of the woman client, as she will have to give a statement and this can put her at risk, either at the time or at a future date. Also, she has to want to be involved, and this is often not the case.

Partner violence is usually not an isolated action but rather a pattern of behaviour, the underpinning of male control. Any pattern of behaviour will not be changed quickly and there will be relapses into former undesirable actions. Having worked with clients who committed theft offences, were heroin users, or had unprotected sex when sexually infected, it is tempting to react and call in the authorities. However, this may not be successful and certainly deters others from trying to get help. Of course, if the client is under a legal order such as probation, then the counsellor has no option but to act on an offence.

However, usually it is preferable that women, rather than counsellors, take legal action against their partners, so that action is not counselling confined but is applicable to the clients' full lives.

If the result seems rather indeterminate and lacking in simple answers, then this reflects the counselling reality, and it is a reality that should be shared with clients. Clients can follow the reasoning, and talking about the Law welds the counselling context firmly to the real world, rather than the world of excuses, minimization, and rationalization. At times I have even had a copy of the Criminal Law to hand, so the penalties for assault can be read by clients.

In the end, we return to the earlier question of who benefits from the introduction of rules about counselling in couples or individually, whether there should be general rules or whether each case should be taken on its merits. In my opinion, rules are useful if they are employed in a learning context by clients. We have to be careful that they are not simply for the benefit of the agency or counsellors, though both of these also incur a small degree of risk through the nature of the work.

Reacting to male control

Counselling work is directed towards benefiting clients, but counsellors themselves and the agency cannot be ignored. For counsellors there can be a degree of risk in working with clients in very poor relationships, but even this should be used as a learning experience for clients. Usually, the trouble comes not from actual violence but from threats of violence, so clients have to learn not only that such behaviour will not be tolerated but also that it is ineffective in the long run.

Aspects of this can be glimpsed in a case where I was working with a woman client in one-to-one counselling, about the relationship she had with her partner. This was so bad that she wanted to ask about divorce, seeking some measure of support. A few days later her partner phoned from Manchester, threatening to shoot me for my 'interference'. This man had extensive criminal connections, so the threat was not to be taken lightly. The phone call went approximately as follows:

'Where are you phoning from, Ed?'

'Manchester.'

'Right. And from the background noise I reckon you are in a pub.'

'So what? It's none of yor business where I am.'

'You are in a pub, probably sitting at the bar, and you've had a few.'

'How d'you know that?'

'I'm quite willing to talk things over with you, but not when you've been drinking. When you are back in Edinburgh, you can make an appointment. In the meantime have a good day, and don't fall off that bar-stool.'

When under threat, counsellors have to seize the initiative, which means saying what has to be said and not responding to client questions, objections or digressions. Once a counsellor is seen as being unable to exert control, then the risks to female clients increase. This means that invoking the Law must be done in the context of knowing male clients' perceptions. To some, that would be an admission of a loss of control.

What began as a question of whether to choose individual or couples counselling has taken a rather circuitous route, and there is no easy answer. To some extent it is linked with the aims of the counselling, as clients wishing to remain in a relationship might be seen together, but if the woman client is contemplating leaving then individual counselling is required – though even this does not guarantee client safety. Whatever the choice, counsellors should ensure that clients have an escape or warning procedure in the event of violence and danger to themselves.

Although couples work is not common with clients in violent relationships, we should allow women to make their own decisions – and the outcome is not necessarily negative.

Carol: 'It was the first time I really felt able to talk to Dod, and it felt good. I was able to say what was on my mind and felt safe. He had to sit there and listen. Usually he just walks out of the room.'

The role of the man and counselling

The final problem, and sometimes it is a major problem, is that of the involvement of the woman's partner in any counselling arrangements. Some workers tend to ignore violent partners and some counsellors seem to have difficulties engaging those who inflict violence. Yet the truth is that women in violent relationships are linked with their partners and to simply ignore such an important part of the situation is unrealistic. For this reason my preference is to try and engage male partners, though this does not mean they should be involved in the counselling. Sometimes knowing what is happening can be sufficient. Sometimes they can give permission for their partners to attend counselling, and if this reduces the risk of violence, if the partners are happy enough for the women to attend, then this can be helpful –

however much the idea of getting permission for someone to come to counselling leaves me uneasy.

There is always tension in counselling women in violent relationships in that it sounds as if this is aimed solely at women, whereas clients make no such differentiation. They often see themselves as part of a couple, and to ignore their partner makes them uncomfortable. Thus counsellors have to be flexible, to be conscious that all cases are different, and they have to keep the welfare of the client as paramount, as opposed to their own feelings. As a believer in non-violence, I still believe it is right that as a counsellor I try to engage violent partners. What also has to be accepted is that male partners are seldom overjoyed with the idea of counselling.

Fortunately, I have had experience of working with family support groups and came across the same problem of trying to engage men in looking at relationship difficulties. This involves trying to get men to go beyond their macho role, to see that their behaviour might not be acceptable but that they are accepted as a person. One thing that I try to impress on male partners is that they have a right to make their views heard, that they are important, and that their involvement in the counselling is a reflection of their role in the situation.

Peter: 'I have to admit I was not keen to come along here. I thought you would be all for Tanya. But when the two of us got talking then I thought at least you were listening. At last there was someone who was listening to my part of the story. I did not like you, but I respected you. I felt you were OK. And that was a shock. I had you marked out as a goody-goody interfering bastard. And now? I don't know ... I've got to think this all out.'

What is important is that counsellors are sensitive to everyone who is involved in a problematic situation and are able to put aside their own feelings. Counsellors are not in control of the process that is going on, but they are part of it. Thus there is less control in counselling than might be imagined. This is no drawback to its effectiveness, provided counsellors acknowledge their limitations and those of counselling itself.

Reasons for coming to counselling

It is worthwhile discussing why couples with violent relationships have come for counselling. Clients will often give what they think the answers are or what they think the answers should be: the woman is being subjected to violence and wants this to stop and wants the relationship to improve; the man comes along to see if he can be helped as regards his violence and also wants things to get better. This is all possible, but in my experience couples come along with a variety of agendas. The couple want to improve their relationship, but there is a great likelihood that they will end up arguing during the session. In short, they fall into old patterns of behaviour. At times the counsellor might even wonder whether the office is merely another venue for a shouting match. So one of the counsellor's tasks is to work out what the clients' agendas are and then to introduce them as areas of work at a later stage.

From the male client's perspective, coming to counselling may be the result of partner pressure – I'll stay with you as long as you agree we go for help.' The result of such pressure can be resentment, which can be taken out against his partner, the counsellor, or the counselling itself, by trying to sabotage it. Counsellors should home in on the resentment and the man's feelings around being pressurized into coming for counselling. What the resentment also indicates is a power imbalance and struggle, a struggle that continues through the counselling. The male client will pressurize his partner and often the counsellor as well. He can affect the counselling by trying to monopolize the conversation, by implicit threats, or simply by creating a threatening atmosphere. However, such obvious attempts are more easily countered, as opposed to less blatant tactics such as not speaking in the session, which eventually can cause tension.

What can be difficult for counsellors to deal with is the male clients' use of reasonableness. They say they are being quite reasonable, talk in a controlled manner, and contrast themselves with their partners who are unstable, hysterical and unable to act logically. This is best done with female partners who are easily upset by such tactics and make the mistake of reacting emotively, thereby appearing to confirm their partners' assertions. If the female partners are more restrained then it is easier to concentrate on the subject of violence. The male partners now use reason to minimize what has happened, to rationalize the violence, and to claim that it was provoked. An extension of the male process can be to forward unfounded reasons for the violence, such as false justification, placing the responsibility on the woman, or externalizing the situation and placing the responsibility on outside forces such as drink or past relationships, as if these are totally unrelated to the male partner.

Couples counselling – the beginning

Suppose there is an agreement that the counselling should take place with both client and partner present. There has to be a negotiation about the work to be contracted for the future. In particular, should the couple only be seen together by the counsellor? This seems a very reasonable arrangement, but it is open to power play. If the going gets tough, then it is usually the male partner who fails to come to the counselling. And with all such failures, it is easy enough to manufacture reasons to explain why it was impossible to come. But this then means his partner, the client, cannot come for counselling. In effect, he can sabotage the counselling. It is not surprising that the drop-out rate for couples is greater than that of individual counselling (Allgood and Crane, 1991). Another point is that women may be afraid to fully disclose what is happening in front of their partner, and by insisting on always working with couples, counsellors may simply never discover the reality of their clients' lives together. Some women clients manoeuvre events so that their partners are unable to attend. So it can be easier to say that couples counselling is not essential, and either party can also be seen individually. Of course, this is no perfect answer as it sets up its own dynamic and further potential problems. With issues of power, jealousy and recognition already apparent, who is seen by the counsellor can become a further contentious issue.

The structure of counselling sessions

In my opinion, it is best to contract for a number of sessions, twelve at the most, and then have a review and a break. The reason for so doing, and this procedure is recommended for individual counselling as well, is to provide clear structure and a chance to evaluate progress. It also provides the opportunity for a change to individual counselling. I noticed some time ago that introducing a month's break after the review, if the couple wanted to continue, was surprisingly productive. This break gives couples the opportunity to inwardly digest and put into practice what has been said and what has been learned during counselling. There can be a renegotiation of the counselling contract, and there is much to be said for this plan. It brings a sense of ending, which itself provides a useful resonance and material for those in relationships that may be coming to an end. Also, a sense of closure is easier to contemplate for abuser clients and lessens their anxiety, which is likely to prove beneficial for their partners. Abusers attending counselling can feel themselves under attack and find their counselling is not the most pleasant experience. However, it is easier to bear if there is at least a foreseeable end.

Counsellor and reality

The first requirement for the counsellor working with clients in violent relationships is to be realistic. This is not just a product of counsellors' experience but is echoed by clients themselves (Oldfield, 1983:73). Couples who have been behaving in set ways are not going to suddenly change, even if they want to. Months or years of arguing, being mutually verbally abusive and then the man being physically abusive is not likely to end overnight. But there is going to be no change unless certain behaviour is indicated as being unacceptable. Yet if every objectionable action is picked up, there will be very little learning. Two or three points made and discussed are going to be more effective than twenty. If too much learning is attempted, clients can feel overhelmed, even under attack.

To avoid behavioural ruts, we have to avoid situations where it is easy to trigger off accustomed action and reaction patterns. Working with couples, we expect them to be able to talk through issues logically, identify problems and work on their solution. But this is precisely what violence-affected couples cannot do. They are liable to end up arguing or being kept away from contentious areas by the worker, so feel the real substance of their difficulties is not being addressed. Ordinary counselling, useful for low emotional situations, fails where there is high emotion. Here a much more structured approach is needed, with the emphasis on client learning.

The reality of helping

Sometimes, as counsellors, we read about working with couples and even read a bit of actual session work done by others. We then try to do the same, but things in reality seem so much messier. The following shows some of the difficulties in such work. At this early session, the couple have agreed to the rules, yet it is not long before they become history.

Me: 'Well ...'

Anna: 'We get on fine, don't we?'

Me: 'Sorry, I thought we had agreed that there were some difficulties?'

Gary: 'What difficulties?'

Me: 'Those the two of you had spoken about earlier. Look, I'm beginning to feel a bit uncomfortable, as if I'm walking into forbidden territory.'

Gary: 'I don't know what you are fucking talking about!'

Me: 'Anger. I feel you are getting angry.'

Gary: 'No fucking wonder!'

Anna: 'Shut up, Gary!'

Gary: 'You, shut your puss!'

Me: 'Let's stop right there! We agreed to there being no verbal abuse ...'

Gary: 'Errrmmm.' [Indistinct mumbling]

Me: 'Sorry, you were saying, Gary?'

Gary: 'FUCKING POOF!!'

Anna: 'He's married. You're fucking ignorant, you know that?'

Gary: 'Fancy him, do you?'

Anna: 'Aw, piss off!'

Me: 'OK, OK. Let's all calm down. Gary, you seem unhappy with the way things are developing in this session ...'

Anna: 'See, that's what I have to put up with all the time.'

Me: 'Gary, how are you feeling right now?'

Gary: 'Pissed off with all this talk. What's the point?'

Anna: 'The point is we are trying to work things out.'

Me: 'Do you want to work things out and the two of you get on better together, Gary?'

The first point to make is that working with such couples can be exhausting and as the worker's energy falls, so it becomes harder to guide the session. But there is a further point in that Gary did have a point. For men who are used to dominating women physically, just talking may seem not just pointless, but also dangerous from their controlling stance. Indeed, some men will react physically because their partners are verbally more accomplished. This is a very general characteristic; men are brought up to be active, whereas women are brought up to care and relate verbally. So men accustomed to dominating may well be placed in a situation where they feel outgunned. The chief concern must be with the victims of violence, so making the helping process easier for men is done only to ensure that they feel happier and are thus less likely to be violent towards their partner. In this way, a result can be achieved and the violence, one way or another, can be stopped.

Role of the worker

Insisting on structure seems simple enough, but this aim may conflict with client behaviour. The latter can be a continuation of power struggles, which is now transplanted into counselling. Counsellors may well experience both parties wanting the worker as an ally against their partner. This can be evidenced in several ways.

- Direct appeals to the worker looking for agreement with the client's view.

- Trying to engage in a close relationship with the worker, so the latter is seen as acting as a support to the particular client. This can be done by agreeing with the worker, asking for the worker's opinion or advice.

- Speaking to the worker rather than his or her partner and trying to get the continuing attention of the worker.

If these manoeuvres prove ineffective, clients may continue their warfare and the counsellor may be ignored or treated as an enemy. The latter may not be obvious as methods other than overt aggression may be used. This can take the form of emotional blackmail, with openings such as, 'I thought it was your job to help people like me.' In fact, anything directed to the counsellor has to be viewed as a possible attempt to influence, whatever its apparent content or objective. In addition, a client may court influence by acting as a victim, as helpless, or as wronged when this is not the case.

Making alliances

It may seem that counsellors have to take a neutral line and favour neither party, yet this merely reinforces the power imbalance. An alternative is for the counsellor to make an alliance with the woman as the less powerful, weaker client, rather in the manner of structural family therapy. However, this overt support of the woman can endanger her. Her partner may feel embattled and become more defensive, and this can result in violence. However, there are more indirect means of helping the woman client and yet still safeguarding her position.

1. The woman client can be asked to start first.

2. Names are used constantly, as this shows respect.

3. The session is monitored for signs of oppression and appropriate action taken.

4. Concepts such as control, respect, and oppression are named and linked up with the here-and-now events in the session.

5. The worker should not overreact but remember the male client should also be treated with respect.

What is important, especially in the early stages of counselling, is to weave a passage through promoting change and possible counteractions against such change. Most often, clients do not come about their violent and abusive relationship, but this emerges after some time. What is required is a partial renegotiation of the contracted counselling. This may require overriding the desires of one or even both clients. This leads to some counsellors feeling very uneasy, as they see client wants and needs as paramount. However, in violent relationships, couples are likely to have very different wants and needs, and these may well conflict. Furthermore, we tend to see the person-centred approach based on Western individual values rather than the betterment of the group. This does not mean the interests of the group have to be necessarily pursued, but it does mean there are others to consider, and society as a whole, usually in the form of the Law and its enforcement.

Client expectations

Thus, expectations are not simply what the clients say they want but are subject to negotiation with the counsellor. Very few couples are likely to agree to talk about their violence, just like that. This means the worker has to devise a positive way of presenting possible areas of discussion and action. There is no set way of doing so, as the counsellor has to judge what clients can take without walking out or failing to return for the next session.

Me: 'We have arrived at a difficult area, one that I did not expect, that of violence. The two of you came here about your debts; the question is where do we go from here? Do you think it is worth looking ...'

Lorraine: 'Aye, definitely ...'

Me: 'You haven't said anything, Mark. Do you think it is worth taking some time to look at the difficulties both of you have?'

Mark: 'I don't see it is any of your business.'

Me: 'Unfortunately, now I have been told about the violence it is my business. If that is going on then you are committing common assault and breaking the Law. But is involving the Law going to help?'

Lorraine: 'I don't want the Law, police ...'

Me: 'So we all agree we do not want the police in, right?'

Mark: 'Who told you, said I was lifting my hand anyway?'

Me: 'Hold on, can I get agreement or not about the police. Do we want them to be involved or not?'

Lorraine: 'No.'

Mark: 'No.'

Me: 'Good, so we all agree on that. Going back to your question, Mark, I think it's a good one. What I know, or think I know, comes from what the two of you tell me, directly or indirectly. Now Lorraine mentioned being hit and you, Mark, did not argue.'

Mark: 'That was just a fucking accident ...'

Lorraine: 'Some accident! Boomph! A fist accidently lands in my face. That'll be right!'

Me: 'It strikes me that there are several problems both of you face and continue to face. They don't seem to go away. Violence or at least Lorraine imagining there is violence is one of them.'

Lorraine: 'Imagining!'

Me: 'I say that, Lorraine, because my job is not to take sides but to help both of you look at what is happening, to help both of you to have your say, and for both of you to listen to the other person. Whether this succeeds is up to the two of you. At the end of this interview you might walk out and say,"Well, that was a bloody waste of time!" and not return. I hope not, as I would like to help, but it's your decision.'

Lorraine: 'Well, I think we need help.'

Me: 'So the question now is what do you, Lorraine, and you, Mark, want to happen and what do you expect to happen? Let's look at wants first. Lorraine?'

Lorraine: 'I just want him to act like we were married. He thinks he's still single, does what he likes, and treats me like a doormat.'

Mark: 'You let people walk all over you! Buy any old rubbish.'

Lorraine: 'Never takes me out.'

Me: 'We will come to these points later. Mark, what do you want out of coming here?'

Mark: 'I just want her to stop getting into debt.'

Lorraine: 'You spend all the money!'

Me: 'OK. Now I notice one thing about your wants; they referred to the other person. Lorraine, you wanted Mark to take you out, to share life with you more. Mark, you wanted Lorraine to stop getting into debt. Right? And why hasn't this happened? Because neither of you can totally control the other one. So however much we want a person to change, it means nothing, nothing at all, unless that person wants to change. You can change yourself, but in the end you can't force others to change.'

Lorraine: 'You mean I've got to change for him?'

Me: 'No. You've got to change for each other. If there is not movement on both sides then we are all wasting our time.'

Lorraine: 'I still think it's wrong that he hits me and it's me who has to change.'

Me: 'It's your decision whether to change and what kind of change. Some women who have been hit by their partners have decided to leave, or decided to learn martial arts, or ...'

Lorraine: 'That I fancy! Kung fu, you bastard!'

Mark: 'That'll be right!'

Me: 'Before the two of you troop off to watch Bruce Lee, do you understand what I am saying? Both of you have got to be prepared to change and to get away from what seems to have been happening.'

Lorraine: '... no use if things stay the same.'

Me: 'So don't sit back and wait for the other to change, otherwise nothing will happen.'

Some counsellors prefer not to work in a way that is so directive. Indeed, some may see it as hardly person-centred. First, this tends to be the perception of counsellors, not clients. This does, however, assume that all clients are the same, which is clearly not the case. So counsellors have to be able to sense what would be seen by their clients as directive. The former often exaggerate the influence they have. If this is not the case, then the likelihood of dependency on counselling and oppression by the counsellor would be even greater threats to real helpfulness. There is a tendency to downgrade client potential and abilities, which can act against counselling. Part of the problem comes with counsellors seeing directiveness as being very much bound up with verbal communication, with grammatical syntax, rather than non-verbal aspects such as tone, context and working relationship. Haley was more realistic when he saw that any statements have connotations of power (Haley, 1976), so directiveness is not absolute but a matter of degree.

Another aspect that should be noted is the matter of the Law, which cannot be ignored. Counselling is usually seen as private and confidential to those involved, which can mean those not involved are seen as being largely irrelevant. In particular, social concerns can remain hidden from the general public. However, violence against women is not just a private but also a social issue. Treating it just as the former leaves counsellors open to manipulation as counselling can be used as a substitute for justice. The question of whether counselling comes before or after a possible legal conviction has to be considered. As we have noted, legal action is the best way to stop battering; it cannot simply be ignored.

We also glimpsed a common criticism of working with couples, namely, that it is the woman who appears to have to make compromises whereas it is her partner who is causing the problem. There seems little justice in this. What we have to bear in mind are the following points.

- Abused clients are used to making compromises, so for many they readily accept that doing so is preferable to possibly antagonizing their partners.

- The counsellor has to plan for the long term and this may require compromises in the beginning, and for counsellors as well as women clients. This I see as acceptable provided it is more than counter-balanced by working toward the real empowerment of women clients in the end.

- Though outsiders might see the crucial issue as being one of justice, women clients usually see it more personally, as their partners trying to put one over them. This makes it easier to turn the situation round, as any empowering action by the counsellor is seen as an adequate counteraction.

- Client perceptions should be checked out later on, and due attention given to feelings and clients understanding precisely what is happening.

Finally, rather than worrying about being directive, it is sometimes more productive to consider the question of control, which actually mirrors the basic client concern. Counsellors can be directive – in fact it is difficult not to be so – but it is not necessary to be controlling. For instance, the counsellor should never get angry or annoyed, as this is a loss of control. To aid this process, there are some basic procedures that may be employed.

1. Be firm to the point of usefulness. Insistence on a point of view or on agreement when this is not going to occur is a waste of time. Remember the issue and re-introduce it in a later session.

2. Never prove clients wrong. They do not change their minds but 'develop their outlook'; they are not wrong but 'have their own perspectives'; no one loses but everyone wins. The counsellor has to avoid being sucked into the clients' ways of thinking. Counsellors are not right, but they have been helpful to clients.

3. Losing face is more damaging than losing the argument. Clients have to be given support and some way of retaining self-esteem in counselling, whether abuser or abused. Self-direction rarely comes from low self-esteem. Thus any point against a client has to be followed by positive input for that person. This is not just for the counselling but also models ways in which clients can interact more productively.

What is left unsaid

Violence against a client may be forgotten by the counsellor. This may seem extraordinary, but results from counsellors knowing intellectually of the violence but not being able to link it emotionally with the person sitting in the room. Many counsellors are disarmed by the fact that violent men can be very pleasant and sound very reasonable. They are so because it is a very good way to control counsellors. The opposite side is when the counsellor takes the facade at face value and tries to go against what the man wants. The client can then turn quite abruptly to bullying tactics. If being nice does not work, then another tactic is employed. However, the important task for the counsellor is to look not just to his or her relationship with the male client, but also to that between the couple. One way of moving to this perspective and ignoring confrontation with the counsellor is for the latter to understand that violent bullying tactics are just that – tactics. Many male clients have been very angry with me and left me anxious about the session, yet by the next time they have forgotten the verbal abuse simply because it was a reaction and not personal. This should be contrasted with their reactions against partners which are personal and nothing appears to be forgotten. So counsellors in turn do not have to forget and never mention these incidents, as boundaries have to be maintained, but neither do they have to take abuse personally.

The counsellor puts such confrontation behind and attends not to his agenda but to the couple and their interactions, particularly the non-verbal signals as these are harder to disguise. With violent relationships, so much is unsaid so the counsellor has to grasp the total understanding, intellectual and emotional, of the possible situation and orientate to the couple's life-situation; not only to listen actively but also to watch for signals. These can be overt, such as when the woman looks to the man before replying. The difficulty then lies in working out the significance of this move, as couples who are very sharing will also react in this way. Another signal is the time taken to reply to questions, as this is usually a bit longer when people are covering up. Again, this slight delay has to be differentiated from time needed for clients to think about the answer or simply being unsure which of them will answer. Another indication can be over-compensation or overreaction to questions. When one client was asked how she would describe her partner, she replied:

Anita: 'He is everything to me, the best person in the world. We will probably settle down and get married, be together for ever. I don't see us ever being apart.'

However, this simply did not ring true, and Anita's partner did not seem totally at ease, nor did he react like a person in an ecstatic relationship. To some extent the counsellor's gut feelings should not be dismissed, nor simply accepted, but analysed and seen as one possible perspective on clients. As it happened, this relationship ended in a matter of months.

Entering into the counselling

Saying that counsellors should be aware of the power of relationships, including their own, in the counselling session, and mark gender inequality and counsellor–client inequality to achieve honesty and self-responsibility, has to be seen as an ongoing process. It begins from the very start. If there has been violence, then simply asking clients, 'Can you tell me the problem?', the usual counselling gambit, ignores the power differential and the difficulty women have in answering honestly. What is more, starting off in this way, it may sound as if the counsellor is going to solve that problem.

To begin correctly is important, as once a certain line has been taken by the counsellor it is difficult to take clients along with an abrupt change. So a certain line is taken and it is best to be quite explicit about it.

Me: 'Right, now, in what way can I help the two of you?'

Don: 'You tell us ...'

Chantel: 'I thought, well, you tell us ... get things sorted out.'

Me: 'I get worried, like I am now, when people ask me to sort things out, and I'll tell you why. In the end, only the two of you can really do that. I can help but not tell you what to do, solve things for you. Most of it is up to you. Does that sound reasonable?'

Chantel: 'I think you're right. It's up to us in the end to get things worked out. We can't do it on our own.'

Me: 'You haven't been able to up to now, at least not easily. But the two of you managed to come along here together so the two of you can work some things out, agree in some respects ... Don, you don't look totally convinced about what has been said. Is there something with which you disagree or are you unsure ...?'

Don: '... wait and see.'

Me: 'I appreciate your honesty, Don. It's easy to simply agree, not so easy at times to hold back. Let me tell you, I think you have struck on an important point. Why should you trust me or what might happen? Let's see how things work out and then form our own judgements. So perhaps that is something for the three of us to remember: all of this will take a bit of time. How do you feel about that, Chantel?'

Chantel: 'I'm not a very patient person.'

Me: 'So do you think you will be able to stick with it?'

Chantel: 'Oh, yes! It's easy here ... There's no pressure.'

Me: 'It will not be easy all the time. The three of us have to be aware that we have a lot to get through and the going may be tough ... As usual, I've veered off the subject a bit. I started out asking how I could help, but then rather said it was up to you. Perhaps I should ask if you have any more of an idea what you expect of me. Don, any thoughts?'

Don: 'No, I'm easy.'

Me: 'Chantel?'

Chantel: 'I would prefer you to go on like you've been doing.'

Me: 'What I suggest is that we look at your own different reasons for coming for help and what you expect. Is that OK? Chantel?'

Chantel: 'That's fine.'

Me: 'Don?'

Don: 'OK.'

Me: 'Chantel, can you tell me what you want from the counselling? You mentioned getting things sorted out. Can you be precise and say exactly what things?'

Comments on the introductory stage

It is important to have the roles of the worker and the clients clear and acknowledged as soon as possible. Clients have to be ultimately responsible for themselves and the worker for what happens in the counselling session. Very reasonably, most people not accustomed to counselling have the expectation that it might be like a medical consultation, the closest comparison in their eyes. There is a natural expectation that the counsellor will tell them what is wrong, will produce a remedy and tell them how to carry out it out. Such expectations are very often present, even when unspoken, so the worker has to make the situation quite clear.

Although rules and guidelines may be outlined, these do not mean very much unless they are bedded into an adequate working relationship. For this reason, the worker is also trying to build up that relationship and has to take time to do so. What may seem to be irrelevancies are often responses to the demands of the working relationship. Such demands are sensed by the worker and have to be balanced against the clients beginning to lose interest is the proceedings.

Another point to be made is that it is worth making minimal self-disclosure such as, 'I get worried ...', as in the above extract. The couple are not prepared for any great degree of worker self-disclosure, but it is important to include it minimally as it does help to give a pointer to the style of counselling.

Finally, no worker can do everything correctly or cover all points. For this reason, a recording of the sessions is important so the counselling can be reviewed and amendments made during the next session.

Specific points about couples counselling

The couple, whatever their difficulties and strains, have come as a couple and so are treated as such. Within this dyad, it is also important to reinforce individuality and ask both members questions rather than speaking indirectly 'to the couple'. Treating clients solely as individuals increases the risks to the woman client and can involve power struggles in the counselling, whereas addressing just the couple reinforces the ongoing gender inequality and resultant behaviour.

There is a need from the start for some positive reinforcement. The counsellor also has to take account of who is being reinforced and the effect of the clients' relationship. This applies equally to the asking of questions: which of the clients is asked first. The less powerful client, the woman, is often likely to agree automatically with her partner over contentious issues if asked second. However, always asking her first is likely to be seen as an overt attempt at influencing the relationship, and even favouring her. Account should also be taken of the tactic of not answering questions put in general to the couple. This may force the worker to ask that person specifically and can represent a way for that client to gain control.

Ending and learning

Sir Thomas Beecham said of conducting that as long as the orchestra started together and ended together, people would ignore much of what went on in between. Counselling can be like that. Usually there is emphasis put on starting sessions or starting the counselling in general, but less on endings. In other forms of counselling, endings are impor-tant, but they are potentially extremely valuable with clients in violent relationships, as ending is often an underlying agenda, especially if much of the counselling of violence-affected couples relies on the clients learning new patterns of behaviour. Learning is an important aspect of the counselling process. Though Rogers (Rogers, C., 1967: 351) saw self-actualization as an inherent tendency, it is more realistic to see it working through social learning (Wexler, 1974). This means the ending of the session is important as a means of reinforcing that learning. This can be done in various ways, inlcuding those below.

1. Relaxing tension to make learning more effective. This can be done by acknowledging the difficulties encountered in the session, commenting generally on some positive advances, and thanking the clients for having put in hard work in coming to grips with the various issues.

2. By having a short review of some of the main points covered in the session. It is best to concentrate on just two or three; more than this results in less final learning. The review should not be cognitive; it should also refer to feelings during the session and, as the worker, I should state how I feel. This also allows me to turn the session into a positive experience for myself, so I can say what I have learnt. However the session goes, it helps to view difficulties

as steps to learning, so even the most difficult time can be turned to good use. It is unhelpful if clients go away from the session feeling bad.

3. The counsellor should be aware of difficulties clients can have with endings and their reactions. This can vary between skipping through the ending process, to delaying it by bringing up new material or problems. It is best to leave matters but then raise the issue at the early part of the next session.

Continuation through the ending

The session comes to an end, but recognition should be made of the fact that there will be further work ahead. This can be done indirectly by:

1. Asking the couple whether they think anything could have been done differently and better in future sessions.

2. Asking them if there is anything that they feel should be discussed the next time.

3. Recognizing any unfinished issues and agreeing that they should be brought up and examined during the next session.

By referring to the future the worker not only increases the chance of the sessions continuing, if required, but moves the clients to think of the future, rather than constantly thinking back to the past and all its problems. Ultimately, the aim must be to enable clients to function without any recourse to counselling, to act with responsibility which includes not just themselves but their obligations to others (Brayfield, 1962). Paradoxically, this means that some of the ending comes at the start. Counsellors should think about ending when they start; they should never leave it to the end of the session.

6 FEELINGS, RISKS AND CONSCIOUSNESS-RAISING

Long-term work

Those who come for help tend to do so because their difficulties are long-standing and they have failed to solve or to work through them. Where relationship violence is concerned, the difficulties are even more likely to have a considerable history. This means that there is often much long-term multi-problem work to be done, and there is a real danger of being submerged by the many cumulative difficulties, of being diverted from course by ongoing difficulties, and so allowing events to control the counselling and clients. To counteract such dangers counsellors should have an overall plan to fall back on, a basic guide to ensure overall progress.

The art of using plans is to ensure that they are as brief as possible, and helpful rather than directive. If they cannot be remembered by the counsellor then they are of little use. The counsellor has to be able to remember and implement them during the counselling.

Content of an overall plan

The following plan is no more than a list of different aspects that might be considered. They are those which relate to violent relationships, but it should be remembered that there are going to be other areas of work which are not directly related to violence. Thus the following is merely supplementary to other ongoing work.

Working with feelings
Risk assessment
Consciousness-raising
Work on communication
Boundary-setting
Male abusers and treatment
Violence and alcohol
Love and affective issues
Self-esteem
Separation
The role of children
Identity

Counselling has been divided into individual and couples counselling, but in the pursuit of brevity the above sections will be divided between the two. However this does not imply that they do not apply to both forms of counselling. It will be noticed that there is no work done on violence itself. This is because such work does not concern women clients but men, and such work should be done individually or in male abuser groups, not with partners.

WORKING WITH FEELINGS

Feelings as an agenda

Person-centred counselling is very much about working with feelings, so it might seem redundant to see this topic as deserving a special mention. However, this is not such an easy area, partly because emotions can become so heightened that everyone is wary of dealing with them. Here the importance of boundaries should be stressed, as they may seem to be barriers but they also provide safety. An analogy would be a dog on a leash that tries to fight every passing dog, whatever its size. Its bravery comes from being on the leash and knowing that its owner will intervene. Take it off the lead and the dog's behaviour is likely to be very different.

Counsellors have to be prepared to allow clients to express themselves, even though the outcome can be upsetting at times. To know how clients feel, counsellors have to be empathic. This comes from interpreting and verifying verbal and non-verbal language. However, this cannot be done all the time, so after a time counsellors rely on sensing how clients are feeling. Most of the information is given non-verbally, usually facially, but as such it not only relates to feelings but is also determined by the social context (Hess et al., 1991) and the person's intent (Chovil, 1991). So there has to be careful interpretation of facial and other non-verbal expressions. This process is made easier if there are repeated interactions with the person (Ickes et al., 1990). Not surprisingly, we tend to be more empathic with friends than with strangers. To increase empathy, apart from being with people more often, it helps to check verbally how they are feeling. This shows whether our evaluation is accurate or not (Marangoni et al., 1995).

In practice, it is easier to gauge negative emotions than those which are positive (Gaelick et al., 1985) and situations which are important or threatening (Sillars et al., 1984). All this would suggest that women in violent relationships should be able to sense impending trouble, but it seems that those in insecure relationships who find their partners attractive are likely to give poor empathic responses (Simpson et al., 1995). In fact, empathy can be affected by a person's expectations. What has to be said is that empathy is not easy to gauge correctly in situations of high affect, and counsellors would be unwise to rely too much on their empathy. This in turn requires them to ask about feelings and check them out.

Identification of feelings

It is easy to presume that we know how others feel and think, but this can be incorrect and also relies on our feelings about clients and the stereotypical pictures we have of them. We see male clients as angry. This might well be correct, but fails to acknowledge that male abusive partners can fall into certain patterns of emotional expression, and one of the most acceptable to them is anger. In complex scenarios clients are likely to have many feelings, and part of their problem is that these are contradictory and often unidentified. By being empathic, we might pick up some of these different feelings, or not. The important task is to work with them if they are genuinely experienced by the clients.

Graham: 'I do lose the rag with Della. She acts daft, makes a fool of herself, puts herself at risk, goes out and will do whatever after a drink.'

Me: 'So were you angry or were you worried about her?'

Graham: 'Both, I suppose.'

Me: 'So part of it was worry, worry about what might happen to her. It sounds as if you care for Della.'

Graham: 'Yes.'

Me: 'Is that a definite "Yes" or is that a polite "Yes"? I'll tell you right now, I prefer honesty to politeness.'

Graham: 'Of course I care for her! Why do you think ... do you think it's easy ...?'

Me: 'But do you think Della knows you care? Do you think getting angry shows that you care for her? I mean, have you told her that you care?'

Graham: 'I've told her, I've told her! I said to her, "This is just because you're important. Don't you understand, you silly idiot!" ... I could have put it better.'

Me: 'I reckon you should put it better. What comes over to me is a very mixed message. At this very moment I don't know what your feelings for Della are, so she might be having the same problem. Your words say one thing but your whole tone and behaviour says something different. I love you; shout. I love you; biff. Do you see what I mean?'

Graham: 'I suppose so.'

There can be a difficulty in that apparently contrary emotions can be evoked, which leads to confusion as to what really is felt. This is often the case with intimates, who can produce feelings of both love and hate at the same time, resulting in anxiety about that confusion. When we think we know how clients feel, we would do well to remember that this is frequently more than the clients do themselves.

Expression of feelings

Once a client has thought and reflected on what feelings are being experienced, then there is the question of how best they might be expressed. With Graham, we saw a common difficulty for men, the expression of softer feelings. For women, especially those who have been abused, there is some trepidation about expressing any feelings, partly through fear of the consequences. After a time, this becomes an ingrained habit so it then becomes independent of any immediate consequences. Yet feelings cannot be entirely suppressed. It is emotionally and even physically draining constantly having to keep the lid on one's feelings, and sometimes these will erupt. Those abused women who feel murderous towards their partners do so because of an accumulation of feelings, past and present, which can hardly be restrained.

Me: 'Normally, do you find it quite difficult to say how you feel?'

Leigh: 'I've got to get angry before I say what I feel. I put up with quite a lot, but it all builds up. And something silly can trigger it off, and whoosh! It comes out.'

Me: 'It all comes out then.'

Leigh: 'Yes. Once I start then I'm hard to stop.'

It is worth noting that abused women can be afraid not only of their abusers but also of themselves. Though violence comes from male partners, feelings of violence come from both men and women.

Counselling sessions and feelings

One of the difficult questions for counsellors is the extent to which they should encourage, allow or restrain the expression of feelings with couples. If clients come to the counselling session with strong feelings, as is often the case, then those feelings are likely to interfere with their ability to listen and concentrate, to reason and to interact with their partners in a constructive manner. So the process of ventilation, allowing clients to express overwhelming feelings, appears best. However, such feelings often involve their partners and what can happen is that it results in an acrimonious argument, which with some couples can be lengthy and hard to stop. Even intervention by the counsellor is not always effective.

Me: 'OK, so the two of you are upset over the money. You have both had your say, so I would like the three of us to look a bit further and ...'

Bill: 'You must not use that money! You must not use that money!'

Sandra: 'Dick!'

Me: 'Have the two of you finished? Look, I don't want to keep interrupting the two of you, but I think it is time to move on. Is that OK?'

Bill: 'Fine by me!'

Sandra: 'If he shuts up.'

Bill: 'You can't leave it, can you? Must have the last ...'

Sandra: 'It's the only time I do have a say! Paul knows that.'

Me: 'Everyone will have their say. I would like to have mine right now.'

Bill: 'If it stops Sandra.'

Sandra: 'That's what you would like!'

Most counsellors have probably encountered such situations, where client couples indulge in sniping and the counsellor feels increasingly physically and emotionally drained but is conscious that any coherent plan is slipping away from the session. It is at this point the counsellor must act, as the clients are not likely to alter their behaviour.

Me: 'Have either of you been on television?'

Bill: 'Eh?'

Me: 'No? Because it just occurred to me, suppose the three of us had been secretly televised, then what would the viewers have seen? The two of you having goes at each other over the last five minutes and me – totally unsuccessfully – trying to stop the two of you.'

Sanda: 'Wasn't my fault!'

Me: 'No, it was not your fault Sandra, neither was it Bill's fault. It was my fault, and I would like to explain. If we had been on television, then viewers would have noticed that I was caught up in what was happening as much as the two of you. None of us was able to change the discussion and make it more helpful because none of us sat back and thought, "Hold on a minute, what exactly is going on here? Why are we", and this includes me, "why are we unable to help each other?" I believe all of us do want things to get better, otherwise why should the two of you bother to come to see me and why should I bother to see the two of you? So however bad things have been, however bad things are for you, yet in some way there are feelings for each other and both of you wish things were better. Am I right?'

Bill: 'Yes.'

Sandra: 'Right.'

Me: 'So let's look back over the five minutes of arguing. None of us was able to change matters as all three of us were caught up in it. It was my fault as I should be able to make things better, but because I too was caught up I couldn't. So no matter who it is, or what feelings are about, we can hit a brick wall. Now if you were running towards a brick wall what would you do?'

Bill: 'Stop.'

Me: 'Exactly. And have a quick look and then go round it. Change direction. What were the three of us doing? Not changing direction. Repeating the pattern of behaviour again and again. Here's a nice brick wall. Bang! Didn't get through it that time. Bang! Nor that. But if I run into this wall a thousand times, then I'm going to get through it eventually. Do you believe that!'

Sandra: 'You're nuts.'

Me: 'I'll get a professional opinion on that later. But, seriously, do you see what I'm getting at? Same pattern of arguing and we get nowhere.'

Bill: 'I can see what you're getting at. I agree. But what do we do?'

Me: 'You do what I'm doing now and what I should have done earlier. Think about what was really going on. Bill, you mentioned Sandra had to have the last word, but I was doing exactly the same. While Sandra, you were saying that you hardly ever had a chance to have your say, but I was stopping you. So I wasn't helping the situation. However, now I can do something about it by getting the two of you to talk not about the money, as I reckon the two of you have argued enough times about that. Let's consider what I mentioned. Sandra, you have to have the last word, and you, Bill, tend to stop Sandra from speaking. I mean, what is more important, money or the relationship between the two of you? So are we all going to look at, look seriously at what happens between the two of you?'

So ventilation is useful in the short term. If it continues too long it can change into client arguments, but these are also of use provided they are used as a source of material for counselling. A second point is that of having breaks in counselling. These are usually taken to allow all parties to regain their composure and calm down. However, we can also use breaks to allow clients to internalize what has been said or to introduce a change when the counselling does not seem to be getting anywhere.

Me: 'Look, we have been going at this for about half an hour. Do you fancy having a quick break, have some coffee and biscuits?'

Robin: 'Suits me.'

Me: 'Carla?'

Carla: 'Sure, why not?'

[Later]

Me: 'Here we are then. Actually, I was beginning to wilt a bit. You know, it's like I hear myself talking and then I think, "Did I really say that?" Does that sound a bit weird?'

Robin: 'We all say things and then wonder about it. Me, I say things and they come out wrong.'

Me: 'Only this morning the police were diverting cars around this accident in the road and I had been thinking of going to the supermarket. This policeman comes up, and I wind down the window and I swear to God I meant to say "What's up, officer?" but said "Radishes" ...'

Robin: 'He probably thought you were swearing at him.'

Me: 'I never thought of that!'

Robin: 'It's easy to pick things up wrong. I have to admit I do that at times ...'

Here we see that the normally monosyllabic Robin has become quite chatty and also quite revealing, as he has relaxed and no longer feels he is under scrutiny, no longer has to be defensive. So it can be helpful not to counsel clients, or at least give that impression.

Role of the worker

We have noted that women clients can and often are inhibited in what they say by the presence of their partners. Counsellors should remember this, and be extra sure that they are not just accepting and empathic but seen to be so by clients. This has to be integrated with counsellors' abilities to be truly themselves and to be true to themselves. The latter involves being realistic about themselves and others. Reality-grounding, though not considered basic counselling by Rogers, was highlighted by Carkhuff and Berenson (1967) after their research, and is highly relevant when dealing with violence or any form of abuse. This criterion applies not only to counsellors but also to the counselling itself. Reality is often not immediately apparent but sometimes to be discovered, investigated, extended, refined and checked with others.

Mandy: 'It's good to talk to you as you don't just agree. When I done daft things I remember you said, "This is another fine mess you got yourself in", Laurel and Hardy like. I laughed, but I also knew you were serious. I needed to be told because I'm always making excuses. I know when I've fucked up, and feel better if you tell me so as well. How am I going to learn if there's no one to come out and tell me?'

Roy: 'For me, I need an anchor, someone with a line to reality. Sometimes my head's up my arse, and people trying to help is no use. But I can come to see you and there is no need to pretend. I can admit I am in a mess.'

Working with feelings may be viewed as a purely internal affair, but this is insufficient. Feelings have to be put into context, they have to be viewed against the world.

The role of working with feelings

Much of counselling is working with feelings, but in abusive relationships they play an important role with regard to behaviour. Abusers behave in a way that maintains patriarchal control in intimate relationships, but this is not usually a conscious decision. Men will keep control as that is their social role, as they see it, and often as many women also view it. However, reactions come with a diminution of power, so they are losing control. This might be sensed directly, or indirectly, as is the case when he believes his partner 'is getting cheeky, keeps answering back' or 'keeps arguing' – rather than letting him win, presumably. Finally, there can be deep-seated fears such as that of his partner leaving, which is really a fear of abandonment. Feelings disclosed and understood, not interpretations, are the basis for helping and for the ability to be helped.

Dealing with feelings exhibited as anger is especially important, as clients can learn how to distinguish between damaging and non-damaging anger, between personal hostility and annoyance (Cahill, 1981). It is essential that male clients learn to express their anger in ways that are acceptable. This runs beyond dealing just with feelings and their expression, to include consideration of their audience (Welpton, 1973). But this takes some time, so the counsellor has to be prepared for high affect during the early sessions. Indeed, part of the counselling role is that of letting clients access their feelings and express them, but in the context of overall communication, so what is said is also heard (Greenberg and Johnson, 1988). Feelings may come out as anger, but this is of little account until the meaning of that anger is discovered and conveyed to everyone present.

In conclusion, though the emphasis has been on working with feelings, yet we should not forget that they are of prime importance during counselling as far as clients are concerned, more than the problems presented (Maluccio, 1979). Thus feelings are not to be addressed just with regard to counselling work, but are the whole context for doing any work.

RISK ASSESSMENT

Introductory work

Partner violence is so prevalent that counsellors who work with women are quite likely to be working with abused women, even if they do not realize the fact. So the first step is the identification of relationship violence, which requires counsellors to bear in mind its possibility, that it is a common occurrence.

The first step in identification rests on observation, such as noting any bruising, which might be largely covered by heavy make-up. Absence of bruising is not a negative sign, as many men will punch and kick where any marks can be covered by clothing. Other signs can include difficulty in walking and a general jumpiness. Often it is possible to judge that the couple are not happy together from the way they interact, their mutual distance, their watching each other (Rambo et al., 1993:106). There can also be indirect signs, such as being unable to come for counselling or often being ill for two or three days.

All of these can be possible signs and leave the door open for the counsellor to open up the topic of partner violence. Asking clients directly whether they have been hit is actually forcing most of them to deny it, even when a good working relationship has been set up and the woman client appears to feel safe. An abused woman will usually feel safe only when separated from her partner, so if a couple is being seen, it helps to part them, even if for a few minutes. Asking about possible violence is best done gently, by firstly making a statement such as, 'That's a bit of a bruise you've got there.' If the client does not say there is any violence, then rather than just accepting the statement, it can help to say something in the manner of, 'I was just wondering. Sometimes clients come who have been hit, and that concerns me.' Clients are given opportunities to say what has happened, without them being forced to do so. The reason for identification of violence is that there has to be an assessment done to avoid high risks and possible injury to clients.

Identifying the basics

Such an assessment should be part of the overall person-centred style, and thus should be part of a discussion rather than sounding as if the counsellor is using a questionnaire. Talking about violence should be for the benefit of clients, not counsellors, so it should be said that there will be no referral to the police or doctor. Any such action is the responsibility of the clients, unless there is a real physical risk.

What is of most interest are the triggers and patterns of violence. By using these it should be possible to gain some rough idea as to the possible risks to clients. What is needed is precise information, and it should be remembered that clients will often minimize injuries they have sustained. Of particular interest are the following:

- Where did the acts of violence take place: in private? in public? in front of family or friends?

- When did the acts of violence take place: after arguments? after drinking?

- What form did the violence take: fists? feet? belt? stick? knife?

- Were the assaults unforeseen, possible, inevitable?

- Are there particular triggers that set off the the assault?

- Are the acts of violence changing; becoming more overt? more frequent? more severe?

- What were the pre-assault state of the female client: asleep? drunk? pregnant? standing? running away?

- What was the aftermath of the assault: partner apologized? partner refused to allow the woman to see a doctor? no communication?

- Afterwards, did the partner admit responsibility for his actions?

- Finally, there can be signs that demand immediate safety. Some of these are:

  (a) a pet belonging to the woman is killed
  (b) the woman sustains multiple injuries from the attacks
  (c) the woman is locked in the house
  (d) the bringing of weapons such as guns into the house (Browne, 1987)

Leigh: 'Jimmy tore up my birth lines and marriage certificate. He destroyed photographs of us. Then I heard he got a gun – I found out later he really did have one. I never thought it dangerous until you pointed it out. It was lucky I ran away when I did.'

It is possible to get some idea of future risks from past violence, but it is worth paying attention to extreme verbal aggression. For example, concern is raised if the woman is called names such as 'whore', 'bitch' or similar; if the woman is told she is ugly, stupid or similar; or if the woman is compared unfavourably with other women (Burstow, 1992:151).

Role of violence assessment

Normally, assessments are used to make some form of expert diagnosis or prognosis, but in counselling in violent relationships the assessments are made in order that they can be shared with clients or couples. It is irresponsible for the counsellor to realize the risks to clients and not share such knowledge. In addition, clients are helped by talking through what the counsellor and clients see as the risks. In such discussions, counsellors will find that a lot of information is given and this should be used to help clients reflect on their lives.

Talking about violent incidents can be helpful in getting clients to sense imminent attacks and to be able to react in the most useful manner. Again, advice can be given, such as, 'Threaten to call the police if he looks as if he is about to start on you', but women rarely do; usually because they are terrified or are only too aware what the consequences will be. One safer option is for the woman simply to get out of the house if possible to avoid immediate injury.

Leigh: 'How did I know Jimmy was about to explode? He became more quiet – brooding. But he also became more aggressive when speaking. If offering me a roll-up, he would say, 'Have a roll-up!', and throw it at me. It was also the look of him, looking through me as if I was nothing. He had that look of hatred and disgust. It was the atmosphere as well; if there were other folk about they would get out of the road. Usually there was no sudden attack but a build-up over several days. Then he would take a drink and I knew I was for it. Later on, it would happen without the drink.'

Me: 'Were there other ways you would recognize the build-up?'

Leigh: 'You could see him tensing his shoulders, he would slouch about. The least thing and he would have a go at me. Every word I said annoyed him more.'

Me: 'What kind of things did you say when you tried to talk him down?'

Leigh: 'Oh, things like, "I can see you are getting wound up. Talk to me about it." He would just say, "Fuck off!", and then add other things like, "Bitch!"'

Me: 'Do you think he may have been looking for an opportunity ..?

Leigh: 'Yes. He wanted an excuse to start. Afterwards he used to say that it was the drink, and for years I believed this. Then I realized the drink was just an excuse to batter me ... Of course, sometimes I would misjudge it, and Jimmy would erupt quite spontaneously.'

Me: 'And if you met a young lassie whose man had started to hit her, what sort of things would you tell her to watch out for to try and avoid being hit?'

As can be seen, assessment should meld into counselling, not be something different for the client. Only by talking through the exact nature of what goes on can clients become more realistic about their situation. At the end, Leigh was almost put into a teaching position – what would she say to the young girl? One way of ensuring knowledge is retained is to get clients to 'teach' it to others. This is also empowerimg for clients.

Counselling should then move on and concentrate on the fact that the abuse happened within a relationship, and so looking at the nature of that relationship. This can be done by looking at specific aspects, such as a lack of fairness within it (Walster et al., 1973), or the breaking of trust. Another view is looking at verbal abuse (Walker, 1985) and how it relates to the violence. Stress is a further possible concern, looking at the woman's sleeplessness, irritability and suicidal thoughts (Stanko, 1985). Clearly, there are myriad possible continuations. The important point is to use the assessment to raise consciousness of risks and then place such risks in the context of clients' relationships and lives.

Reactions to violence

A different approach to violence is to look at reactions to it. These can be short term or long term. The former may come in three main forms.

1. No apparent reaction, just allowing oneself to be hit and waiting till it is over.

2. Reacting by arguing, pleading, or trying to escape the violence either through words or running away.

3. The woman might fight back.

Talking through their specific reactions helps women to come to terms with their own behaviour. Counsellors can help through affirmative support in helping clients see what they did as perfectly normal. Those who do nothing, who wait out the storm, often worry that they should have done something, and mentally go through what they think they might have done. Another aspect is that violence by their partners can leave women clients in a state of shock.

Debbie: 'The first time he hit me I went into shock. I was alternatively laughing and crying, but I simply could not speak for ages.'

After this initial stage, denial can take over. Alternatively, the woman can feel ashamed about telling anyone, or fears the consequences of doing so (Giles-Sim, 1983). Merely discussing what happened, going through every small action, thought and feeling, breaks through the shock. Reassurance is also needed, emphasizing the fact that frequently action by the woman merely worsens the situation, and not reacting can be the safest course.

Similarly, trying to escape, whether by pleading or running away, can be felt as humiliation, and the counsellor has to reframe the woman's actions as being smart, as doing the right thing, as ultimately being more in control than her partner.

Retaliation

Western women have been socialized into being passive and caring, unlike other societies such as Native Americans, whose women are far more likely to retaliate (Becker et al., 1990). As a result, Western women clients find retaliation difficult, apart from the fact that they are likely to be lighter, smaller, and weaker than their male partner. Signals of distress may well lessen or stop low aggression or violence, but they fail in cases of high violence (Baron, 1979), so hoping that her partner will stop his violence because of her obvious pain and distress is likely to fail women. This means that retaliation may be a possibility, even though it will probably make the perpetrators feel guilty.

First, guilt is misplaced as retaliation is a defensive reaction; far from being seen as bad by the abuser, it may be welcomed.

Ben: 'It is better if the woman hits back, as they could not hurt you. It is like fighting a ten-year-old.'

This means that retaliation is likely to be successful only if it is extreme. Normal retaliation is likely to be interpreted as a desire for a continuing physical confrontation. So the client relies on surprise and extreme reaction, often with violent verbal abuse.

Debbie: 'In the pub he threw his pint over me, so I threw mine over him. He then hit me, so I hit him back. There were even times when he said he was scared of me as I would fight back.'

The danger is that to redress the physical imbalance, the woman will use weapons; often household objects such as pokers or kitchen knives. This can lead to severe injury or even death, which raises further problems for the woman. First, women have to make themselves prepared for retaliation, and this involves pumping themselves up to be in a rage. But doing this can end up frightening the woman as much as her partner.

Leigh: 'I'm frightened of myself. I very nearly wrote a letter to the hospital saying they were going to have to do something. The way I'm going now, I'll land up in jail or in a locked ward. I felt so angry. I was going to kill Jimmy.'

There is an additional difficulty that can arise here, as those who are afraid of their anger might be treated for it. This is often done through drugs, such as benzodiazepines. Such minor tranquillizers can batten down extreme emotions, but there is no saying that this will be permanent. In fact, anger can break out, and when it does the reaction can be very violent. This means that long-term use can result in violence from the victimized woman. The use of tranquillizers can also be risky in the short term as they can have paradoxical effects and increase violence. I know of one man who carried diazepam in his shirt pocket and chewed the tablets regularly, and this caused him to stay in a fighting mood.

This fear of internal anger is lessened once the counsellor goes through the experience of violence and subsequent retaliation with the client, putting both in context. Counsellors will also have to deal with client guilt which can be extreme, whatever its justification. They can also help by checking on clients' feelings of revenge and fantasies about killing their partners. These may metamorphose into reality, with subsequent difficulties for the client, and thus are best prevented if possible.

Retaliation and resistance are the most effective ways of preventing partner or ex-partner rape, except under the most extreme circumstances, and are less risky than submission (Klech and Sayles, 1990). Resistance and fighting back will also make the woman less likely to be blamed (Shotland and Goodstein, 1983). However, we do come up against the problem that the most effective way to resist is to use weapons (Klech and Sayles, 1990), which is a risky option.

Attacks on the person

Attacks on the person can be either verbal or physical, and the question arises as to what women should do when they happen. It should be remembered that once there have been some attacks then there are likely to be further examples. There is no simple answer as to what is best; it varies for each individual. It must be for each person to decide what she sees as being best for her. What the worker can usefully do is to suggest that women clients decide what to do before the next attack, which can be anything from walking out there and then on the partner relationship, to deciding what to do if either form of attack occurs.

Many clients see the more difficult choice as that of knowing how to react to verbal attacks, as these are not seen, usually, as sufficient to warrant separation, yet they can be deeply wounding. Talking through reactions to verbal attacks – and this is not to imagine that women are incapable of initiating such attacks – is helpful not just to be able to withstand attacks better, but also to provide another perspective on the partner relationship.

There are three principal options with regard to reacting to verbal attacks: ignoring, accepting or retaliating.

1. Attacks on the woman can simply be ignored by her, and this would appear to give no reason for her partner to continue. However matters are often not so simple in practice, and silence may be followed up by remarks such as, 'You deaf or something?' The point is that ignoring comments can be interpreted as a form of silent aggression.

2. Attacks may be accepted, using a molifying statement like, 'I agree, you're right', and then trying to defuse the situation. This may work in the short term, but this tactic in time may also be

interpreted as a form of silent aggression and simply irritate the man further.

3. Retaliation brings obvious risks of escalation and possible physical aggression. The advantage is that women clients have said that they felt better at the time and also experienced less long-term humiliation.

Perhaps the hardest part is for clients to stop themselves from reacting automatically, as many couples have well developed verbal attack patterns. Women also have to reflect on whether the remarks passed are realistic and, if wounding, whether they were meant to be helpful, or were purely a form of attack. It helps to acknowledge what may be or probably is true or honestly meant, and what is quite unhelpful. In addition, a combination of methods may be used according to those involved and the situation.

CONSCIOUSNESS-RAISING

Its introduction

For clients to be empowered and able to change, they may have to be given basic information about violent relationships. Part of this will have been done during the previous risk assessment stage when the consequences of physical injuries were discussed. However, giving information has to be done discreetly, so consciousness-raising is not a concentrated time-limited stage but a thread that runs through early counselling. It should also be interactive, so clients have to be brought into the process, and asked for their views and experiences. Information given has to be related to counselling purposes, such as affecting client perspective, being supportive or preparing the way for planning options. There can be arguments as to what is an acceptable fact, or what constitutes knowledge in the province of violent relationships, but there are some matters which are largely agreed and which coincide with my own experience.

Degree of consciousness-raising

The form and degree of consciousness-raising depends largely on whether a couple or an individual woman client is being seen. Giving information has usually been directed to abused women in the past, but it is important that abusive men are also told the basics and have the opportunity to talk them over. In particular, information can be used to begin to break down some of the patriarchal myths that clients – but especially men – hold.

There is one point that needs to be decided by counsellors. Clients may present for help but not for help with partner abuse. If the counsellor discovers such abuse then the client or clients may be asked if she or they want to work on the problem. The possible difficulty comes if the answer is in the negative. Should the client or clients undergo consciousness-raising in order to appreciate the fact that they have a problem? Although this might be tempting, it amounts to little more than a professional exerting power in the situation. If clients come for help with a specific problem then it is hardly ethical to ignore this point and try to move the agenda. However, working on such a problem can and should establish a useful counselling realtionship which itself can lead in time to attention being given to any violence.

Some of the information that might be put over includes the following:

- Physical force is usually initiated by men, who are bigger, heavier and stronger. Sometimes I have likened this to putting a light-weight boxer in the ring with a heavyweight. This is not allowed, yet this is precisely what happens in the home.

- Although a third of women are subjected to battering, yet this still leaves the majority who are not subjected to such behaviour. For men, it is neither necessary nor right to act in this way; for women, there is no need to accept such treatment.

- As time proceeds, the batterings are likely to increase both in severity and frequency. And the most common venue for murder and rape is not on the streets, but in the home.

- The violence can affect others, such as the children, relatives and friends. It can happen that these might themselves be subjected to verbal abuse and even violence.

- The violence tends to be embedded in the context of male controlling behaviour, particularly jealousy and possessiveness.

- Promises that the man will not behave violently will not be kept unless there is true honesty, taking of responsibility, apologies, and planned changes in the male partner's behaviour.

- Actions come from people, and cannot simply be blamed on others, provocation, alcohol or drugs. Again, my ploy is to liken the situation to dealing with young children and illegitimately blaming their battering on the same sources.

Clearly, how such information and topics are put across to clients depends on the judgement of counsellors. Too often, information given by helpers is used to scare or threaten, rather than to be affirming. My experience has been that knowing that other women have similar experiences is valued by abused clients – they no longer see themselves as being at fault, as having something wrong with them, or as being singled out as victims.

7 COMMUNICATION AND BOUNDARIES

What are we dealing with?

It is worth underlining the fact that people communicate all the time. In fact, it is difficult to think of a person not communicating (Watzlawick et al., 1967); even silence can be eloquent. In relationships, communication is seen as very important. Indeed, the main goal of marital therapy may be seen as that of producing clear and open communication between partners (L'Abate and McHenry, 1983). Furthermore, the predictors of a good outcome of work with marital difficulties are communication, tenderness and sexual intercourse (Halweg et al., 1984). Perhaps it is significant that difficulties with communication in couples with marital problems are typical of husbands rather than wives (Noller, 1985).

This might lead us to expect that just talking about the situation would ease matters. In fact, most of the communication between people tends to be non-verbal (Mehrabian, 1972) and it is this aspect that requires most attention, helping partners to avoid misreading each other's messages (Gottman, 1976). We find that in unsatisfactory relationships, there tends to be an over-confidence in the ability to interpret non-verbal messages given and received (Noller and Venardos, 1986). Thus simply talking things out is not enough as it concentrates on the cognitive over the affective (Archer and Akert, 1977). Where affect is high, communication is conveyed non-verbally for the most part (Newton and Burgoon, 1990).

Practicalities of working with communication

Communication is especially important in violent relationships as it may take the form of verbal abuse, which can prove more damaging to the person than actual physical assaults. However, it is simpler not to concentrate on such abuse alone, but to look at the whole of the couple's communication. This avoids defining what is or is not abusive, as frequently the clients will not agree.

Communication can be verbal or non-verbal, and there can be a lack of communication. From my many tape-recordings, it seems to me that communication is more chaotic than we might imagine both from novels and books on counselling. This is particularly the case between couples. A lot can be left unsaid, which is bridged by mutual experiences and understandings. A second characteristic is that affective communication shows a move away from verbal to non-verbal communication, with an increasing breakdown in the former. The final thought is that counsellors rarely see clients at their worst, so the latter's behaviour is modified by being in the presence of helpers. Yet what is needed is not reasonable behaviour in the counselling room, but reasonable behaviour outside it. We want to know what really goes on when couples are together. One method is to ask couples to tape-record their discussions and even their arguments. In the following example, we encounter a situation of high emotion, close to violence.

Steve: 'No, wait a minute! Fucking stop, eh. Gi' us a fucking break!'

Melanie: 'I can't take it any longer. That's it! I've had enough!'

Steve: 'Right.'

Melanie: 'I'm going ...'

Steve: 'No, it's not got to be that.'

Melanie: 'Yes, it has. It's got to be this.'

Steve: 'Look ...'

Melanie: 'Nah.'

Steve: 'Nah, nah, nah. What has it got to be?'

Melanie: 'It's got to be me leaving the house and I can't fucking handle it any more ...'

What is important to appreciate is that although we can all get somewhat incoherent when emotionally aroused, this can be more of a pattern for those living in high affective situations. It can almost become a habit, and this increases the chance of mutual miscommunication.

Following the above example, it was not Melanie but Steve who left the house, to return later. The two of them then attempted to talk together, but found this no easy task.

Steve: 'Let's talk. Let's just ... sit down ... and communicate ... Let's take ... '

Melanie: 'For instance?'

Steve: 'No. Let's just ... No, right ...Why does it always happen on a Sunday? Right.'

Melanie: 'I don't ...'

Steve: 'On you go then.'

Melanie: 'I haven't ... I don't know why on a Sunday ... It could have been a Monday. It could have been a Tuesday, Wednesday, what happened.'

Steve: 'What?'

Melanie: 'What happened today. I know what happened today. I'm not repeating it.'

Steve: 'Repeating yourself. Part of it is to say ...'

Melanie: 'I've had enough.'

Steve: 'Had enough. Sure you've had enough?'

Melanie: 'I know why I did what I done.'

Steve: 'Tell me.'

Melanie: 'No, I'm not repeating it. I'm getting frustrated and annoyed here. I just want some peace.'

[Long silence]

Steve: 'Are you just playing a game? What's wrong with you?'

Melanie: 'No, I'm sick of playing games. This is reality.'

Steve: 'I canna ... fuck, shit, cunt, bastard.'

Yet we should not see couples as being unable to gain control of what is happening. As the affective level declines, so we find both are able to begin to look at things more clearly. The problem is not an inability to communicate but an inability to deal with affective issues.

Melanie: 'We've been like this for an hour.'

Steve: 'Well, let's stick with that. We've been at this longer than that.'

Melanie: 'You've told me too much. I don't know where to start.'

Steve: 'Too much, far too much, far too much.'

Melanie: 'To keep it in.'

Steve: 'But, but ... why is there always a but?'

Melanie: 'I never said but.'

[Inaudible for twelve seconds]

Steve: 'You know, two fucking idiots, us.'

Melanie: 'Yes.'

From a working point of view, there is a need, as Melanie herself appreciated, to get through to reality. The difficulty is that as counsellors we tend to set up situations which protect us and our clients from total reality. We have to do this for ethical reasons. Counselling violence-affected couples does not mean that we should allow violence to take place. However, this also means that as counsellors we are insulated from what actually can take place. Of special interest is the extent to which workers can permit verbal as opposed to physical violence. Verbal, as opposed to physical violence, tends to be bi-directional in couples. Although it is less upsetting if direct language is not permitted in counselling, yet promoting a completely artificial scenario may prevent clients from ventilating, from expressing themselves openly, from ridding themselves of unhelpful, retained feelings. Some clients do so and in different ways.

Me: 'You write stuff down. Do you find that helpful?'

Leigh: 'Very much so. Like I'm doing just now, at the moment. I'm angry with this guy. When I'm like that then I write it down. It's like therapy.'

Me: 'I notice you read it afterwards. Does that help?'

Leigh: 'Yeh, I'll read it and say, "Yeh! I like it!"'

The other aspect to this is that by stopping a straightforward expression of feelings, we may never really know what goes on and so be less able to help.

Jacqui: 'We argue about loads of things. The two of us get really het up at times.'

Roddy: 'And everything comes out.'

Jacqui: 'And everything comes out. It just comes tumbling out of your mouth, things you really regret saying afterwards.'

Roddy: 'When we've said something really bad we have always apologized.'

Jacqui: 'We don't really.'

Roddy: 'We do! We do!'

Again, the emphasis must be on being realistic. Workers can hardly expect clients to suddenly change their behaviour overnight, at least not without serious self-inhibition. Also, we have to realize that many clients have different language usage. For instance, words such as 'fucking' to some clients have virtually lost all meaning, except as a method of emphasizing. The best tactic is to discuss the subject of language with clients, while making one's own feelings clear. What I want to avoid is clients using language that diminishes each other, that is wounding. Often this can include the tone used rather than the actual words.

Working on client communication

One of the reasons for introducing the long quote from Steve and Melanie was to point out the fact that what seems virtually incomprehensible to outsiders is clear to those directly involved. Some workers such as Satir (1978) have pointed to personal problems in family settings as having arisen from faulty communication, but this strikes me as a simplification of what transpires. Good communication is helpful, but bad communication does not mean that those involved do not know how to communicate. They have chosen to communicate in certain ways for their own ends.

Much of the writing about communication is highly cognitive and sees communication as a rational process, thereby ignoring the affective aspect. As the Steve and Melanie quote shows, with the entrance of strong feelings the rules begin to break down. This is well known to lyrical poets who can produce emotional results from the deliberate breaking of grammatical rules. The over-cognitive approach to communication rests on a belief that, with rules as to clarity, conciseness and directness, communication should be quite understandable. However, in difficult relationships, even apparently good communication is likely to be insufficient as there is likely to be a lack of trust. This means that what is said might not be believed, or partners may look for possible hidden meanings.

Me: 'So you are saying Jimmy does not trust you. Do you trust Jimmy?'

Leigh: 'I did until he started mistrusting me. And then I would cry to myself, but would not speak. Then everything would build up and finally I would explode. And that's when things would be said that should not have been said.'

In fact, this tends to ignore the role of non-verbal language, and that language, as Wittgenstein noted, is not a simple set of actions but a complex game. If we turn to violent partner relationships, then this game is aligned to the exercise and maintenance of power, upholding Haley's (1967) dictum that all communication involves aspects of power. This power-play can be supplemented by violence. For this reason, merely getting communication onto a more even keel is insufficient. The long-term aim must be the dismantling of the processes of power.

Forms of communication and power imposition

If workers monitor the form and dynamics of communication in couples, then they will notice several different processes that take place, including the following.

Interruptions
One client interrupting the other may be seen as poor communication, or it can be viewed as an attempt at domination. If the latter is the case, then the worker can impose some order by stopping the interruptions and getting clients to discuss what exactly is going on and how they feel about what is happening. Some groupworkers use 'talking sticks', a stick to be held by the person allowed to talk, and then passed to the other party. However, such devices tend to be unavailing in situations of high affect.

Speaking for each other
The habit of speaking for the other person – 'You always say ...' or 'What you mean is ...' – is not just a method of preventing the other person from speaking, of intimating superior knowledge, and not being prepared to listen, but also of showing a degree of disrespect. As usual, merely getting clients to stop the habit is insufficient and it requires discussion and relating to the power situation.

Generalizing
Some clients will over-generalize, and this may be recognized by the use of words such as 'everyone', 'all', or 'never', as in statements such as, 'You always say' or 'Everyone knows ...'. This may be linked with thinking in stereotypes and possible prejudicial views. Some instances are worth examining in order for clients to get a better grasp of the mode of thinking.

Indirect speech
This is a method of speaking without owning what is said and thus avoiding responsibility. It may be identified by phrases such as, 'People say ...' or 'It is well known that ...'. Over-use of such utterances should be challenged as they leave everyone unsure where the speaker stands.

Non-verbal signals
These are very important in high affect confrontations and can vary from standing too close, to a fixed stare, to a generally tensed-up posture or stance. It is often best to get clients to relax such signals before further talk or discussion. Other signs are those of tone, making statements in such a way as brook no argument.

Silence
Silence can be very pointed, and though not so common in sessions, it is more common outside. Silences may differ, from a simple refusal to answer, to a sullen silence, and are an important form of non-verbal communication.

Communication and relationships

We have seen that communication, and poor comunication in particular, plays an important part in the behaviour of couples. The task for counsellors is to help clients to improve their situation. Sometimes counsellors will ensure an improvement by keeping to the agreed rules of the counselling sessions. In addition, communication is improved by helping clients to understand in what ways they are interacting poorly and how they can build up a better relationship on the foundation of good communication. However, good client communication within the counselling session may well not be transferred to the outside, as communication is just one part of the client relationship and may only be advanced through concentrating purely on social skills. It is not only a matter of how people communicate, but also what they say to each other. And what is said should, from time to time, reflect positively on the relationship, providing positive reinforcement to the ongoing personal interactions.

Part of this reinforcement process is getting clients to know what will please their partner and to communicate it. Clients also have to know how to accept such positive reinforcement. This can take some time as partners can be suspicious of each other.

Jacqui: 'So I look nice. What's brought this on?'

Roddy: 'You wanted me to be more, more pleasant – or whatever.

You complained I didn't bother about you. Well, I'm just saying you look nice, which you do.'

Jacqui: 'But you don't mean it. You're just saying that.'

Roddy: 'Of course I'm saying it. What do you want me to say?'

Jacqui: 'What's the point of saying it if you don't mean it?'

Roddy: 'What's the point of saying it if you call me a fucking liar?'

Jacqui: 'You said it!'

Here we are returned to the nature of the underlying relationship, which is characterized by a degree of mistrust. Good communication between couples is not just a matter of skill but of values such as trust and honesty, sharing and loyalty. Student counsellors may wonder whether with such a client relationship they should concern themselves with communication. However, there is no one avenue to helping. By attending to both communication and the relationship, both can slowly improve. This might be a slow process at first, so it is useful to set very modest goals in such a case.

BOUNDARY-SETTING

The role of boundary-setting

The counsellor will find that stopping the violence requires the male client exerting control over himself. Counsellors who expect that their asking, suggesting, or using threats will stop clients from being violent are most likely to be disappointed. But by attending to boundary-setting within counselling, the counsellor can help to lay the grounds for the male clients to be able to reflect on their behaviour and exert greater self-control. The boundary-setting can be applied to many different incidents in counselling. The two following examples refer to clients' verbal content and to the clients' use of power.

Oppression and its context

Violence is not an irrational form of male behaviour but one that is aimed to establish and maintain control in the relationship. To eliminate violence, the couple both have to be aware of such control and its various manifestations. The counsellor's aim is to help them make the links between actions and forms of behaviour and their underlying significance. This is done partly through the rules constructed in counselling, and partly through the content of those rules, especially when the man starts to become oppressive.

Sometimes counsellors will stop clients from behaving in certain ways, reproving them for what they say. But this is little more than counter-oppression unless clients are given a more appropriate way of behaving, of learning that there are alternatives and putting them into practice.

Sylvia: 'I don't know what I want.'

John: 'You never fucking do! Madam Know-fuck-all.'

Me: 'Hold it right there! Why did you say that?'

John: 'Because she knows fuck all, that's why.'

Me: 'But we all know lots of things, as does Sylvia. So why did you feel it necessary to insult her in that way? Why did you do it?'

John: 'What do you mean, why did I do it?'

Me: 'Why did you insult Sylvia that way and do it in front of another person, namely myself?'

John: 'I wasn't insulting ...'

Sylvia: 'Ha!'

Me: 'Look, I'm not getting at you, but can you tell me why you acted like that? Why did you react to Sylvia that way?'

John: 'She annoys me, that's why.'

Me: 'Right. We are beginning to get somewhere. So why did she annoy you? I mean, all she said was, "I don't know what I want." [To Sylvia] Is that right? Was that what you said, Sylvia?'

Sylvia: 'Yes, yes.'

Me: 'So, John, did Sylvia get under your skin and, if so, in what way? Why did you get so irritated?'

John: [Fiddling with his chair] 'Seat ... uncomfortable.'

Me: 'Sorry about that. Yes, the seats could be more comfortable. Now, as I asked, why did Sylvia annoy you as she did?'

Sylvia: '... always doing it ...'

Me: 'Excuse me, Sylvia, but give John a chance to reply. OK, John.'

John: 'Well ... well ..., I don't ...'

Me: 'It can be difficult when we have to say why we do things. Can I make a suggestion? Do you have certain expectations as to how you think Sylvia should behave, act? Perhaps you find she does not come up to your expectations?'

Sylvia: 'Yes, ...'

Me: 'Hold on. OK, John, on you go.'

John: 'Well, it's only right ... I'm reasonable, but she gets on my wick when she can never make up her mind ...'

Me: 'Right. Now can you turn to Sylvia and tell her that? Yes, don't tell me, tell her.'

John: 'You can never make up your bl ... your mind.'

Sylvia: 'That's because you always get onto me, whatever I say.'

As can be seen, the process can take a long time. In addition, there can be pressure from the couple not to continue, and this can take various forms such as denial, avoidance, deflection, rationalizing, intellectualizing, fantasizing, blaming and self-blaming. Such tactics have to be challenged at the appropriate moment. In the above example, getting John to talk directly to Sylvia not only constituted part of the learning process but stopped the couple from distancing themselves from the episode. Both abused and abusers will often function by distancing themselves from what has happened in order to continue to live together, but this is, at the very least, a physically risky policy.

Power struggles against the counsellor

One aspect of the breaking of boundaries in counselling is that it represents a power struggle between clients – very often men – and the counsellor. This can be used to advantage by the counsellor to look at the question of power in relationships, admittedly a rather indirect method. Directly challenging power imbalance in client relationships can so often be unproductive, the man simply denying there is any such imbalance, so less straightforward methods may have to be employed.

Working with couples, the power struggle can be felt when a negative feeling begins to suffuse the counselling. This can arise from the male partner continually asking questions, expressing vague doubts, asking about the counsellor's experience or understanding of the clients' situation, or simply through minimal participation. When asked for positive contributions – 'In what way are you unsure ...?' or 'In what way do you think I have not fully grasped your situation ...?' – the client does not give any relevant or precise answer. Under the circumstances, the counsellor can feel somewhat undermined and initial reactions can be to justify actions to date or to counter-attack and call the client for being negative. Neither of these actions is likely to be helpful; justification can lead to further attacks, while attacking the client merely moves the counsellor to grounds where he feels it is legitimate to be openly aggressive.

The counsellor is better advised to ignore the overt client behaviour and try to move to reasons for it. Sometimes counter-statements, such as, 'You seem rather negative to me. I am wondering whether that could be because ...' can be effective, but they can also be ignored as the client feels safer in his attacking negative mode. What is often required is the setting of boundaries, allowing questions, statements or doubts, but not if they are done for the negative purpose of ultimately sabotaging the counselling. As the client has been so vague and indirect, the best option is that of using directness. After commenting on the client seeming to be negative, then the direct questions can be put, questions such as: 'Are you not willing to continue with counselling ...?' or 'Do you think I am not doing my job correctly ...?' It might be observed that questions that the client might more easily answer, such as, 'Would you be prepared not to come to counselling?' or 'Do you want another counsellor?' are avoided as they are framed in such a way that makes it easy for the client to avoid addressing the problem of power imbalance.

What usually happens is that the client reluctantly submits to the counsellor after the direct question is put to him, such as: 'I'm not saying I wouldn't come', or 'Well, I suppose you know what you're doing.' The counsellor can take the reply as a sign of cooperation and can move counselling on, the previous line of client power-play having been brought to an end. In the momentary lull, the counsellor can then ask, 'It seems to me that you do have a point here, and perhaps what we are really talking about is trust, trust in the relationship between the two of us. Would that be correct?' By looking at the counselling relationship, the suggestion can then be made that the same characteristics might apply to the clients' relationship. If this is the case, then they are connected to the idea of power. It is easy to deny that power issues apply to the way in which clients interact, but it is less easy if there is an instance to hand of the man acting in a power-mongering fashion during the counselling.

Women clients and power struggles

Women can be involved in fighting against the counsellor and, as an expression of their own empowerment, this is a positive sign. Indeed, it could be asked, why bother at all?, if women clients exert their power. Resisting would be no more than the counsellor oppressing the client, returning her to her accustomed state. In practice, the situation is more complex.

The first difficulty can be the way that women clients bid for their legitimate power in the counselling. Many of them will have had to modify their behaviour when talking with their partners, and this can continue into the counselling sessions. Rather than trying to enforce power, they can try to seek it more subtly. This can be done by making themselves out to be victims during the counselling; or trying seduction if the counsellor is male, and appealing to sisterhood if the counsellor is female. They might put on naive or little-girl-lost faces. Such methods might work with their partners but can be less successful with counsellors, not only because counsellors may be well aware of what is happening but also as a result of their partners' presence. Being seductive in the presence of their partners is likely to cause problems, though for some women clients the chance of annoying their partners may be quite welcome. However, the role of the counsellor does become more difficult, especially as any reaction to these ploys can be misinterpreted by both partners.

The second snag is that the constant use of such devices can turn them from temporary manoeuvres into more permanent roles. For instance, the over-use of the woman as a victim can eventually end up with her believing that to be the case, which means that her behaviour then becomes conditioned by her self-perceived role.

8 WORK WITH INDIVIDUALS

Introduction

Counselling individuals differs to some extent from work with couples, chiefly through different emphases rather than separate content. These are magnified by the difference of power in the clients' and counsellors' relationships. When deciding about the possibilities of individual or couples work, the following points about individual counselling, as opposed to that of couples, might be usefully borne in mind.

1. It can be either more or less revealing than couples work.

   (a) It can be more revealing as there is no pressure from the client's partner being present, pressure which can affect both client and counsellor.

   (b) Women clients who may well have been socially isolated by their partners and unable to talk to people, now find someone who is a listening ear. With her partner present, it is less obvious that there is active listening as everyone is more likely to seem to be caught up in ongoing interactions.

   (c) A good counselling relationship is stronger in one-to-one work compared with couples work, where the clients' relationship interferes. A good strong working relationship provides a sense of safety for the client and encourages disclosure, though it also increases the possibility of client dependency.

   (d) However, individual counselling can be less revealing in that the counsellor cannot see the couple's interactions, especially those of a non-verbal nature.

   (e) Sometimes the fact of the client's partner not being present can mean the client is unsure what to say and biases her account according to what she thinks her partner would want her to say.

   (f) Clients can use counselling to their individual purposes, speaking more as to a lawyer than a counsellor. At times, this is not always obvious with the client's partner absent.

2. The counselling boundaries are those between counsellor and client, rather than between the client couple in the main.

(a) The boundaries are qualitatively different, in that between counsellor and single client they are often less obvious and so more difficult to maintain.

(b) Implementation of boundary-setting by the counsellor is power-dependent, and usually easier in one-to-one situations. There is a hidden danger here, as this can make the counsellor too willing to use power in counselling.

(c) Single-client counselling requires counsellors to be very much aware of themselves, both as regards counselling and their reactions to counselling, whereas couples counselling requires more of a groupwork approach.

3. The client and her roles become more important.

(a) Gender-role interactions with the counsellor can be positive, as when the client's sexual identity and self-identity are affirmed. There can be negative aspects, such as greater chances of transference and countertransference.

(b) The social role of women as carers and putting others first, especially if there are children, can become more important and this can mean the client, as herself, might be overlooked.

(c) The role of the woman as victim is one that is hard to avoid at times, especially if the client is treated as such by others, like relatives or doctors. It may be used by clients to gain attention, which may be quite justified, but can lead to problems if the role becomes fixed. However, the role can be helpful, in that it can be supportive to feel one of many abused women and not a unique abnormality. However there is a danger that being a victim invites sympathy, and if internalized this can act as a bar to the client taking action.

4. The biasing of counselling interactions may be greater.

(a) It can be harder for counsellors to avoid taking sides, as client pressure is usually more overt with couples, and partners will also monitor each other's actions.

(b) Single counselling tends to reinforce the slant to individualist perceptions and concerns.

(c) The client has greater power in the counselling interactions, which can be for good or for bad. An example of the latter is the giving of false accounts about the client's situation.

5. Goals are restricted.

(a) With partners absent, clients cannot plan for the couple and those plans made can be sabotaged by the partner.

(b) Planning for single clients can be easier when considering sensitive actions such as leaving the relationship.

6. Time for reflection is increased.

(a) More time can be given to helping single clients understand the process of the counselling encounter, so they can empower themselves.

(b) It is easier for single clients and counsellors to understand what is happening in one-to-one counselling situations, though this does not mean they are necessarily correct.

These are some possible variations between single and couple counselling as applied to clients in violent relationships. They do not determine the form of counselling but are useful to bear in mind during conselling and subsequent reviews and supervision.

Following the General Plan as outlined earlier, we find there are areas of work that require more specific attention.

ENDING MALE VIOLENCE

Stopping the violence

One thought that battered women often hold on to is that their partners might change and stop behaving in a violent manner. However, experience has shown that hoping for any ingrained behavioural patterns such as heavy drinking, gambling, drug use or partner violence to stop is not enough. Such behaviour may eventually come to an end, but it can take a long time, and is characterized by periods of non-violence and then another violent outburst. Meanwhile, considerable and even irreparable damage may have been inflicted. Change rarely comes unless change is made to come and incorporated into the couple's everyday life.

Sally: 'My man hasn't hit me in five years now. He's calmed down.

Part of it is he's cut down on the drink but he also knows what I would do if he started again.'

For violence to end, the man has to want it to end, be prepared to make it end and then work at achieving that goal. This may require outside help and support.

Ben: 'You get worse and worse, get more and more violent. I did four stabbings in two days and then realized I had to get myself sorted out. I realized the violence was not going to go away and the way I was going I would never have any proper relationships with women.'

However, any help offered has to be effective if it is to be of use. If help is ineffective, women partners can be lulled into a sense of false security or unrealistic hope, which can put them at risk.

Help for male partners

The rational policy for women wanting their partners to end their violence is to persuade these men to get help for themselves. Such partners rarely seek help voluntarily but are either persuaded to do so or legally obliged via a Court order (Segel-Evans, 1994). Even persuasion is difficult as they tend to lie or minimize their actions and place blame elsewhere (Ganley, 1981). Abusive men also describe any assault as unintentional, ignoring the multiplicity of attacking actions, the pattern of violent behaviour and the ignoring of the woman's attempts to stop the assault. Batterers have to work through their self-justification and resentment if pressurized to seek help, and they are rarely willing to do so (Koval et al., 1982). When they do come for help, this is in the context of the violence being supplementary to other problems, such as heavy drinking or childhood abuse (Ptacek, 1988). Moreover, men with such severe problems are those most likely to drop out of treatment programmes (Hamberger and Hastings, 1989).

It has to be remembered that we might see ourselves as helping and doing good, but the abuser might well see us as merely interfering.

Ben: 'If someone interfered then I would just set about him.'

This means we have to put across the fact that we will be helping him and that we take a non-judgemental view of him as a person. It also means that often violent men are not at the stage when they want to be helped and as counsellors we have to accept this. If they are not willing to change then our intervention is unlikely to be effective. In short, we are probably wasting their and our time.

Expert help

Abusive male partners who want to stay in a relationship may promise to go for help, and may actually do so. This move may be supported by professional experts, without full consideration for the risks to the women partners. Psychiatrists feel they are able to predict a cessation of violence after treatment, though there is little reason to have confidence in such an assertion (Cocozza and Steadman, 1977). Indeed, there are weaknesses in all clinical methods of predicting violence (Steadman and Morrissey, 1982). In addition, we should be wary of those methods which depend on symptom relief rather than a change in the person.

Leigh: 'At first the drugs that Jimmy was prescribed were a blessing as he calmed down a lot and life was a lot better. But after a time they were not so effective, and anyway it depended on whether he took them or not. The drugs dampened things down but they did not change anything. Underneath it all, he was just the same kind of person.'

In fact, psychiatry may only confuse the situation and externalize responsibility for violent behaviour by labelling abusers as borderline personalities (Saunders, 1987) or trying to trace alleged causes in childhood trauma (van der Kolk, 1987). This ignores the fact that experiments have shown that anyone is capable of behaving violently, especially if he or she can project responsibility onto another person (Milgram, 1976:76; Sabini and Silver, 1982). Also, there is no guarantee that any treatment will necessarily be effective (Jacobson, 1993). On the other hand, help for abusers should not be dismissed simply because success cannot be guaranteed. Interviews with those who have been through treatment programmes for men do show a decrease in violence and verbal aggression in a large number of cases (Dutton, 1986). Most of the improvement comes in the first three months so there is little need for programmes of much greater length (Shepard, 1987). Yet we do have to be very careful of research results, as much of the research methodology is open to criticism.

Help is only meaningful if three criteria are satisfied (Jenkins, 1990).

1. The man acknowledges what he has done, physically and mentally to the woman.

2. The man takes responsibility for what he has done, recognizes he has the problem and that it arises from satisfying his own needs

rather than those of others, and also understands how others view his violence.

3. The man helps his partner by taking responsibility for his actions: he understands the rights of others, and learns and carries out alternative non-violent ways of behaving subsequently.

If the man fails these three criteria then there is no real way he can be helped, as he has shown he does not want to be helped. The stress put on taking responsibility contrasts with other attempts at helping such as mediation. Mediators are trained not to be neutral where there is partner violence, emphasis being put on violence being a legal offence and the woman being able to bring legal sanctions at any time (Orenstein, 1982). However, the man is not asked to admit having been violent, but merely warned not to do it again (Wright, 1991:70). This does not get to the underlying reasons for the behaviour and so make sense to clients. Abused women frequently want to know the reason for the violence, and in the absence of reasons are more likely to see themselves as to blame.

A further danger with violent men is that they are often very much in control of themselves and come over well in the initial interview. The abused woman is likely to be in a state of high anxiety, which can make her forgetful, emotional and liable to contradict herself. So it can happen that the man comes over much more convincingly than her partner, and is seen as reasonable and cooperative. Workers might think that the three criteria mentioned above are not really required or they are relaxed. We should remember that the couple may give different accounts of what has happened (Browning and Dutton, 1986), and it may be that the man is believed rather than the woman. This is usually a product of the form of interview, of not being firm and pressing the abusive man. Counsellors can be worried about the session getting out of control and even of violence occurring, so are sometimes reluctant to press hard. Pressing hard can be done as long as the counsellor is prepared to be seen as the one pressing, is able to keep the situation within bounds, and at the end ensures the man feels reasonably at ease.

Me: 'OK, so you, Colin, are saying that nothing happened and Joy says you hit her. Two quite different accounts. Which one do I believe? Do you know what I do? I ask myself which person has a better reason not to tell the truth. In general, and I stress in general, it is men who have the better reasons to cover up. I mean, why should Joy say this, bother to come to counselling to say this? Do you see my point, Colin?'

Colin: 'She says things like that. Tends to exaggerate.'

Me: 'I'm sorry, Joy, I'm not ignoring you but I feel I want to get the situation clear in my head. So if Joy does exaggerate, what was being exaggerated? You didn't hit her hard at all, but she makes a meal of it?'

Colin: 'I might have caught her by accident.'

Me: 'So you did hit her.'

Joy: 'And it wasn't by accident!'

Me: 'I think we will leave that point till a bit later. The picture I now have, which is still very hazy, is that you were hit, Joy. I'm not here to judge you or Joy, I'm just here to help. So can we start from the position that Joy was hit by you, Colin? OK, that's what happened. Do the both of you agree? ... I'm taking the silence as agreement. I know this is not easy. Well, it certainly isn't for me, but at least agreement is a good start.'

Treatment schemes are best if carried out by or accountable to women in organizations such as the local Women's Aid refuge. Programmes heavily reliant on male workers are likely to be less successful (Hart, 1988) as feminist insights may be lost and male collusion becomes a real danger. The few successful cases known to me went through schemes which had female treatment staff present in numbers. The system used was one of appropriate confrontation and feminist insights (Ganley, 1981; Sonkin et al., 1985) – a vigorous arrangement that broke through the denial, victim blaming, justification and distortion (Purdy and Nickel, 1981).

Ben: 'You make excuses, you say it was an accident. But if you are allowed to get away with it, then the violence gets worse and worse. But you promise not to do it again, and at the time you really believe it. You make all sorts of excuses: "I can't remember it"; "I had a blackout"; "I'm ill and I need help." Sometimes you tell yourself it's because you love her that much, but really it's a fear of being alone.'

If the man gets through the scheme then there should be ongoing monitoring and support of the man. The emphasis is always on his non-violent behaviour – not whether he has attended for treatment or completed a non-violence course. However, I would go even further. The man has to understand why he might be acting as he does. Merely telling a person not to behave in a certain way is seldom effective unless there are reasons given and the man brought into the whole process of treatment as a responsible participant.

Control and action

Everyone has the option of self-control under all but the most exceptional circumstances. Men might get very angry, but they are capable of
letting themselves get angry, of using that anger to get or maintain
control (Pence and Paynor, 1993). Conflict comes where authority is
questioned and power shifts in the partnership (Steinmetz, 1977), or
when men perceive their control of the relationship slipping away. This
perception may only be that there is a change in emotional distance
between the couple, which explains the greater likelihood of violence
just after marriage or during pregnancy (Rounsville, 1978). Men try to
redefine their perception of what the relationship should be (Dutton
and Browning, 1987) and re-impose control. This is more likely to be
through violence if their verbal skills are poor (Dutton and Strachan,
1987).

We should not be surprised that partner violence is more common
in cohabiting than married couples (Yllo and Straus, 1981), as
marriage can be seen by men as furthering their possession and
control. It is worth noting that power in a relationship is a reflection of
not only the couple's relationship but also their economic power,
status and level of education (Houseknecht and Spanier, 1980). The
closer these are for husband and wife, the less the violence
(McDonald, 1980; Vogler and Pahl, 1994).

Work with abusive men in general

Whether abusive men are helped individually or as part of a couple, they
are likely to employ neutralization techniques. These are likely to be:

- Denial of responsibility
- Denying anyone was hurt
- Claiming the victim deserved it
- Attacking those critical of the action
- Claiming some good resulted from the action

It is important to realize that such techniques are quite usual. They
are also used in cases of child abuse (Milner and Chilamkurti, 1991),
in particular the ruse of blaming the partner (Dutton and Painter,
1980). Nor is it unusual for abused women to agree with their
partners, sometimes because that is the safest option, but sometimes
they have been so conditioned by the violence and their partner's
control that they really do believe what has been said.

Specifics when working with men

When working with abusive men, it is not only their behaviour but also their attitudes and beliefs that have to change. Simple behaviourist programmes that rely on teaching men impulse control or anger management are insufficient as they work to a stereotype of abusers being out of control, whereas this is not the case. Abusers let themselves get out of control or direct their actions in order to control. It has been rightly noted that abusive men are rarely physically abusive against their employers (Wood and Middleman, 1990) and although clients have threatened me and been abusive, I have never been hit by a client. So if abusers want to end their violence, then their attitudes and beliefs that support violence have to be altered. Basic anger management courses (Deschner, 1984) are usually insufficient as they are gender non-specific and fail to give a social understanding to violent behaviour. For this reason it is not political correctness but rather part of the overall process that examples of sexist attitudes are picked up.

Chas: 'It was just a joke! A cow with no tits ... You've got to have a laugh sometimes.'

Me: 'But it's not funny.'

Chas: 'Well, don't blame me if you've no sense of humour.'

Me: 'But it is simply not funny. It is unfunny, offensive, sexist, and, frankly, to my mind intended to be hurtful.'

Chas: 'OK, perhaps it wasn't that funny, thinking about it.'

Me: 'You think about it some more, and then tell me it's not offensive.'

However, this has to be balanced against openness and acceptance of the male abuser, so he feels able to open up and explain things. Part of this comes from listening to such accounts without moralizing.

Ben: 'You don't enjoy being violent. Straight after I would feel guilty and would try to make it up by buying flowers or giving gifts, but these material things don't mean the same.'

This might be seen as the counsellor listening to and silently condoning male justifications. However, the real purpose is for men to be able to hear themselves and work through their attitudes and beliefs. Once men feel able to open up, then they can begin to identify when they might be abusive and understand the whole process.

Ben: 'With some women I was OK, but some would set me off. Those who were quick off the mark or who would not back off. If she would not let up, kept arguing, then I would end up hitting her ... I came to recognize what set me off. I realized I could not stand screaming kids or if my wife came in late, especially if she said some man had tried to chat her up. I would not do anything, but you would store it up at the back of your head. All these incidents would build up and up. Finally it would all come out.'

Insight seldom comes from mere introspection. It is usually better to interact with other people, especially non-violent men and women. Violent men can hide behind their defences and see the world how they want to see it, but the presence of others helps them to see reality.

Ben: 'The hardest thing was being told I was a bully, and coming to recognize the fact.'

We should also be careful not to overrate men's confessions about their abusive behaviour as mere confession is easy (Hearn, 1994), changing that behaviour less easy. Abusers can learn the right language and sound penitent, but confession can then be clearing the ground to feel free to abuse again. Also, not being violent is insufficient. Violent men have to learn how to externalize and express their feelings, especially their anger. Male sex socialization makes it easier to express anger than other feelings such as love, caring or fear (Gondolf, 1985). Conflict is a characteristic of relationships, so good conflict management is also an important skill to acquire. Conflict need not lead to violence, but it can lead to verbal aggression, and this might lead to physical action (Murphy and O'Leary, 1987). It is important for the abuser to listen to himself and see if the dispute is becoming personalized, as many batterers see conflict as attacks upon themselves (Ganley, 1981), and thus retaliate.

As with the treatment of child abusers, all positive behaviour should be positively reinforced (Nicol, 1988). Merely telling violent men how they should behave is not likely in itself to prove successful. Understanding them and supporting their non-violence are required. Finally, abusive men have to come to terms with being non-violent, which can demand a change in life-style and friends.

Ben: 'I find it difficult to spend time with old mates if they are violent. And I also find myself having to say something if they are being sexist.'

There are also adjustments to be made by the partner to someone who is no longer abusive. This can affect the partner, who can now risk behaving in a normal way, without having to repress feelings, thoughts and actions.

Ben: 'After I got help for myself it was like me and my wife changed places. She started becoming violent and I wasn't. But in a way I could understand that as she had a lot to get out of her system.'

If men are the problem, if they are physically abusive towards their partners, then it seems only right that it is they who should have to change. The difficulty is that any change is likely to be seen by them as a loss of partner control and a threat not only to their role but also to themselves as people. Most women want their partner but not the abuse, so are attracted to the idea of helping programmes, medication for their partners, or some form of therapy. However, if there is to be change, then the man has to want it, and has to take responsibility for himself and his actions, and separate from his partner for a time. The last condition is recommended as staying with his partner makes it tempting to fall back into old patterns of behaviour and be controlling. However, the likelihood of both partners agreeing to such a separation is not high.

Although what has been discussed so far in this chapter might seem very negative, it is important to go through the findings and conclusions, to let women clients know that very often it is they who have to act as their partner will not voluntarily change. Even those men who try and end their violence may not be successful, so promises of change should be regarded with suspicion.

ALCOHOL AND VIOLENCE

Use of alcohol
One of the main factors associated with partner violence is the use of alcohol (Roberts, 1987; Leonard and Jacob, 1988; Schurger and Reigle, 1988). Its disinhibiting effect allows for greater ease in social interaction. For this reason, it has become a socially accepted drug in Western countries and it is often difficult at times to avoid its use. Its use is often associated with work, such as selling or heavy industry, with some sports clubs, with social gatherings and with formal settings. For many people, especially men, the pub is the local meeting place and going out for a drink is a pleasure. In addition, many men have been brought up to regard drinking, and usually heavy drinking, as a sign of manliness. Thus men can find themselves in a drinking environment which may be hard to resist.

But no one forces men to drink. They do so because the disinhibiting effects of alcohol not only reduce anxiety but also make communication easier because the social restraints are lowered. The result can be that an enjoyable time can be had by everyone. Violence is not the necessary accompaniment of alcohol. To understand the full picture, then we should appreciate that the effects of taking alcohol are not simple, but are in part dose-related. A small amount has a calming effect; increasing the dose generally increases communication and social interaction, so people seem more lively. Still greater amounts decrease physical coordination, impair judgement and permit the expression of inner feelings. It is at this stage that there is a risk of violence (Taylor and Gammon, 1975), especially if the drinker carries a lot of repressed anger or others in the drinking environment carry such anger, combining to produce a subculture of violence (Kantor and Straus, 1987). Even so, violence is still not inevitable. People who are normally non-violent are not likely to become violent with drink (Jeavons and Taylor, 1985).

If someone uses alcohol to be either relaxed, sociable, merry or violent then they have to drink the correct amount, but, more than that, they have to maintain the level. The human body slowly metabolizes the alcohol, so drinkers continually have to top up to stay at the same level of intoxication. All this means that men do not happen to get drunk and become violent; nor is 'I was drunk' an adequate excuse for violence. To arrive at such a state, they have chosen to go for a drink, decided to have a drink, then another, and another. They have kept their alcohol intake at a certain level and then gone home at a certain level of intoxication.

However, the situation is even more complicated. Alcohol, like most drugs, is unpleasant to take initially, and its effects can be unpleasant, even frightening. To lose control, to fall about, to make a fool of oneself, can be embarrassing. These are overcome by social learning. Most first-time drinkers later learn to interpret the taste of drink as pleasant, the effects as good, and any unfortunate behaviour as seen by others as a good laugh and a bonus for the group. Thus a circle of drinking friends, as can be found in a pub, is a useful social medium for allowing a person to get drunk and be accepted. The group in a pub, furthermore, has its own nature. Frequently it is male or male dominated, and provides a place where male and often macho views and beliefs are exchanged, resulting in mutual reinforcement. These social groups also serve to normalize the perception of the abusive male, as others see him as a sociable person they get on with, a person with whom they can laugh and joke. This bolsters the abuser's self-image and can even give him the feeling that what he does – acts of violence – is acceptable and normal.

Drink and excuses

All too often alcohol use is used as a mitigating factor, even when violence is severe. It may be employed as an excuse for the violence (Gelles, 1988), but this is hardly sustainable. As we have seen, no one suddenly becomes drunk, out of control and violent. There are hundreds of steps that lead up to the final state, and at any point the drinker can decide to stop. Perhaps I should add that I take a drink and go into pubs, so my intention is not one of advocating abstinence but merely one of looking at what actually happens. Never having been violent after drinking, like many other people, male and female, I have always been doubtful of the simplistic connecting of alcohol with violence, and even more doubtful when it is stated that alcohol is a cause of violence. My view is that alcohol is a liquid that stays in its bottle or cask unless removed. Personal violence is caused by people, with or without alcohol.

Leigh: 'Jimmy used to say that the arguments and trouble were the result of drink and I accepted this. But after I time I came to realize that he would drink to be able to be violent. The violence came not from drink but from him.'

We should remember that violence is rarely a set of isolated outbursts but is a regular pattern of behaviour. The use of alcohol is part of the overall pattern. Indeed, just as drinkers top up their level of alcohol, so abusers will do the same to keep up their level of released resentment and anger.

Annmarie: 'He always did his antics on a Saturday. He would cause arguments so he could storm out and get to the pub, instead of saying, "Look, I'm out for a pint." He was never like that, saying things normal.'

Alcohol use and the man

There is little doubt that alcohol can worsen a strained relationship and makes righting matters more difficult. This is due in part to the fact that alcohol affects drinkers' judgement (Pernanen, 1976). They can no longer properly appreciate situations, they frequently miss subtleties, especially non-verbal messages (Borrill et al., 1987). Nor are they easily able to retrieve situations as they fail to be fully aware of their own behaviour and might be less amenable to rational argument. But all this rests on the premise that things happen to the drinker. We have to appreciate that abusive drinkers can want things to happen, they want certain effects – the regard from certain people, a particular way of life – and all of this is related to them, the people they are or the people they want to be.

Pearl: 'He used to drink. Most of the violence was related to drink. He would drink whisky straight from the bottle and say, "No one can drink as much whisky as I can." He thought he was a man doing that, but actually folks would see him drinking in the street and think, "What a prick!"'

One strong argument for the minor role played by alcohol is that it aggravates a poor situation, but fights can start without it. Indeed, once a pattern of violence has been established it can become incidental.

Pearl: 'At first the beatings would come after the drink, but later they would just come, drink or no.'

This is a common feature, that the pattern of violence becomes self-perpetuating and there is little apparent reason or cause to set off violence.

Views around alcohol use

From a counselling perspective it is essential to recognize that alcohol frequently is a factor in partner violence, but it is not a cause and not an excuse. This may not be the view of the abuser, nor of those who are abused and other professional helpers. Blaming drink is incidental to seeing that person, the drinker, as being responsible.

Counsellors have to be sure of their own views, especially as they are likely to be subjected to different opinions by others, including other professional helpers. One of the professional myths that may be heard is that of the out-of-control drinker who is consequently violent. In fact, the only drinker out of control is one who is asleep or unconscious: drinkers always have some meaure of control. The point at issue is whether they want to employ that control. Of course, we should not feel too superior about drinkers who avoid taking responsi-bility for their actions as society tends to do the same. We allow behaviour under the influence of drink that we would not allow if the person was sober (MacAndrew and Edgerton, 1969).

Abuser alcohol use

As they do not easily take responsibility, abusive male partners who are heavy or regular alcohol users are usually resistant to getting help for their violent behaviour but may be more likely to respond to dealing with their drinking (Nace, 1982). This might seem quite contrary to what has gone before, as drinking is not the basic problem which is the person who inflicts violence. Even if the counsellor can help clients to reduce or stop their drinking, this does not mean the violence is stopped (Richardson and Campbell, 1980).

In practice the situation is not so clear cut. If a male abuser agrees to get help for his drinking then this might not necessarily help directly, but getting a client to become more receptive can increase the chance of later work on his violent behaviour (Sedlak, 1988). The fact that there has been progress in one area makes all those concerned with the problem of the violence more confident that it too can be changed.

Coping through alcohol use

One of the difficulties about drinking is that it may be that the woman in the violent relationship also drinks. This raises an immediate problem in that her behaviour is likened to that of her partner. It is less easy to blame the man and his use of alcohol as leading to violence if his partner does the same. But the two instances of drinking should not be compared but contrasted. The abuser drinks as it can help him be and continue to be violent, whereas the woman drinks mainly to help her cope with the situation.

Maria: 'When he was constantly attacking me, I used to get drunk so the physical attacks were less painful, the body was relaxed and there was less likelihood of bones being broken.'

But in the main, those battered have to cope not just with the physical pain but with their feelings, a mixture of apprehension, anxiety and emotional pain. These feelings are reduced by drugs such as alcohol. In fact, battered women are fifteen times more likely to drink heavily compared with non-battered women (Stark, 1984). Yet drink brings its own problems for abused women. As with abusive men, their judgement and ability to recognize potential trouble is impaired, as is their capacity to take evasive or preventative actions. They can also be more inclined to violence themselves, though in my experience this is often retaliatory.

Fleur: 'I gave Danny a good keeker [black eye]. Well, he hit me in the eye first. You know I don't like anyone who lays a finger on me like that. Danny's all right until he's been drinking and then he gets out of order. We were both downing the vodka and things got out of hand.'

If the violence is frequent and takes place over a long time, then abused women may find they need the support of drink almost constantly, and this leads to psychological dependence.

Leigh: 'I used to be so tense and anxious that I had no energy. So I would take a couple of strong lagers to be able to get up and do things. But having a drink changed me, even one drink would be enough to do it. And then I began to rely on the drink; I needed it. It gave me Dutch courage.'

The dependence can grow apart from the violence, so abused women drink, whether or not they are subjected to violence.

Drinking as an illness

In some cases of violence the women may stay with their partners even though they are abusive. This may reflect their role as carer. They feel unable to leave partners who have a pattern of drinking, especially if they view the drinking as an illness. However, once those partners have settled down and no longer drink, or drink in a very controlled way, they feel their partners can look after themselves and there is no reason for them to stay. Furthermore, if both partners drink heavily, then they can become co-dependent. This makes the reasons for working on the drinking greater. Co-dependency can distort the clients' patterns of behaviour, which become so intertwined, that knowing what will happen becomes extremely difficult.

Work around alcohol use

From the counselling perspective, prioritizing the alcohol use above the violence when helping can divert attention from the latter. This carries risks. What is required is a dual approach that covers both the drinking and the violence, and the interaction of the two. In addition, often counselling can be too narrow, concentrating just on violence or on drinking rather than the whole situation in context. Some of the broad view can be seen in the following.

Me: 'So let me get this right. Douglas, your partner, used to drink heavily but virtually stopped six months ago. That sounds quite a change.'

Bess: 'He had ulcers, bleeding inside. The doctor said he would be dead within the year if he kept it up.'

Me: 'Even with ulcers it is still something to have stopped the drinking. It must have been hard for him, hard for everyone perhaps.'

Bess: 'He got more violent. They say drink makes you violent, but it was the lack of drink with him. Always on edge. His family did not help, either. His father used to be the same, a drinker and violent, and I believe his brothers as well.'

Me: 'So he would occasionally hit you when he was drinking, but after he stopped it was worse. How did you feel about that?'

Bess: 'I thought once he ended with the drink it would be all right. It sounds terrible to say this, but I prefer him drunk than sober. At least he would be a bit of a laugh and he would talk, even if most of it was rubbish. But recently he seems just bitter, and holds me responsible – for what I don't really know.'

Me: 'It sounds as if the two of you don't really talk then.'

Bess: 'I tried, but now I've given up. It just seems to make him angry.'

Me: 'Is there anything that sets him off?'

Bess: 'I've wondered about that. There doesn't seem to be any reason as far as I can tell.'

Me: 'Mmm.'

Bess: 'On the other hand I can sometimes tell when he is about to explode. He goes very quiet and you can feel the tension.'

Me: 'And what do you do when that happens, you feel the tension rising?'

Bess: 'I try and calm him down, do what he wants.'

Me: 'Yes.'

Bess: 'It doesn't really work though ... I thought everything would be fine once he stopped the drinking.'

Me: 'Did he always drink from the time you first knew him?'

Bess: 'Yes. Not much at first, but it got worse ... Or perhaps I never knew how much he did drink initially. It's as if I have never really known him. Perhaps he is changing. I wake up in the morning and wonder who this man is I'm lying next to. Part of it is the violence. The drinking, well, men do it, women do it as well, but I accepted it. It was him. But the violence, in some way I did not see it as part of him. I just cannot accept it. Even the violence with the drink was difficult to take, but violence without it ... No, I can't take it. For me, it breaks all the rules, all trust.'

Me: 'And how do the children see it?'

Bess: 'That's another bit. When he was drinking he would make a fuss of them, play the fool, and they liked it. Did not understand. But now, the violence and his ill-temper, the atmosphere ... they are unsettled.'

Me: 'Do you see them being at risk?'

Bess: 'No, it's just me he has a go at. If the kids were at risk, I would take them and go.'

Me: 'You sound very definite on that point.'

Bess: 'Yes, I'm quite certain in my own mind about that.'

Me: 'The children mean a lot to you.'

Bess: 'They are just kids. It's not fair on them. They mean everything to me.'

The above was an extract from the only session we had. It is interesting in that alcohol is a problem, but not in the usual way. In addition, there were several other indicative points which were suggestive. However, none of these could be followed up. It seems, especially after the letter I received from her, that Bess had made up her mind what she wanted to do and counselling was no more than a means of affirmation and also a justification in some measure for her decision to leave – though, of course, there was never any prompting from myself that she should do so.

WORKING WITH SELF-ESTEEM

Self-esteem

For those not directly involved in counselling or similar helping activities, it can be difficult to understand how rigid but unpredictable male control in a relationship can reduce a woman's self-esteem, especially if she is isolated from other people. Control is usually obtained through both physical and verbal abuse, but the latter can be especially destructive.

Annmarie: 'Mental abuse; I was this, I was that. And it got to the stage when I believed it. You used to believe it. Your ego was so low you would believe it.'

Physical abuse can make you feel low and bad about yourself, but verbal abuse is specific, gives reasons why you should feel bad about yourself. Even if the violence ends, abused women still feel bad about themselves for a considerable time. So it is important that counsellors have a grasp of the nature of low self-esteem if they are to be of help.

Low self-esteem

Clients in a state of low esteem may be characterized by the following.

- A dependence on what clients think others think of them.

- Their self-esteem may be covered up or disguised to impress others.

- Low self-esteem cripples their autonomy and individuality.

- They have great expectations of others but also great fears, expecting to be put down, and so find it difficult to trust others. (Satir, 1978:8)

The result is that decisions, especially those which require long-term adherence, are difficult to make and harder to maintain. Women submitted to abuse will seem very variable in their behaviour, and are easily influenced by their partner, and this is a result of the abuse and subsequent low self-esteem.

Another aspect of low self-esteem is how those affected interpret what is happening, even if no one is telling them directly. Quite innocent remarks can be interpreted by the abused as being personal, as directed against them. They believe that the world is against them and this allows a rationalization of the treatment meted out to them. Low self-esteem can be a prison for the woman, unless she realizes what her real state is. And it does not have to be a permanent state. For instance, the self-esteem of women violence victims returned to normal if they left the relationship within a year of the violence starting (Andrews, 1987).

It is also important to remember that self-image is connected to self-esteem, and being hit in the face is likely to damage not merely a woman's appearance but also her self-image. However, it is of interest to note that abused women's self-esteem is less damaged by fighting back, though retaliation is likely to escalate the conflict and increase the severity of the male attack (Bowker, 1983). For some women, the additional pain is worth the price of maintaining self-esteem and even a sense of self.

Finally, low self-esteem in battered women is often associated with guilt. Clients with whom I have worked will constantly make excuses or apologize for the actions of others and for themselves. One such client would always apologise for being late for our meetings, though this was never the case. I then purposely arrived a few minutes late, and she apologized for being early. After that, I insisted she should never apologize to me or make excuses – though it was several weeks before she could stop herself.

The role of self-esteem

Though one of the main effects of violence on women partners is to reduce their self-esteem, a lack of belief in themselves and a lack of confidence in their actions is largely the result of verbal abuse and belittling. However, we should not overlook the effect of the male partners' unpredictable behaviour. By failing to give a consistent idea of what behaviour is acceptable, by complaining about behaviour that was previously acceptable, men can force their partners into a state of anxiety. The abused partners feel they can never get things right, and it must be their fault. They spend time and effort in trying to do what is right, not realizing that they cannot succeed with a partner who changes the rules arbitrarily in order to stay in control. Such a strategem of control is usually effective simply because it is continually applied and it can also reinforce any existing low self-esteem. We might also note that the abusive male is locked into this strategy of control. He cannot afford to let his grip on the relationship slacken. Control is not a sign of strength but of weakness, a fear of letting others do as they wish and not being able to deal with the consequences. As a result, those who use violence in my experience often have low self-esteem as well (Pillemer and Moore, 1989).

Raising self-esteem is necessary, not so much to allow clients to feel better about themselves – though this is certainly desirable – but because low self-esteem makes it difficult to take a realistic view of what is happening, makes decision-making more difficult, and the decisions made may not be in the interests of the abused woman. Furthermore, even if the right decision is made, those with low self-esteem are easily persuaded, inveigled, threatened or frightened into changing it.

Finally, it should be added that low self-esteem is not always obvious. Some women can present a facade of competence, even argue their point with their partner, but ultimately always submit to him. A variation is for men to allow their partners competence and some decision-making in certain fields, almost always domestic, but they are denied any influence in others such as financial, social, sexual and work. Of course, having some power in domestic matters does not shield the woman from partner criticism.

Self-work

Low self-esteem is a reflection of how people view themselves and so behave towards themselves. If they see themselves as incompetent, as always making mistakes, as unable to deal with ongoing problems, then they can become unduly self-critical and self-censuring. One outcome is that in time abused women with low self-esteem are controlled to their male partner's advantage without the latter having to do anything. Even if abused women are separated from their abusive partner, yet they are often still under partner control. Should both meet up then it is quite likely that the men can persuade their partners to return. Abused women have great difficulty in resisting their partner's entreaties as they lack the self-esteem and consequent self-confidence to be able to do so.

Counsellors can help women clients to recognize that they do self-criticize and this is a regular pattern of behaviour. To change this pattern, clients are asked to describe a situation and are then asked how they feel about it. The decription should be firmly held in the here-and-now, rather than being related to how they felt at the time. Counsellors then pick up on any self-criticism and help the client to look at it and then to see the described situation in a more realistic manner.

Me: 'Just stop yourself, Mandy. That's the second time you have criticized yourself. Did you realize that? Do you realize you criticize yourself a lot?'

Mandy: 'It was my fault the meal was burnt.'

Me: 'That's not the real point. You keep describing yourself as useless, which is wrong. After all, you are capable of cooking a meal. Right?'

Mandy: 'Uh huh.'

Me: 'Is that Norwegian for "You're talking bullshit"?'

Mandy: 'Yes, you're right. Of course, I can cook.'

Me: 'Sorry to interrupt but can I hear that again?'

Mandy: 'I said you were right.'

Me: 'The other bit, the other bit! I could have sworn you said something about cooking.'

Mandy: 'I ... can ... cook.'

Me: 'Is that useless? I think not.'

Mandy: 'I know that really.'

Me: 'I'm sure you do, deep down. When you stop and think about it, then you know you are not useless, but how often do you do that? How often do you think you're no good, then think about it for a minute and say to yourself, "No, that's rubbish. I can cook." Instead of going with what Rab tells you, look to reality.'

Mandy: 'But I did burn his meal. I wasn't surprised he hit me. I'm always doing things like that.'

Me: 'Always? Every time you make a meal you burn it?'

Mandy: 'No ... Though I have in the past. I suppose it has only been once before. Same thing, he came in late and I forgot it was in the oven. Got thumped that time, too.'

Me: 'So of the hundreds and hundreds of meals you've cooked for him, this was the second time it was burnt. And the only reason was he came in late. Did he phone you to say he would be in late?'

Mandy: 'No.'

Me: 'So whose problem is it? ... It's his, isn't it?'

Mandy: 'It's mine if he hits me.'

Me: 'That's both your problem. But Rab was unrealistic and that's his problem. I mean, does he thank you when the meal is cooked and served to him?'

Mandy: 'Never!'

Me: 'So you cook for him. No thanks. But if things go wrong – and it's his mistake – you not only get the blame but you believe it really is your fault. Is that the situation?'

Mandy: 'Put like that ... you're right! I'm an idiot!'

Me: 'Excuse me?'

Mandy: 'Oh, shit! He's the idiot. I'm brilliant! Satisfied?'

Me: 'Probably understated, but good enough!'

From the quote above we can also see the importance of getting clients to look at situations objectively, to avoid polarized thinking such as 'I always', 'I never', and for clients not to take on problems which belong to someone else. Although it might sound simplistic, it does help if clients actually say positive things about themselves.

Further work on self-esteem

Work on self-esteem can be extended to include the following. These are best avoided by abused clients.

- Making excuses for others, especially partners. This includes the habit of rationalizing and minimizing their abusive actions. People will often see themselves in comparison with others, especially those close or important to them. If clients wrongly judge those persons' behaviour, making it better than it is, then this indirectly decreases clients' estimation of themselves.

- Saying, 'I can't ...', when they really mean 'I don't want to ...'. For example, 'I can't go out at night', should be changed to, 'I don't want to go out at night (because my partner will leather me).' This opens up the possibility of change, of going out at night, provided the behaviour of the woman's partner changes or action is taken to ensure he will not be physically abusive.

- Some clients will insist on saying, 'It was my fault', about any incident that is brought to their attention or which they bring to their own attention. To get past this, I ask clients to stop themselves and substitute the question, 'Is it my fault?' Initially, clients will answer themselves in the affirmative but eventually they stop blaming themselves and even put the blame where it should lie.

- Abused clients often gain some comfort by comparing themselves with others, and putting others down to make themselves feel better. Though this makes them feel better in the short term, it does mean the process interferes with making or maintaining good relationships. This is important for those who are in a poor relationship. Whenever clients are dismissive of acquaintances, then I ask them also to say one good or positive thing about that person. This does get clients to seriously consider their acquaintances, to think about others rather than themselves.

- Clients should be advised to take their time. This is in practice not an easy task as so many clients will have got into the habit of reacting, especially with regard to their partner. Indeed, partners often expect an immediate reaction as opposed to a considered and measured reaction, as this allows the abuser easier control. Indeed, abusers will often provoke their partners to get an immediate response. Part of the need for clients to take their time is that they can jump to conclusions. For example, they may indulge in 'mind-reading', imagining they know what another person is thinking, often incorrectly. By waiting for a few moments, clients allow themselves to hear what the other person says.

- Connected with the previous point is that of clients relying overly on their 'gut feelings', and not taking a cognitive appraisal of the situation. Even when some clients hear what others say, they still dismiss it and go with their feelings. It should be stressed that useful understanding comes from a combination of the affective and the cognitive, and relying solely on one or the other leads to difficulties.

Clients' needs

Everyone has certain basic needs, physical, psychological and social, and a lack of them will affect personal self-esteem. Physical needs include adequate housing, clothing and financial income; psychological needs include love, respect, trust, understanding and purpose; social needs include friendship, fulfilling social roles, and independence.

Another avenue to helping with client self-esteem is to talk through with them such needs, checking on whether clients see themselves as having such needs met; and both aspects are important. Too often the emphasis is on unmet needs, which gives an unbalanced picture, and clients who think they have no needs met, who feel that nothing has gone their way, are more inclined to take an overly pessimistic view of themselves.

Discussing unmet needs is useful in that it can be linked with the idea of human rights and what members of society may be legitimately entitled to as well as their obligations. Some clients do not see themselves as having any rights, but see themselves as being just objects in life blown this way and that. Rights are balanced with obligations and duties, as clients then find they carry out their duties and obligations in life. What is missing is the other side of the equation, namely, rights for themselves.

Clients should always have the final say as to what they see their different needs as being and whether they are being satisfied. Sometimes helpers and even counsellors are inclined to insist on what client rights should be, presumably forgetting that a right to be heard is one of them. Clients often have their reasons for wanting and seeing themselves entitled to things others might count as being relatively unimportant.

Jacqui: 'I want my own place and I want it kept smart.'

Me: 'You want it looking nice.'

Jacqui: 'I want it spotless. Anyone coming into it would see I kept a clean house.'

Me: 'So you would be proud of it.'

Jacqui: 'Yes! To show I'm no wee daft lassie. And to show Roddy that I can live on my own, live better on my own in fact.'

Me: 'So your house says something about the person living there.'

Jacqui: 'Definitely! Well, I think it does. If I get the house right then that's a start.'

Me: 'I agree.'

Suicide

An extreme aspect of low self-esteem is that of women who self-mutilate, self-harm or attempt suicide. Women in abusive relations are likely to be very angry at their treatment, as evidenced in their arguing and retaliation. However, some women dare not express their anger because of the likely consequences. Their anger is internalized and over time this becomes the pattern of how they deal with their feelings. As contained anger mounts, it may boil over and one possible result is self-mutilation. This gives relief as anger subsides, and so self-harming may become a way of gaining relief. *In extremis*, the woman may attempt or commit suicide (Carmen et al., 1984). This should be of special concern to counsellors, as attempted suicide is five times more common among women who have been battered compared with those non-battered (Stark, 1984). Research of known cases in a Casualty Department showed that about half of the attempts occurred on the same day as the battering, suggesting a strong causal link (Stark and Flitcraft, 1996). This also suggests that attempted suicide is not the product of a woman's individual pathology, but an intense reaction to being subjected to violence.

Part of the counsellor's remit may be seen as preventing clients reaching such an extreme as self-harming. This can be done by asking clients if they have ever had suicidal thoughts and encouraging them to talk them through. As suicide is a product of internalized feelings, there is little point in waiting for clients to mention them; the counsellor has to take the initiative. It should be said that, in my experience, most abused women have had suicidal thoughts at some time. What is unhelpful is for counsellors to try and dissuade or argue against suicide. Suicidal feelings do not necessarily lead to self-damaging acts. Also, what is happening is that it is the counsellor who has the problem – what happens if my client commits suicide? – and this interferes with the counselling. It communicates counsellor anxiety and shows the counsellor has not come to terms with the fact that there is no way he or she can prevent a determined client from acting in a particular manner. Only the client can do that. Some counselling acquaintances have argued that talking against suicide does show concern for the client and should be attempted. Personally, this might show but it hardly communicates concern, which is much better done through listening to the client and trying to understand her. It helps to acknowledge that the client's feelings can go very low and have done so. This is put in the personal context, and seen as a reaction to a situation and not some personal abnormality. The positive aspects also should be highlighted, such as the client coming for counselling, talking about negative feelings and about suicide itself. What can be helpful is disovering out how the client is feeling and whether she is agreeable to continuing to talk on about such dark feelings or whether she feels the situation is getting beyond her control. Clients should always be encouraged to make their own decisions, even if as counsellors we might not agree with them.

9 SEPARATION AND LEAVING

Women clients and guilt

One of the factors that can inhibit abused women from doing what they really want is a feeling of guilt. Unfortunately, this may be overlooked by helpers who, trying to be supportive, insist that women have no need to feel guilty as it is their abusive partners who are to blame for the ongoing problems and difficulties. But blaming a partner does not make the woman feel free of guilt and when combined with low self-esteem, the message is not accepted – whatever outward appearances may suggest.

Guilt is a feeling that may be felt but not named by women clients. This reflects the fact that what they feel, they interpret as quite normal, and thus not worthy of any special note. However, it is often identifiable from what they say; phrases such as:

'He just couldn't cope on his own ...'

'The children need their father ...'

'I provoked him ...'

'We could try harder at making the marriage work ...'

One of these can be a useful entry into a discussion with the client which covers identification of relevant feelings, naming the feelings, and connecting guilt to events or stages in the client's life. These can vary to a general guilt produced by male expectations of women and their social role, to guilt being inculcated in the female partner as a means of male control, to guilt being associated with feelings of loss. Again, as guilt is mainly a feeling, it is not helpful to rely on a purely cognitive approach. Even trying to connect guilt to episodes in a person's life poses difficulties, and it can then be of use to discover whether the client feels guilt over a great number of things or whether it is more specific. Then the client can be asked to determine whether anyone close to her had the same or similar guilt feelings.

Ending the relationship

In general, the ending of any close relationship usually takes time and can be a painful process (Rose and Serafica, 1986). In fact ending is often more complicated than appears initially, as people tend to reflect on the relationship (Duck, 1982), rewrite its history (Duck and Miell, 1986) and tell others what seems to be the more acceptable account. All of this indicates a process of trying to maintain an acceptable self-image (Harvey et al., 1986) and so not compromise personal identity. From the counselling viewpoint, we have to realize that the whole process of separation is likely to be accompanied by a degree of biased perceptions.

Clients can be realistic about their relationships but still find separation difficult. Abused women have to deal with the idea of the loss of not only a partner, but what also can seem like a loss of part of their life.

Me: 'I wonder where you see yourself for the rest of your life.'

Tracy: 'I see myself on my own. If I knew twelve years ago my life was going to be like this, I would have left him eleven years ago, pissed off to London and had a life.'

However, for many women who have been physically abused, there are difficulties in that they are reluctant to be realistic about their situation and then do something about it. Yet only when they are realistic is there a likelihood of real improvement.

Annmarie: 'Mum says, "What are you going back for?" I says, "Look Mum, I'm going back for my bairns. That's all I want, the bairns. I'm never going to learn him. He's never going to turn round to me and say to me I was the greatest thing or even be nice to me. I'm just going back and just annoy him. Deliberately annoy him. And if he lifts his hand I'll chase him. I'll get him out of the house one way or another." So I went back and I nagged and nagged him. Then this Sunday he came back from the ice-hockey practice and said, "I'm moving out." He said he had his own flat. Fair enough. I didn't think he would go, mind you. I didn't want him to go. I didn't want him to stay either. He went and for two years that was brilliant. He came for the bairns every now and then. I enjoyed being on my own with the bairns.'

Grief

If the separation of a couple had occurred through the death of the man, then his partner would be given time to grieve, and expected to do so. When a relationship ends badly, the woman is often expected to put the separated partner out of her mind, to forget about him. This is impractical as he might return. Alternatively, he might not return, but might continue to have contact with the children, or the financial arrangements are such as to make a complete separation impossible. However, what is needed is some form of grief work, whatever the situation, to work towards an acceptance of the separation.

Mere reflection on what has happened is unlikely to be beneficial, and might even develop into an almost obsessional state (Pennebaker and O'Heeron, 1984), as the woman finds her thoughts going round and round and she feels unable to progress. To ensure going forward, it is helpful to aim for three main objectives (Stroebe and Stroebe, 1987).

1. Try to discover the meaning of the whole past experience.

2. Try to regain mastery over one's life.

3. Try to gain and maintain high self-esteem.

Thus counselling around separation can be helped by encouraging women clients to recall the past relationship, from start to present. The first step is to get the framework of that relationship, to arrive at a brief description that is as factual as possible. Often the counsellor has to assist the client, who will inject feelings, opinions and hindsight into the account. Such accounts are of use to clients as they tend to see their relationship as if through a mist. A factual summary of what has happened does help them focus and get way from the ongoing disputes or difficulties.

Once the framework has been set up then counsellor and client can look at the process of change that has happened within the relationship. This can be divided into the following:

1. *Relationships in general*

This applies at first to relationships with parents and also the parental relationship. Both of these might influence clients in later life, though they do not determine what happens.

> *Tina*: 'My Mum left us when we were young and my Dad couldn't look after us. So we were brought up by two aunts. They were alcoholics. All I wanted to do was leave home as soon as possible, so I got pregnant when I was sixteen. I left the father a few weeks after the baby was born. None of my relationships have been very long-lasting. Perhaps that has made the men I have stayed with almost expect me to go. Yes, some men lift their hands. That's what you expect.'

2. *Expectations of the relationship*

Men and women bring their expectations, which are not necessarily shared, into an intimate relationship. Often expectations are portrayed as idealistic, the product of romanticism, but I would suggest these are not so much expectations as hopes. My experience has been that actual expectations are not as high as hopes. They are much more realistic, and linked in part with jobs, money, getting accommodation, and starting or raising a family. It should be remembered that many intimate relationships or marriages are not the client's first.

> *Leigh*: 'I had left Chris but he was after me and I knew if he caught up with me I was in for a serious doing. So I ended up with Jimmy, thinking he could take care of himself and he would protect me. Well, he saw off Chris, but what I didn't realize was that he was even worse and would batter me.'

3. *Moving in or marriage*

The moment when two people decide to become a couple, whether by living together or getting engaged and then married is a significant time as it now becomes more difficult to move out of the relationship. Again, the picture of two people in love – if that is the case – is too simple. Any fear or ambivalence is covered up and events may even have a momentum of their own, so the two people are not fully in control.

> *Rena*: 'I look back on the years of being battered and realize it could have been different. Even on my marriage day I was uncertain. My Dad saw it and asked if I was all right. I said I was. He said I didn't have to go through with it, but I said that I wanted to get married. And that was it. I believed in those days that if you married it was for life, so it took years ...'

The following comments by clients show some of the variation, not just in reasons, but also hint at different accompanying feelings when it came to settling down in a relationship.

'We were in love.'

'I loved him.'

'I had just finished with a former boyfriend.'

'All my pals were getting married.'

'I just wanted to be married.'

'I was pregnant at the time.'

These statements are all worthy of further examination with the respective client involved. In particular, what were the different feelings and how did they change over time.

4. *Children*

Children do change any couple or family. The fact of a couple not being able to have their own children can be a factor. The fact that children belong to a previous relationship has its consequences. The birth of the first child can alter the couple's relationship as the woman's affection and attention is partly diverted to that child. What is a source of pride for some men can be a threat for others.

> *Claire*: 'It really started when I was pregnant. Kevin started punching me and jumping on my stomach. I thought that he must realize that that was dangerous, me being pregnant. Then I tippled it was intended. It was like I had changed from a wife into a mother. His mother even. He was acting like a wee boy who could not get his way. I don't know whether I suddenly grew up or he started being a child again.'

The four above-mentioned factors do help to fix various points, which make examination of the couple's changing relationship easier. These are not the only significant factors; others might include the man losing his job, the woman getting a job, the children being able to talk, and the onset of puberty for the children. All of these represent potential threats to male control. But relationships can change imperceptibly, without any identifiable point which can be linked to changes in the man's behaviour. These may require the asking of rather different questions.

1. Regarding the woman, such as: How have the woman's feelings for her partner altered?

2. Regarding her partner, such as: Does his behaviour seem to have changed?

3. Regarding the two of them, such as: How much time is spent together?

4. Regarding others, such as: How much, and what kind of, contact is there with in-laws?

The meaning of the past relationship

By talking through the changes in the relationships, the events and the feelings, then clients can make sense of what has happened. A common mistake is that of searching for meaning rather than waiting for meaning to make itself apparent. Naturally, any meaning has to be a meaning for the client. Interpretations of what has happened are not helpful.

By arriving at the meaning of what has gone before, clients are then better able to move on. Counsellors might disagree with the meaning, but this is unimportant. The object is for clients to find some meaning in their past life so they are able to close it off and progress. This is the first step in working through the grief of ending a relationship, and there is the task of regaining mastery over life, and this usually begins when there is separation of abuser and abused.

Getting out

Helping women is often made more difficult in that some women do not leave abusive relationships. They are prepared to risk their health and end up badly physically injured, rather than leave. There are some points to make about this curious situation.

- Partners are expected to remain in relationships, not leave them. Thus leaving a relationship is an expectation put on them by others (Loseke and Cahill, 1984), including commentators on abuse. If there is a problem then we have to be sure to whom it belongs, to us or to the abused person.

- Those who do not leave abusive relationships are more likely to come to official attention, so we tend to overlook those who do leave – 80 per cent in Pagelow's sample (Pagelow, 1981), and those wanting to leave amounted to 90 per cent in Roy's sample (Roy, 1977).

- There is the presumption that women in such situtions will get out immediately. If they do not do so, then it is assumed that there is something wrong with them. What can be missed is that women do leave such relationships, though the separation can occur after some time, maybe months or years. Thus women often do get out of violent situations, but it takes time.

- The situation is used by many helpers as a vehicle for their own agendas and theories rather than attending to what actually happens as seen from the involved woman's perspective. Unfortunately, theoretical oppression then occurs and physically abused women are seen as objects in cognitive schema rather than individual people in human situations. Emphasis is placed on what is rational and the affective aspects are largely ignored. Client comments such as 'But I love him', are given short shrift rather than being accepted.

When we look at the situation of the woman leaving a violent relationship there are four principal aspects to consider. First, there is the process of ending a relationship, any relationship. Second, there is the emotional involvement of both parties. Third, there are those reasons which apply particularly to the abused women and are controllable by them that make leaving difficult. Fourth, there are those reasons which involve other people and which are much less easy to control.

Ending a relationship

Ending any partner relationship, even one where there has been no violence, is not easy. Such relationships may be seen as an ongoing process whereby two individuals renegotiate their life with respect to one another and the world around them (Berger and Kellner, 1964). However, in time there also has to be renegotiation about the couple's separate individualities. Two people come together to be as one, but then have to rediscover their own selves, so they do not become lost as individuals.

This renegotiation can be a private process, healthy for the relationship, but difficulties can arise when partners gently hint at their desire for some form of change in that relationship (Bok, 1982). This change may be an adjustment – and it is likely that many adjustments will be required over time. Problems only arise when the couple cannot individually respond to perceived required changes. In extreme cases, one party might be trying to save the relationship, and even secretly talk the matter over with friends (Brannen and Collard, 1982).

In poor relationships, matters are likely to further deteriorate, and each partner tends to magnify the flaws in the other (Johnson, 1982) and reinterpret the relationship (Davis, 1973), and in such a way to maintain the consistency between the past and the present (Unruh, 1983). By now, the relationship does not seem worth saving, and one or both may pass hints to this effect in public to friends (Scanzoni, 1972). Such friends might become allies of one or other of the partners, or may prefer to avoid any involvement in what seems to them to be purely private business. Public involvement is always risky, as it can reduce the standing of the 'wrongdoer', but it might also reduce that of the complainant (Goffman, 1968:106).

Finally, there can be open confrontation about the state of the relationship. Even at this stage, matters can be improved by refocusing on the good aspects of the relationship and reinterpreting it in a more positive light, and then making plans to change behaviours. At the same time, more attention is given to the possibility of separation, and even the seeking out of those who themselves have separated.

This illustrates the point that separation is not an act but a process which can last for months or even years. The time and energy put into a relationship, any relationship, is not simply thrown away without some attempt to save the situation.

Emotional needs

Another aspect of intimate relationships is that they may fulfil both parties' emotional needs. However, often this is not the case for one or both members. Relationships may begin on a false basis as both partners put up a front, acting in a way that they think will attract and maintain the other. This might represent unconscious needs or it might be conscious behaviour. Only after a while do such couples discover that they are not really suited. This may be no problem, as couples then drift apart and seek new partners.

But for some couples separation is seen not as a solution but as the worst that can happen. This can arise from one or both parties being emotionally immature in that they have not broken away completely from their family of origin. This can happen when the parents have their own difficulties

Internal reasons

However when considering a violent relationship, there can be particular difficulties which appear to present barriers to a woman leaving.

1. Some women, especially if they are teenagers, are unsure what to expect from a long-term relationship and take what happens as normal. This may be reinforced by outsiders, such as parents, who say she 'has to take the rough with the smooth', or, 'You have to work at the marriage.'

2. The man may stay with the woman for some time, say three months, before starting to use any violence. This allows mutual attachment bonds to develop and makes breaking the relationship difficult.

3. Some women whose parents have had a poor relationship or who have had a poor relationship with their parents may find an unsatisfactory relationship hard to break, resembling a break of or with their own parents.

4. The woman may still love her male partner. This affective state can continue despite the abusive behaviour that takes place.

5. The woman can make excuses for her partner. This is not perverse behaviour but represents one way of coping with an overwhelming

situation. However, the excuses, though helpful in the short term, can be unhelpful in a long-term relationship. These excuses, such as, 'He didn't mean it', 'I deserved it', 'It was just the drink', lay the grounds for continuing difficulties.

6. The woman has to come to terms with being a battered woman, further lowering her self-esteem and taking on a possible survivor role. She might not want to see herself in such a light, even if it is correct.

7. A frequent response is that the woman says her partner will change (Gelles and Cornell, 1985), a belief frequently resulting from promises that he has made.

8. Women might well wonder why, if the men in their life are causing the difficulties through being violent, they should have to move out of the house. This seems to be rewarding those who behave in an insupportable manner.

9. Sometimes the woman is realistic and knows that the relationhip has broken down, but then reacts by staying in it as her family have always warned her what was going to happen. Generally, telling women to leave is ineffective. Indeed, if this is continued, the woman can become resistant and either hide or deny to others what is taking place, or the woman simply becomes more determined to make the relationship work.

10. Sometimes the woman has real difficulty in knowing what to do about the situation or how a relationship should be ended. This can be the case even if she has had past broken relationships in her life. Fear of leaving is increased if she has poor social skills and does not make friends easily (Cook, 1977).

11. Women might be well aware of the dangers but still not want to admit to themselves that they have made a mistake in choosing to stay with their partner.

12. Women may have made a heavy personal investment in the relationship and so find it difficult to leave (Rusbult, 1983). In addition, there may seem to be no good alternative person with whom to start a relationship (Sabini and Silver, 1982).

13. Friends and relations will expect and even advise her to stay with an abusive partner, often disbelieving or playing down the actual dangers of what is happening. If they do want to help, then women may experience difficulties if the abuser oppresses them as he does his partner. Men may find the situation difficult as often they have

trouble dealing with their own feelings and so either over-react with extreme anger or avoid feelings and attempt a totally cognitive approach. Many outside helpers, men or women, are inclined to offer conditional help – they will assist as long as the woman leaves the relationship for good. Many women have not reached this stage, their feelings are still paramount, and this leads to difficulties between the abused woman and friends or relatives. In addition, abused women have their own particular needs and will not react so well if these needs are not addressed.

14. To many women the idea of adult life outside marriage and the family is not one desired, perhaps a thought that applies particularly to some women in ethnic minorities (Gifford, 1990). These women in addition are unprepared for such an extra-marital life.

15. The woman with children sees them as needing a father and she also believes that the needs of her children are paramount, whereas her needs must be secondary. Sometimes there can be a fear that leaving her partner might also result in her losing her children, a fear that her partner could be reinforcing.

16. The woman may fear that her leaving will result in her partner's breakdown and this concern might be increased by his threats to kill himself if she does leave.

17. Because of her own experiences, the woman may strongly identify with her partner's distress and want to care for him. This desire to stay can be further augmented by periods of reconciliation, when the woman thinks her care for him has changed the situation.

18. Finally, the woman may decide there is more to the relationship than the violence, and that there are enough positives to continue (Kirkwood, 1993).

These are just some of the reasons why women continue in bad relationships, but there are others. This does not end the personal reasons for finding leaving difficult, as often the male partner is aware of the woman's inhibitions about leaving and will reinforce them, not only making their separation more difficult but adding to his overall domination of her. He might also seek out allies, such as members of the family who will further reinforce the process.

Counsellors have to be aware of such difficulties, even actively to search for them, as not all clients will mention them. There is often pressure on counsellors to do something about women in abusive situations, some of that pressure coming from themselves. It is not easy to explain that any departure is up to the clients and may take some considerable time, during which she continues to be at risk.

Emotional work

There is one less than obvious aspect worthy of remark. Men tend to be poor at expressing emotions, but are more likely to express themselves physically or through their work or life-style. This means that the affective aspect of the relationship and its management is left to the woman, who through her socialization is likely to take it up (Marsden, 1978). This is permitted by the man as it acts as a source of power for him. He feels less constrained about ensuring the life of the relationship, relying on his partner to repair any fractures in it. She, on the other hand, because of her gender caring role, usually carries out such tasks.

However, often she finds herself with an impossible task. Rather than giving critical feedback, her socialization tends to make her work for reconciliation where there is none to be had (Eagly, 1978). She is likely to be aware that critical women are not popular (Hull and Schroeder, 1979), and her attempts to right a poor relationship may well be viewed by her partner as criticism. Unfortunately, there can be a danger that this process is continued in counselling. I have known counsellors suggest that women can do more to preserve the relationship, ignoring the fact that they are the ones who have kept it going. In addition, it is assumed that this is a task that can be given to women and somehow the male partners are only indirectly involved. Women should not be expected to carry the affective burden for the couple or the family.

External reasons which affect leaving

A pattern of physical abuse is difficult to stop and abused women require protection, even if only for a while until the relationship and behaviour are greatly altered. However, there are numerous external reasons why leaving a violent relationship presents difficulties.

1. Women who separate are usually placed in a poor financial position, and their possessions might be destroyed, or retrievable only with the cooperation of the male partner – and this cooperation is usually absent. Possessions might be retrieved with police help, but this may only be possible if the woman has first obtained a legal order. These financial constraints are also to be found in divorce cases, where employed as opposed to unemployed women are more likely to consider divorce (Huber and Spitze, 1980) and less likely to return to their ex-partners (Kitson and Langlie, 1984).

2. Accommodation is a difficulty experienced by about 60 per cent of women who leave violent relationships (Binney et al., 1981). Women have to leave their homes in most cases, rather than the man, as the house is most likely to be in his name. Relatives and friends may be unwilling to offer shelter as it could be viewed as taking sides in a marital or relationship dispute. This can become aggravated if the male partner searches for his partner and finds her staying with friends. The friends can then be subject to abuse, both verbal and physical.

   Local authorities should house battered women under the Housing (Homeless Persons) Act, 1977, but there is no assurance that they will do so, as they can argue that the woman made herself intentionally homeless, and they can also insist on evidence such as a court injunction or criminal conviction (Binney et al., 1981; Bryan, 1984). Women's Aid refuges provide a very useful halfway house and are staffed with workers who have an appreciation of the practical needs of abused women. This is different from the help given by other agencies such as social workers who espouse empowerment (Kirkwood, 1993, p. 90) but are often reluctant to give out relevant information or advise what should be done at a time when some clients are unable to make decisions for themselves. The downside of refuges is that Women's Aid is underfunded and as a result the refuges are overcrowded, there can be little sense of privacy (Hoff, 1990), and they seldom appeal to the middle-class abused woman.

3. If the woman is in employment then there can be further problems as her ex-partner can contact her place of work and cause difficulties, or simply wait outside the work gates; and the result in extreme cases is that the woman fears her job is in jeopardy. The economic and financial consequences of leaving the home and the relationship make it more likely that the woman will return to the abusive partnership (Aguirre, 1986).

4. The male partner often makes threats against the woman should she try to end the relationship. Furthermore, such threats may well be carried out and in extreme cases can lead to the woman's death.

5. Many women find that their same-sex relationships decline as the couple-based socializing tends to be with male partner friends (Johnson and Leslie, 1982). Women who have been in a violent relationship for some time are likely to be isolated to an extent from all outsiders and be emotionally dependent on their partner.

This means they have a fear of living on their own, which may be greater than their fear of being battered. It should be remembered that women tend to be defined primarily as wives and mothers (Chodorow, 1978) and so have difficulty in maintaining themselves as individuals within intimate relationships (Rubin, 1983). Apart from feeling isolated, women can also be physically isolated, as in rural areas, or as newcomers to a district. Abusers will often increase isolation by not allowing friends in the house and even disconnecting the telephone.

6. Family and friends may be reluctant to offer help, fearing such action may be seen as being little more than interference. In addition, there is a respect for privacy and a disinclination to become involved in other people's lives. Even if friends and neighbours do intervene, they can be uncertain as to how far their actions should go.

    Annmarie: 'I was embarrassed and would cover bruises with make-up and wear dark glasses to hide black eyes. I hid what was happening from my family. I made all sorts of excuses to my doctor. I don't know if he really knew what was happening, but he never said anything. His family lived next door and once I did tell his father what was happening, but his father didn't believe me.'

    Me: 'So he didn't believe you.'

    Annmarie: 'Well, he wouldn't admit it. But John had battered his wife before being with me, so I think his family knew. But John was their blue-eyed boy, couldn't do any wrong.'

    Me: 'Was there any one else who knew what was going on?'

    Annmarie: 'The couple who lived upstairs, above us. The man came down one evening and told John he could hear him hitting me, which tells you the noise the battering made. He told John that if it happened again, he would take him out into the garden and do him over.'

7. Women may see their role as being that of housewife and mother, and their present possible worth in the employment market as being minimal, so what they think about is another, better relationship. But another relationship may not seem possible to them because of the attitude of their present partners, the fact that they have come to see themselves as unattractive and not likely to be wanted by other men, and the fact that it is not so easy for older women to meet the opposite sex (O'Meara, 1994).

8. The decision to leave a relationship can be influenced by other members of the family such as the woman's parents, who might have their own agendas. They might want the couple to stay together. Even when the family wants the woman to leave, the fact that the family wants this can lead the woman to react against the idea.

9. The effect of belief systems such as those of religion can tend to keep partners together. This may be reinforced by the family and friends who belong to the woman's church (West, 1995). Although clients with whom I have worked tended not to be religious, they often had various beliefs such as reincarnation. They felt that there must be another better life and this gave a sense of ultimate hope and meaning, though it could also be used to reinforce the status quo.

10. Perhaps the strongest effect is that of ingrained behaviour of couples, the automatic command and obedience that can characterize abusive relationships. These behavioural patterns can survive the separation, which is why contact with the male partner increases the likelihood of the couple getting back together again.

11. The abused woman's parents can be helpful, but some can be unhelpful and unsupportive. They can reinforce feelings of guilt with remarks such as, 'You must have done something'; they can invoke religious arguments against leaving a marriage partner, they may be concerned about the children and ignore completely the mother's situation. The crisis can also unload past ill-feeling between the abused woman and her parents.

12. The children can become worried by their mother's threats to leave and then angry when the action is not carried out. Leaving can also invoke fear of abandonment in the children, and the mother's apparently inconsistent behaviour may add to their distress.

What is apparent is that battered women have many valid reasons for not seriously contemplating getting out of a violent relationship (Strube and Barbour, 1983; 1984). Their staying does not denote any strange or irrational behaviour. On the contrary, it is the product of existing emotional ties, feelings of duty, fulfilling the role of wife and mother, plus a risk assessment on leaving and being able to live outside the relationship. Leaving the relationship can be a very positive step, but it is not one lightly or easily undertaken. There are undoubtedly many difficulties in leaving a relationship, and this applies to any relationship, not just an abusive one. Women in abusive relationships are little different from those in non-abusive relationships, apart from the behaviour of their partner.

Ambivalence about leaving

Despite there being good reasons for leaving and the woman saying that she wants to leave, we should not assume she will do so. This needs to be discussed. One difficulty for counsellors lies in how clients express the difficulty in leaving, which can be very much bound up in their negativity.

Carla: 'I know what to do, what I should do, but I don't seem to be able to do it. What I want are some courage pills.'

When faced with such a statement, counsellors first have to look to their own understanding and sensitivity. For women clients part of the difficulty is dealing with change, fear of the unknown, of losing the security of a relationship – albeit an abusive relationship. People need time to assimilate the idea of change but at some time they have to make a decision. If the abuse continues for too long, the woman might find she is in no position to make a decision. However, trying to force the woman to make the decision or, even worse, making it for her, is a continuation of the exercise of power over her and may produce resistance with the result that she is less likely to leave. Sometimes the woman can become conscious of her procrastination and this can become a problem in itself. What is important is that such a delay is understood by clients as being quite normal and not a form of weakness or irrationality. Even when all love has gone and the relationship is little more than a shell, women can still feel guilty about leaving.

Marsha: 'I know there is nothing there, but I still wonder if he will be all right, whether he can make it on his own. People say that's his problem. That doesn't stop me feeling bad, even when I know I shouldn't.'

After being in a certain role for years, it is not easy to change. That role is more than a particular way of behaving. It carries memories, hopes, feelings and perceptions of the world. Thus contemplating leaving a relationship leads to a degree of internal conflict, to ambivalence.

Ambivalence is a product of conflicting perceptions and conflicting feelings, which can become so interlocked that the cognitive and the affective inter-react. It becomes difficult for abused women to know what are their true feelings and thoughts, what they really feel and think. As a result, battered women should not simply be seen as obstinately refusing to listen to good advice or being so victimized that they have lost all ability to make a rational choice. Rather, we should see them as trying to work through a situation as best they can.

Professional contra-helping

Outside helpers can sometimes be less than helpful and this can arise from their placing of undue emphasis on theoretical rather than practical explanations, resulting in women being seen and treated as being in some way sick. They might be regarded as suffering from post-traumatic stress (Stark and Flitcraft, 1996) or identify with their abusers through traumatic bonding (Dutton and Painter, 1981). Women are seen as having unrealistic beliefs about the consequences of staying or leaving (Strube, 1988).

This ignoring of what abused women are actually doing in desperate circumstances does raise questions about the helpers or theorists. In a neat spin, Gondolf suggests that it is helpers rather than their clients who actually exhibit real helplessness (Gondolf, 1988). But to me what is missing is an understanding of what it means to be battered, and the ambivalence that can result.

Working through ambivalence

Ambivalence is not about the abusive partner; it concerns the abused woman. The fight is not with the partner; the fight is with herself. For this reason, constantly talking about the partner or the relationship may not be so helpful – though this is often what outsiders do. Instead, the woman requires support and help for herself, help to raise her self-esteem. In one case, a woman client went out to the hairdresser before telling her partner to move out. Though that might be a very simple example, yet in order to be decisive and to avoid going back on what she says, the abused woman has to feel good in herself. A lot of advice at this stage can be negative; the abused person interprets what is meant to be helpful as merely underlining her own deficiencies and failure to act.

The task at this stage is for the attention to be put on the woman's strengths, not on her partner's faults. The role of women who have experienced similar troubles may be helpful, provided they are not caught up in their own agendas or fail to allow everyone to work through to achieve their own aims.

When working through ambivalence it is helpful to bear in mind the following points:

- There is never a good time to end a relationship. The woman can only try to make it as easy for herself as possible.

- There is no nice way of saying a relationship is over. Extending the leaving process by breaking the news gently can, in the long run, be more painful for everyone.

Both these statements I make to clients, though not suggesting that they should leave. However, knowing how best to leave is frequently of more use to clients than being told what to do – however seemingly correct and well meant.

Finally, counsellors when dealing with a case should consider whether they are the best people for the job. I would not counsel anyone from an ethnic minority as, apart from the possible language difficulties, such women can find cultural factors and possibly their ethnic community are against them (Imam, 1994), so they need the help of a counsellor from their own community.

Leaving as a process

Leaving a relationship is often seen as a single irrevocable action, but this is rarely the case. It is often done in stages. The woman says she is leaving but does not do so till a later date. Alternatively, the man is told to get out of the house but fails to go. What is important for the woman and others to see is that even the act of telling a person alters the relationship and puts matters on a different plane.

Tina: 'I told him to go but he wouldn't. He's not speaking to me. That made it easier for me to get on with things, so I went to a lawyer to see how I stood. And I told him. That gave him a shock; he wasn't expecting that!'

Much of the process of separation is marked by ambivalence, by two steps forward and one step back, but each step back is not a failure but a practice run.

Gena: 'I had walked out so many times before and then returned. Idiot! This time I walked out, he even held the door open for me, but this time I kept on walking. Two weeks later I saw him in the street and I was shocked. Really, he was an ugly, pathetic bastard. What did I see in him? Why the fuck did I stay so long? It was like I had been under a spell and now it was broken. "When are you coming back?", he said. Just like that, as if I had been out for some messages [shopping]. "When cows shit gold!" "You're off your head." "No, for the first time in years I've come to my senses." For the first time I felt in control, and it was great!'

Telling a friend that the partner is going to be told at a certain time can be useful as this makes backing down more difficult. However, the woman has to be determined to go through with the process, otherwise it can be seen as another failure.

The final action

The final difficulty about leaving an abusive relationship is simply that of planning and coordinating actions. Thus the woman must have a place of safety to go to – possibly with children – and she must have money and income in her own name. If she is employed then her partner is likely to turn up at her place of work if he cannot find her, so employers may have to be apprised of the situation. The childrens' schools might have to be changed and the rest of the family told what is happening. Preparations to leave have to be made without the man being aware of the situation. And all the time the woman is worrying about what might happen.

Pearl: 'I was scared of him as Josh said he would cut my face from side to side if I left. People said, "You don't want to listen to that", but I think he would have done it.'

Threats to kill the woman by her partner are not uncommon (Hanmer and Saunders, 1983) and should always be taken seriously. They can constitute a real threat and may well be carried out (Saunders and Browne, 1990; Dutton, 1986). Further problems include having to negotiate the physical restraints that might surround her.

Tina: 'He used to lock the door when he went out and I wasn't allowed out. No one was allowed into the house or he said I was carrying on with them. I was a prisoner.'

Even if the woman is allowed out, she is still treated as a prisoner.

Fleur: 'I couldn't go to the chipper [fish and chip shop] or get a Chinese [meal]. I couldn't go anywhere. I had to sit by his side or where he could see me. As long as I was there he didn't bother, would talk to others.'

All the time, battered women are making rational assessments as to the course of action which best preserves their well-being (Tedeschi et al., 1973), and reviewing their feelings in the situation. What is required is that they finally feel able to take responsibility for themselves. In the end, only they can make the decision.

Annmarie: 'Before Christmas I was going downhill; I was quite ill. I

was all black under the eyes from not sleeping. Eventually I got out –
Elaine went on at me and that – but it was more I had to make up my
own mind, my own decision, even though folk were telling me what to
do all the time. Eventually I made my mind up after he tried to put the
door in. That was the last straw. He was breaking into my privacy and
I thought, "Enough is enough!".'

The final action of leaving may have to be done in a secretive way
which may arouse further suspicions in the male partner, such as that
his partner is leaving for another man. The woman should be prepared
for accusations of this sort and see the problem as lying with her
partner, not with her. She does not have to give excuses for the
manner of leaving.

As previously mentioned, the counsellor should not directly advise
a client to leave a relationship, but mentioning it as one option is
acceptable. Even this is subject to timing as unless the woman's
self-esteem has been built up to some extent, talk of leaving can seem
too threatening – however bad her situation might seem. This means
that preliminary work on outstanding and possibly impeding problems, on restoring self-esteem, and on closing the relationship needs
to take place. It can be helpful to run through a rehearsal of leaving
and the attendant practicalities.

- There must be a safe retreat and this might be a Women's Aid
  hostel, though there are not always spare places available. The
  usual alternative for the woman client is to stay with her parents or
  a parent. Parents can be very supportive, though they can also get
  caught up in the situation, take sides, and have expectations about
  what should happen. This is especially the case if children are
  involved. It should be added that it is seldom worthwhile expecting
  council housing to be provided as this will take some time, with
  increased physical risks to the client.

- The whole leaving process is helped if there is absolutely no contact
  with the abusing partner till considerable preparations have been
  made. This is usually given by Women's Aid hostels but not by the
  woman's parental home, which is usually one of the first ports of
  call for the male partner looking for his partner. He is capable not
  only of calling at the house, repeatedly, but also of causing scenes,
  of threatening, and even of causing damage such as breaking
  windows. There is always the danger that the woman will return to
  her partner simply to avoid further upset to her parents.

- Another necessity is that of money. If the woman concerned is not
  in paid employment she needs direct access to money and any

benefits being paid in her name. Matters can often be expedited if there has already been contact with a lawyer, one to whom officials can refer.

- People do not tend to take separations seriously unless a lawyer has been seen. It is best to contact one with previous experience of such cases, so usually Citizens' Advice Bureaux or Social Services Departments have appropriate lists. My experience has been that women lawyers or solicitors tend to be more sympathetic, though clearly this need not apply everywhere.

- If there are children, this can lead to further complications as unless they suddenly change school, they provide an easy way for the mother to be traced. The male partner hanging around the school gates is common in these circumstances.

- Many of the separations are done in haste, so the question often arises for the woman of whether to take all her possessions or leave them. Trying to retrieve them later can be risky, and may need the assistance of the police. Also, the male partner might immediately sell or destroy them. I recommend taking what is meaningful, such as photographs, documentation and items significant to the person. Other items may or may not be taken, but making a list beforehand and knowing what is to be taken is helpful.

- A form should be put in, redirecting mail, preferably to the woman's lawyer or a third party who has a phone. That person could then be contacted by phone about further arrangements about the mail.

She's leaving home

The following is my brief account of one battered mother and how she left her partner. Though not related directly to counselling, it does contain some useful points.

Tina and I had talked through the possibility of her leaving Josh. She had always seemed very ambivalent, despite his treatment of her. However, one afternoon she phoned me up to say she was leaving and needed help to move out. In fact, she had made up her mind and what I had taken as ambivalence was merely caution, waiting for a suitable opportunity. That had now come, as Josh was away for the day. This raised a further difficulty as Tina had no place to go and there proved that day to be no place in a Women's Aid hostel. This was no problem for Tina herself, who was prepared to sleep rough, though she expected to be able to get a bed at the home of one friend or another. The difficulty was getting a place for her son at short notice, and the upshot was that I arranged for him to be taken into short-term foster care. Tina had agreed to this idea as she expected Josh to come after her, and being accompanied by her young son would have made any escape more difficult.

Matters were not so easy for Tina, as being parted from her child caused her to become depressed, so she hardly visited her son in care. This was seen as uncaring by some in the Social Work Department, who then queried whether she was ready to have him back. This had the result of further depressing her. From that point there was a real danger that although she had been abused, Tina was going to be treated as the person needing to change. The suggestion was made that she should prove herself by getting accommodation through the Housing Department without outside help. She had been prescribed the anti-depressant, amiltryptyline, which made her drowsy and disinclined to do anything.

Although Tina's situation was soon righted through directly helping her or doing some of the required tasks for her, yet it does show the risks women with children undergo when trying to escape their predicament. It may be another reason for women to prepare carefully before leaving their partners.

Separation and after

Even after the woman has left the abusive relationship, that is not the end of matters. Leaving any long-term and intimate relationship is difficult and there is the temptation to go back rather than remain on one's own. As a result, women may leave several times, trying to come to terms with the loss of their partners. Violent men usually have even more difficulty in accepting such loss and pressurize their partners to return. Even in very poor relationships, such pressure is often initially successful.

Pearl: 'My Mum and Dad wanted me to leave him and I did so several times. But he would always win me over.'

Taking into account the severe treatment meted out to Pearl by her partner, such a statement can seem almost incomprehensible. Only by seeing leaving as a process does it begin to make sense. There is seldom one clean break, but more often a series of attempts to break away.

Annmarie: 'My confidence began to pick up and left for the second time, but now it was a lot stronger. I had made up my mind to get on with it and moved out. I was more stable and realized it was either my health and my kids or him. I said that if I stayed in town I would have gone back eventually, so I decided to get on with it, move out and start a new life – and that's what I did.'

But what is notable is that men seem to have even greater difficulties in leaving or being left, and accepting the situation.

Leigh: 'I said to Jimmy, "At least we can end up being friends, as we started out as friends." He just said, "No way!"'

As abusers seek control in relationships, the idea of friendship on an equal basis with a member of the opposite sex is difficult for them to contemplate and even harder to accept in practice.

Even after couples have separated, the effect of their meeting up again is very often to bring old behaviour patterns into play, and the couple get back together again. Despite everything that has happened, women may be very ambivalent about ending violent relationships. Part of this may arise from still loving or having positive feelings for their partners; it may come partly from the psychological state to which they have been reduced. They may fear everything, including change. Their induced dependency on their partner can make ending seem frightening. All these can result in ambivalence, which in turn can itself become a problem, with outsiders getting impatient with 'somebody who cannot make their mind up'.

Melanie: 'I was kicked into scaredness. I had butterflies all the time. I wanted to go but I didn't want to go. I wanted him and I didn't want him.'

Counsellors have to attend to clients' ambivalence, not the fact that they have not left, and how clients can be helped to make their own decisions. This, like grief counselling, is often marked by listening to what clients have to say and reassuring them that the chaos they are experiencing is quite normal for someone in their situation. We should remember that what is important is not so much what counsellors bring to counselling as what clients take away.

10 CONTINUANCE, LOVE AND SELF-IDENTITY

Introduction

It might seem that finally getting out of a bad relationship would end the violence, but this assumes that the male partner recognizes that the relationship has ended. In fact, only a minority of male abusers want a separation, preferring the relationship to continue. Some indication of this is given by that fact that reconciliation was wanted by few women who applied for an emergency order under Section 209A of the Massachusetts Abuse Protection Act 1978, yet about half of the male partners wanted it (Wright, 1991:72). Male abusers tend not to recognize the breakdown in a relationship and see violence as the norm. They continue to be violent and this can continue even after the official ending of the relationship. In Britain, of the intimate violent incidents reported to the police, 55 per cent were between husbands and wives or their common law equivalents, but 11 per cent were between ex-husbands and wives or their common law equivalents (Home Office, 1995).

This possibility of continuing violence has to be put in the context of the woman wanting to make a life for herself and even take up a new relationship. This aspect tends to be ignored. Troubles are seen as ending after the abusive relationship is seemingly over, with little thought given to the fact that abused women still have the rest of their life to live, new relationships to make, perhaps even a new family to raise. Though outsiders might not consider this aspect, yet for many women these are relevant thoughts and can even occur while women are still being abused.

Tracy: 'I don't think I am interested in men. My sexual feelings are dead. Mind, if I met someone it might be different. But I think I would have to have four months on my own before I met a guy, and it would be several months before I went with him sexually.'

We see that change is usually a gradual process, and clients need time to work through relationships. New ones are contemplated and old ones are slowly put into the past. Old relationships may have been formally brought to a finish but the memory of them persists and can affect subsequent behaviour. It can take some time for old feelings and memories to disappear.

Leigh: 'I used to have dreams about being back there with Jimmy, but with time they got fainter and fainter. Then suddenly something must haver triggered it off again, as the dream returned, more vivid than ever – really scary.'

So even when the abuser is away for good, he may seem to persist like an invisible presence. Women can be haunted by the ghosts of past relationships.

Hangover effects in new relationships

So even if the women are in new non-violent relationships, this does not put an end to their difficulties. There may be a hangover effect from past bad experiences.

Karen: 'It was not a relationship with Pete: he would just tell me to do this or do that, and I dare not argue. I fell out with the family, and my Mum and Dad asked me to leave him many times, but Pete would always win me over. I left him many times but ended up going back. When I was pregnant I knew it was over. I intended to leave Glasgow and go to Wales, but he would have found me. I'm with George now, and it was difficult at first as I could not trust him. Even now he gets a lot of shit that I should have given to Pete – but couldn't. I know I can get quite nasty but that's all the badness coming out. I was never like that before.'

Counsellors may find that negative feelings attached to past abusers are not only transferred to new partners but can be put on anyone or everyone. For example, there can be a general mistrust.

Me: 'Do you find it difficult to trust people?'

Annmarie: 'You don't trust anyone. You can be sitting and watching the telly and half the time you're not watching it. Your mind is drifting back.'

Bad relationships may be seen by the women involved as failed relationships and so they are more careful and suspicious (Ehrlich and Lipsey, 1969). This in itself can be a problem and can lead to violence, as there is a lack of an easy relationship, providing difficulties for counsellors as to how the violence should be viewed and treated. What is important is that if there is any violence, then it should be quickly brought to an end in the early stages of the new relationship.

Jamie: 'We did fight a lot at first, though it takes a lot to make me start. Estelle, she can start at any time. I tend to go with the flow, but she always speaks her mind and never lets anything go. At first, she would provoke me, go on and on and on. When I hit her it was usually after I had had something to drink. But now there's less violence. She knows for example, if she comes in late she won't get a doing, like what happened with Benny, her previous.'

To some extent the provoking can be seen as a testing-out strategem, Estelle trying to see if her partner will hit her. Unfortunately, she continued as she wanted her own poor view of herself to be confirmed, that she was the sort of person who deserves to get hit. This does not justify the violence, but does shed some light on abused women's adjustment processes. Women themselves may well be conscious of what is happening, but require support that their behaviour is quite rational and is their way of coping.

Annmarie: 'The last three times we have been out I have actually started with a drink inside me. I don't know whether it has been everything coming back to me or whether I want to see if I can push him to see whether he will hit me, or what.'

But testing new relationships to the limit may not just be about the transference of negative feelings. Women might also be taking a practical precaution of wanting to know how the present relationship might develop. However, matters can become complicated as abused women might find themselves reliving past experiences. This may be noticed by their new partner and can add to the difficulty of maintaining the new relationship.

Me: 'I wonder if you have found that Estelle argues, but it's really not with you but as if it is with the person from the previous relationship?'

Jamie: 'It's funny that you should say that because that's exactly what Estelle has said herself. She reacts for no good reason and you begin to understand it's all in her head.'

Adjustment for abused women can be paradoxical in that they might be pushing the new relationship to the limits and yet they want a trouble-free, which initially means a violence-free, time. In addition, though they do not want violence yet its absence can be unsettling.

Nasreen: 'I suddenly found myself in a normal relationship, a relationship where I don't get hit. That was the thing! A normal relationship doesn't have to be an enjoyable one, it doesn't have to be a pleasant one. It is simply one where you don't get hit all the time.'

Hangovers from the previous relationship – the feelings, the memories, the automatic reactions and ways of behaving – can have an effect on new relationships. There is a desire for peace but an expectation of violence. At times the latter can be translated into action.

Elaine: 'You are always on edge, wondering why he is so quiet, what he's thinking about and when he's going to hit you. Once Hal was in front of me and he moved, and I thought he was going to hit me. So I drew back my fist and let him have it. He said,"What the hell did you do that for? I was just going to pick up my take-away from the top of the telly!"'

Moreover, the woman reacts not just to what she sees as violence but also her fear of violence. It is difficult to escape the past completely, and at times it can mould the present.

Leigh: 'That night he came in and had been drinking. That scared the shit out of me. I was afraid he might land me one, because a lot of people who drink beat up on their women. I thought, "Oh God! Is he capable of hitting me?" I've been battered by so many people with drink in them. You look for the least sign of aggression. Later on, I thought,"What else is he capable of?" – forgetting that he had never laid a finger on me.'

In time, the effects of past bad times subside so that the edgy behaviour and mistrust fade away. However, some effects can remain in the abused woman's mind and stay hidden until triggered by something in the present. Then there can be a reliving in memory and feelings of the past.

Leigh: 'Last night Owen and I were larking about and I knocked my head on the side of the table. That bang on the head brought it all back, the times I've been hit.'

For some women, signs of stress such as edginess, poor sleep and disturbing dreams continue after the violence has ended. Such traumatic symptoms generally decline within two or three months. However this may not be the case for a few clients, who exhibit post-traumatic stress.

Annmarie: 'With him I was so mucked up inside I was anorexic, I could not stop shaking, and I ended up with an irritated bowel, which I still have. Even now I'm hyper, neurotic, I cannot sit still. If I sit then my mind wanders and everything comes back. I get flashbacks, so I keep myself on the go, keep myself busy. But when I go to my bed, I did'na sleep well. My mind works overtime.'

But apart from such extreme cases, we should appreciate that there is always likely to be some adjustment required and this is not a simple process, though clients are quite capable of understanding what is going on. What is required from counsellors is continuous support, and giving clients the opportunity to talk over what is happening to them.

Gaye: 'I felt very wary at first, had to cover up, be on the defensive. But then I also felt I had to give Ray the benefit of the doubt, be optimistic, as why should he carry the burden of what someone else had done? Then I would wonder if I should be so optimistic, whether I was over-compensating for what had gone before. Perhaps I had been too naive in the past, too accepting. In the end I wasn't sure what the answer was, and I felt I was going round in circles. And this annoyed me as I was doing it all to myself. If someone is battering you, then there's reason to doubt yourself, but I was doubting myself and Ray never lifted a finger against me. In a way, that made it worse, more reason to doubt myself.'

Counsellors cannot greatly accelerate this process of coming to terms with the loss of a relationship. Through being supportive they can help the client come to terms with new situations and possibly new rules for ongoing relationships. For those clients who have been in a very poor relationship or who have been in a poor relationship for a long time, there has to be a process of closing down completely the past relationship and building up the new, reviewing how the client has changed and what further changes may be needed. For some women, new relationships may be difficult or impossible to contemplate, not just because of what abusive partners have done but also because of what they themselves have done in coping with such partners.

Pearl: 'Afterwards you find you've built walls around yourself and it's a long time before you can trust another person. With some lassies it puts them off men completely.'

Apart from dealing with their anxiety and mistrust, clients have to build up their confidence, so decision-making is easier, but also they have to have confidence in themselves as people. Thus the work required extends to themselves as persons, to their very identity.

Ruth: 'I thought I was a good judge of people, but after all the trouble, all the beatings, then you begin to doubt yourself. Now I'm not so sure of people, and wonder if I do really know what folks are like. And if that's the case, then how do I know myself and how do I really know who I am?'

Sometimes it is suggested that abused women have a mistaken view of their situation, often based on irrational beliefs (Ellis, et al., 1989). This is too simple and judgemental a view. Those who have been subjected to violence in relationships may be seen as having a suspicious and sometimes ill-judged approach to future relationships, but this is a rational product of their perceptions and beliefs which are built of their experiences and so can be seen as quite justified. We might note that those perceptions and beliefs are not static. They are constantly being tested out against reality and slowly changed accordingly.

Leigh: 'I realize that I come on too strong, I know that I'm doing it but don't seem able to stop myself. The good thing is now I am able to sit down and think what I am doing. What it is, I'm afraid of rejection so make myself too available.'

It would be a mistake to think that all women are forever blighted by abuse. Some recover over time and lead their customary lives. We should not pathologize them but remember that, like children who recover from abuse and prove themselves remarkably resilient (Wolfe, 1987), women can be survivors rather than victims. By treating clients as incapable of improving their situation, we collude to ensure that this will be the case.

Counselling around separation

Counselling around separation of partners centres on the idea of change. The woman moves from an old situation and takes on a new one; both aspects need to be addressed.

1. Loss of the old requires clients to work through a grief process for a past or fading relationship, and, as we have seen, to make some personal meaning out of what has happened. Counsellors have to be neutral but realistic. Taking too optimistic a view of matters or condemning an ex-partner for his abuse – rather than the abuse itself – does not actually assist the process of adjustment to the past. It does not help if women either minimize or maximize their distress. There has to be acknowledgement that few relationships are all bad and that there have been some good times.

2. Looking at the past only helps if it is connected to clients; if abused women can investigate their past relationships up to the present and see them related to the various stages of grief, whether denial, blame, self-blame or acceptance. The point is, in part, to turn the grief process into a learning experience so that women can better

understand their own behaviour and so take greater control of their lives.

3. Another part of the process is for women to fully understand the degree of control their partner exerted over them. To some extent they know this – the individual oppressive actions, the possessiveness and the jealousy. However, they may fail to see control as an overall picture and not appreciate the fact that this is not necessary. Part of the difficulty in arriving at this understanding is that intellectually they may know it, but the feelings they have about themselves tends to make them unsure and easily dissuaded – even by themselves. This means that women, after maybe years of domination, have to reassert themselves as individuals and come to know their true selves rather than be the products of their partners' perceptions, expectations and desires.

4. Apart from dealing with relationship loss, clients also have to think about their new situation and be positive about it. If a woman sees her life as being no more than one of being without her abusive partner, then her visions for the future are limited and, in my experience, she is more likely to return to the abuser. Thus clients have to be helped to come to terms with the past, put it behind them, and look to the future in a positive manner.

5. The plans should look at the immediate situation, whether a client wants a single life, life with another partner, or life back with the abusive partner. Clients have to be given a free choice, with the knowledge that much of the pressure in decision-making comes from friends, relatives, and from the client herself. For instance, would a new partner be just that, or merely a substitute for a relationship lost? And if this is the case, then might another abusive partner be chosen?

6. Working through the process of separation takes some time and the effects of past relationships, continuance, can persist and affect present client behaviour. There is often the idea that after the separation, the woman's life will be so much better and virtually problem-free. The reality is that she has to become self-directive, and often face difficulties on her own. The irony is that once abused women have come out of their abusive relationships and are permanently accommodated elsewhere, they are often judged to be all right and no longer in need of help, but this is the very time when they need support the most.

7. There is a danger that in a client's life after an abusive relationship,

all difficulties are seen as being a product of that abuse. This can result in the client denying responsibility for her ongoing actions. What counsellors and clients should understand is that anyone can have problems and these do not have to relate to physical abuse. Some clients may need to be reminded of this fact, otherwise they are in danger of becoming prisoners of their past.

THE LOVE ELEMENT

Much of the investigation into partner abuse is highly cognitive, trying to seek out what those involved are thinking and then looking for reasons why partners behave as they do. This reflects the fact that it is much easier to construct theories and carry out cognitively-based research than to try to grasp affective issues. Yet to ignore feelings, especially love, is to ignore a large part of what actually happens. In particular, feelings can dominate cognitive representations of social relationships (Forgas and Dobosz, 1980) and participants' reactions to interpersonal episodes (Forgas, 1982). However, though love is a concept often discussed by people and sometimes by those abused, it is rarely alluded to by those whose remit it is to help, except as a problem (Framo, 1965).

Cases of passionate attachment

The prime example of passionate attachment is to be seen in women caught up in violent relationships. They are helped out of physical danger, found new and safe accommodation, and they agree that the relationship must end. However, what actually happens is that the woman returns to the abusive relationship, fully aware of the dangers to herself. She explains her decision and action by saying, 'But I still love him.' Often helpers hear this but do not listen. They dismiss the reply as being frivolous, and fail to see such feelings as being perfectly valid as causes of behaviour.

Annmarie: 'I loved him, I mean I adored him when I was young. But a bit of that was being brainwashed. He had made out that I could not get anyone else. I was only twenty-two, a single parent, with a kid. I mean how many single parents are there in the world, how many blokes take on kids nowadays? If someone is continually drumming that into you, you get to the stage when you believe it.'

Yet it is important to accept women's answers as they help to place the behaviour in context. Of those women who leave violent relationships and seek refuge in women's shelters, almost 50 per cent return to the relationship, and over 50 per cent of these will experience further violence within six months (Frude, 1991). The reactions of helpers can range from surprise, disappointment, and a feeling of being let down, to anger with the client. In extreme cases help to the woman might be ended. Yet this reflects our own difficulty at times of knowing what it means for someone else to be in love.

Love and a positive view of a situation may be shown by those abused, even when others see little reason for optimism. This is not peculiar to abused women. Children can show exactly the same behaviour towards their abusive parents (Herzeberger et al., 1981). Rather than dismiss such feelings we have to try and understand them.

Passionate love

Love can be considered as being comprised of three factors: intimacy, passion and commitment (Sternberg, 1986). Passion might be taken as a sensation akin to a chemical 'high' (Liebowitz, 1983), with a degree of idealization of the partner (Tennov, 1979), and with strong attachment (Hazan and Shaver, 1987), often in the context of romantic beliefs such as 'Love conquers all' (Sprecher and Metts, 1989). What may be apparent is that what seemed like an offhand client remark about being in love actually represents a complex situation and one that demands attention. It also requires counsellors to be aware of their own feelings – not just about the client still being in love, not just about their beliefs and attitudes as counsellors and persons to love in general, but their own personal experiences. To my knowledge, the topic of love is not covered in counselling training, or not covered in any depth, nor is it taken up by writers on abused women.

The reason for such attention is that abused women are often not treated well on returning to an abusive relationship, either by their partners or by professional helpers. One of my training exercises consists of trainee counsellors discussing how women should react and behave when faced with difficult behaviour from their children, and comparing this with what they should do when confronted with difficult behaviour from their partners. They then have to discuss the concept of love and how it is or is not applicable to both scenarios.

Love and attachment

Love is in part an attachment process, and couples will spend long periods together initially so that mutual bonds may grow. However, we should be careful about ascribing to any attachment the idea that it reflects childhood relationships with one's parents, and be wary of accompanying simplistic ideas such as the idea that poor parenting could account for present relationship difficulties (Hazan and Shaver, 1987). This view is hard to sustain, except in cases of gross parental deprivation, as adult experiences can compensate for unfortunate childhood experiences (Parker et al., 1992).

In addition, relationship termination and the subsequent separation involve the breakdown of attachment, but this does not necessarily entail the ending of love. The feelings for a partner can continue, and many women will say that they still love their partners but do not want to live with them. Attachment disappears, provided they have no contact with their partner.

Affective analysis

Our interest in love lies in the element of passion. Being in love, especially at first, is a time of high affect and emotional motility, a time of extreme ups and downs. The strength of feelings can be such as to influence the way the world is both seen and experienced. This is caused by various effects which include:

* Cognitive distortions

* False beliefs or myths

* Uncertainty around feelings

* Changes in the form of communication

* Vulnerability of the person

Women in love sometimes face accusations of acting irrationally; they themselves may even agree. But this is a way of dismissing not only their behaviour but also the women themselves. To be rational ourselves, we have to try to understand and appreciate why they might react to their partners as they do.

Cognitive distortions

Distortions to abused women's thinking – which is not to imply that men have undistorted cognition – may arise in part through being unsure of themselves, and this can be one aspect of love. Because of emotional motility, there is a tendency for those in high affect not to know their own feelings or to doubt them. This makes for an uncertain baseline when judging personal situations, as these are likely to have affective components.

The nature of a woman's strong feelings can also influence her thinking, so that an overly optimistic or pessimistic view of things is taken. In addition, reasons, excuses and rationalizations are forwarded to maintain those views. What the woman sees can be partly a product of what she wants to see. Not only is the present distorted, but the same can happen to the past, which can be re-interpreted.

Love myths

Love myths are beliefs that are false in part or in total, and can produce cognitive distortions though their use. They can be romantic, consisting of beliefs such as, 'People should marry because they love each other', or, 'Romantic love is necessary for a satisfactory marriage' (Lazarus, 1985; Beck, 1988). They are romantic in that they guide or instruct people in ways of behaving. Other myths are those of passionate love which give us alleged facts such as:

• Disagreement between partners is destructive to the relationship.

• Partners should be able to sense each other's needs and moods.

• Partners are not capable of changing. (Epstein, 1986)

These myths may be seen as cognitive distortions, but this implies that the person in love is in some way incapable of seeing reality and so is in some way ill and needing help. This is not the case. Another way to view the myths is as products of being in love, products of a certain stage of the relationship. One aspect this raises is the fact that no matter what a woman thinks of her partner now, she did not always feel like that.

Tracy: 'I want Dave out of my life; there are no feelings there. Mind, that wasn't always the case. At one time I thought the sun shone out of his arse.'

Thus women are dealing not just with their feelings but also with their change in feelings, not just with reality but also with a reality that has changed greatly over time.

Uncertainty in feelings – 'Am I in love?'

Another depiction of being in love is that of a combination of a state of physiological arousal combined with an attribution of love to that state (Schachter and Singer, 1962). The question that the subject might ask herself is, 'Am I in love, or should love be attributed to my present state?' And there is no easy answer. Indicators such as commitment and intimacy, what may be termed quite rational indicators, may be overwhelmed by the physiological arousal which arises from passion. This arousal may spring from passionate love but it may also arise from other strong feelings such as rejection or jealousy.

The problem is that arousal of any kind can make others seem more attractive, and this can apply even if those others are quite different from the subject (Brehm, 1985). If the subject has been rejected, she may attribute her experienced state of attraction to love (Jacobs et al., 1971): a case of being 'caught on the rebound'. Similarly, jealousy can also make a woman think she is in love. If she believes or knows her partner has love interests elsewhere or another person has expressed interest in him, then she feels greater attraction to her partner. Not surprisingly, misattributions of love are made in violent relationships, when arousal can be high. Adolescents who are not experienced in attributing love to how they feel are most likely to make mistakes, and apparently fall in and out of love most easily. Misattribution is not necessarily a simple process. People can mistakenly imagine they are aroused rather than actually being physiologically aroused, and this can act as well as arousal in making attributional mistakes of love.

Uncertainty as to whether a person is in love, with consequent doubt about their feelings in general, can lead to mistrust of oneself and even the mistrust of others. This is important as it goes against the basic rule of a good intimate relationship: the requirement of trust and honesty (Argyle and Henderson, 1985). Disregard of this rule can lead to the breakdown of the relationship (Miller et al., 1986).

Changes in verbal communication

High affect, which occurs when people are in love, can affect communication in four ways.

1. There can be an increase in non-verbal communication.

2. There can be a fracturing of the rules of grammar, as verbal language proves insufficient to communicate high affect.

3. There can be a fracturing of the rules of dialogue, so there can be a tendency to speak together or fail to listen properly (Gottman, 1979).

4. Lovers can evolve almost their own private language, and are likely to call each other by private names.

Such changes to communication by their nature signal the states of affect and are not pathological. However, they do represent entry into a private communication world, which can further strengthen the bonds of affection. On the other hand it is a private world which violence can destroy.

Self-disclosure

If high affect can influence cognitive perceptions, then it can also act on behaviour, which in turn has an effect on the relationship itself.

When a couple are in love, they are likely to talk a lot about themselves in order to get to know each other intimately. Such self-disclosure can help and strengthen couples' relationships (Chelune et al., 1985). For this to happen the disclosure should contain affective material and be emotionally focused (Greenberg and Johnson, 1988). It can cover not merely thoughts and feelings but experiences, beliefs and fantasies (Waring et al., 1980). It can be directly verbal or it can be indirect, such as 'I've had a great week!' (Holtgraves, 1990) which gives an opening for further disclosure, or it can be non-verbal (Patterson, 1990). Continuous self-disclosure is not a permanent feature of couples. It usually quickly rises to a peak, becoming deeper and more useful (Altman and Taylor, 1973) and then declines rapidly (Huston et al., 1986).

Self-disclosure and vulnerability

Intimate self-disclosure, typical of those in love, adds to the positive aspect of the relationship. It can make both parties feel good. However, we might also note that people self-disclose in expectation that the other person will do the same (Berg, 1987). A male partner who wishes to control the relationship may disclose little about himself. We might also note that men tend to be worse at this disclosure, so we should not assume that a lack of it necessarily reflects a desire to control. Nevertheless, self-disclosure does introduce a degree of vulnerability, and a person's tolerance of that vulnerability influences whether or not he or she discloses private thoughts or feelings (Kelvin, 1977). If the self-disclosure is ignored, diminished or otherwise dismissed then the result can be the discloser feeling rejected (Bavelas, 1983). This should be contrasted with the positive effects on the counselling relationship which happen when self-disclosure is received positively, and there is a sensitive and under-standing response (Miller and Berg, 1984).

Finally, relationships, even of those in love, are not always even; there can be highs and lows, times of ease and times of stress. These different situations can also affect self-disclosure. For example, under stress both men and women tend to revert to stereotypical gender behaviour: women tend to talk about negative feelings, whereas men tend not to talk about feelings at all (Kobak and Hazan, 1991).

Leigh's diaries

Much of the above is difficult to prove, but is supported by material from Leigh's diaries. She kindly agreed to allow me to quote from them, though the quotes are partial and a lot of material has been omitted. Nevertheless, I do think they provide some insight into what actually took place. They show the thoughts and feelings experienced at the time, as opposed to providing a retrospective view. It should be noted that we tend to recall our behaviours and expectations in ways that increase their consistency with subsequent outcomes (McFarlane and Ross, 1987) and maintain a positive view of ourselves (Conway, 1990), which can be misleading. What the diaries did show was that what Leigh wanted most of the time was not an end to the relationship but an end to the battering (see Giles-Sim, 1983). This was true even when contemplating pressing charges against her partner in respect of the violence (see Lerman, 1986). She rationalized the violence for a long time and did not think of leaving the relationship till such rationalizing was ended (see Ferrero and Johnson, 1982).

The following gives some idea of love and violence in a relationship:

12 December: *Ever since I met Jimmy I have loved him. I don't think I'll ever stop loving him. But for some very cruel reason, which I do not understand, we do not seem to be able to live together.*

15 December: *I left this Thursday. Jimmy had been drinking a lot. Each beating is getting worse and I'm afraid that I won't see the year out. Jimmy, I love you, and pray you will be happy.*

29 December: *I'm on anti-depressants. I went to collect my belongings last week but Jimmy had smashed them up. When am I going to get over this nightmare?*

16 January: *I met Jimmy in a bar. I was glad to see him. I was miserable without him. Though adamant about not going back, I changed my mind when he asked me.*

1 April: *April Fool's Day. What a fool I was. I should never have had Jimmy back.*

31 August: *Now we have a new council flat. Jimmy is good to me. But tonight I have another Jimmy and I don't like him.*

12 September: *I have tried to communicate but it's as if Jimmy doesn't want to know me. We never talk about anything except surface stuff. I have come to the conclusion that I don't really know my husband all that well.*

29 October: *It's as if Jimmy has lost interest in me – he's totally distant.*

2 February: *I want rid of him. The feeling has been building up inside me. I want him to go away but he won't. I thought of killing him. That gave me a fright when I realized I had been serious, thinking of killing him with a sharpened screwdriver.*

Some professional helpers who are accustomed to searching for and working on personal problems might well see Leigh's diary extracts as detailing the behaviour of someone with a disturbed personality. However, I see her as a person in love who is reacting normally to an abnormal situation. How should she deal with a person who is seemingly in love with her and whom she loves, yet is violent towards her? What we see, in my opinion, is Leigh trying to cope in various ways with a basically unsustainable form of partner behaviour. Eventually she was able to improve her situation and put Jimmy out of the house; she was able to improve matters for herself, though only after her feelings for him had radically changed.

Working with clients

The counsellor has to be convinced of the correctness of the underlying theory and concepts before moving to any actual work. Such work consists of listening to women clients talking through their feelings about love for their partners. This might require broaching the subject initially, but once they see this as a fully relevant topic then talking presents no problems.

If the female client is sure of her feelings about the relationship then the counsellor has to accept this fact, whether it means she loves her partner or not. If she does love him and wants to risk staying with him, then it can be profitable to discuss what can be done to lessen the danger. The important point is to engage with clients, not tell them what they should do, and make them more liable to trust solely to feelings.

Another aspect to be considered is that, despite the violence, a woman's love can persist and survive, even after the relationship has ended.

Annmarie: 'I still love him, even after we've been apart for two years. At first, I thought I didn't after I left him, but now I'm not so sure. But if he asked me to go back, I wouldn't.'

This shows two common phenomena. First, love can be reduced by violence but once that violence stops, love returns. If this happens after the couple have separated, the woman might well regret leaving her partner, having diminished, re-interpreted, excused or suppressed his past violent behaviour. This means she is more likely to return to the relationship, even if there is no evidence that her partner will behave less violently.

THE ROLE OF CHILDREN

If there are children in the family, then they too are brought indirectly and sometimes even directly into the abusive situation. A Canadian survey showed that 70 per cent of all women entering Women's Aid shelters had children, and 17 per cent had three or more (McLeod, 1980). And being a mother affects battered women. In particular, separation and staying away from an abusive partner is to some extent subject to the reactions and perceived welfare of the children. We should also note that violence can extend to the children (Bowker et al., 1988), and this can be an ongoing fear for the mother. If this is the case then the woman is much more likely to leave her partner, though a lot of women still subscribe to the belief that a father or father-figure is necessary for a child's upbringing (Binney et al., 1981). This is an important point as charges of irrationality or irresponsibility sometimes brought against women are usually misplaced. Though mothers may feel compelled to submit to violence, rarely do they extend such behaviour to their children.

Violence can involve children of any age. As has been noted, being pregnant is no bar to violence, even at the risk of damage to the unborn child.

Annmarie: 'I caught him in bed with somebody and because I wanted to find out who it was, I was battered when holding his five-month-old son. He clattered my head off the walls and my head must have hit the bairn as his mouth was bleeding. And all the time the lassie was lying in the bed.'

The children themselves, even from as young as twelve months, can be affected by the anger shown between their parents (Christopoulos et al., 1987). Although it is usually thought that children cannot remember in later life anything that occurred before the age of three, this might well be incorrect as there is the possibility that memories are retained from the age of twelve months onwards (Bauer, 1996). Children are not merely auditors or spectators, they become third parties to what is happening, albeit a virtually powerless party (Vuchinich et al., 1988).

As children grow older their presence still tends to be forgotten or overlooked. Half the instances of partner violence take place in front of others. In more than half of these cases, it is the children who witness what is taking place (Dobash and Dobash, 1984). Parents often imagine that their children are unaware of what is happening as they are asleep or outside playing, but this is often incorrect (Rosenberg,

1984) as the children are woken or attracted indoors by the sounds of violence.

Annmarie: 'When Donna was eight or nine, it all came out about when she was young. She could remember when we all stayed in the very first house and she could only have been three, four or five, and she used to lie in her bed and hear it all. And I never ever thought the bairn heard things like that but she did. The last ten years she's wet the bed and just doesn't seem able to stop.'

Children affected

The violence affects the children, and often they may try to intervene in some way (Melville, 1978), only to be frustrated. This can make them feel bad as they realize they are powerless to help. They also can run the risk of being subjected to assault if they persist in attempting to give assistance.

Debbie: 'Lorraine would jump up and shout, "Stop hitting my Mum!", and try and stop him. So he ended up hitting her.'

Children are usually in an even weaker position than women to prevent a man inflicting violence. And like retaliating women, they have to rely on surprise and weapons.

Dawn: 'Jack turned round when John was having a go at me and stabbed him, not bad, but stabbed him.'

So children are not only affected by partner violence but also tend to be drawn into the conflicts, sometimes quite consciously by their mother. This not only increases personal danger but makes any reconciliation or calming down more difficult (Pruitt and Rubin, 1986). Although direct damage comes from abusive husbands, some indirect damage occurs through their partners, who are suffering the effects of battering.

Children's relationships with their parents are often complicated by feelings of guilt. When young, children may think they are the cause of the trouble. When older, they feel bad because they were unable to stop the violence or because their behaviour was given as a reason for the fighting. As a result, children may show behavioural problems such as being aggressive, clinging or depressed (Jaffe et al., 1986). The most affected are reported to be boys if they are pre-school, but girls if they are of school age (Davis and Carlson, 1987). The disturbance in children may be a direct result not of the violence itself but of the tension of their mother or even of having to move into different accommodation or shelters (Wolfe et al., 1985). Children are placed in shelters without a father, with strangers, and often having to share facilities with them. This can lead to the children needing more attention, at a time when their mother is likely to be caught up in legal and other moves to stabilize her separation. The children then may want to return home, unrealistic though this may be, but this does put further pressure on the mother to reconsider their situation.

The whole family is affected by the violence, as are the various family relationships. These feelings do not suddenly go away. They can be present even when the family has split up.

Annmarie: 'Gary is absolutely petrified of his Dad. If his Dad drew up outside and said, "OK son, come on, I'll take you to the shops for a new Rangers strip", he wouldn't go unless I was in the car. It's a shame as Gary is his only son, but the bairn saw what he had done to me and he's close to me.'

It should also be noted that leaving the abusive partner does not necessarily end the troubles. The children are no longer controlled by the abusive situation and so can live for themselves and express themselves rather than having to guard what they say and do. The outcome is that the mother expects everything to be so much better but the children appear to be playing up. In extreme cases, a mother can begin to wonder if the children really do need their 'father' in their lives, whether she should go back to her partner after all.

Brenda: 'Julie would get upset easy. I told her she was bound to miss her dad, tried to keep her mind off it, but nothing seemed to work. Finally, she was round at the neighbours watching telly and she burst into tears and told them what was up. She hadn't said anything to me as she did not want to upset me. At one time things were so bad I wondered if I had done the right thing, but I know now I have. Julie and me talk a lot and it helps the both of us.'

The examples given have assumed a good mother–children relationship. In other cases, this was not so clear and the warfare between mother and father took precedence over the welfare of the children. In such cases, the women have exhibited guilt and rationalization after the relationship has ended, with continuing problems in relation to the children.

Effects on children

The effects on children to a large extent depend on their ages. If they are aged under five and there is no further contact with the abuser, then the effects can be short-lived. From the ages of six to seven there can be problems as the child still has difficulty with the idea of permanent separation. However, if the abuser is seen as 'bad', then this can ease the situation. However, children at this age are egocentric and see the world and events as being related to them. Thus feelings of guilt by such children are common. Unfortunately, abused mothers tend to reassure the children rather than explain what is happening, so the guilt is likely to persist (Crockenberg,1985). There can be additional problems with sons, who identify strongly with their father from the ages of six to eleven, and can be confused in their feelings and seemingly behave erratically. This in turn can confuse, irritate or depress their parents (Hughes, 1982).

Older children want reasons for the break-up and for both parents to stop arguing and fighting if they are still in contact. They want their homes to be safe and their parents to be happy. However, not only are children relatively powerless but they also are likely to be confused and their loyalties to their parents can be stretched (Walczak, 1984). As a result, they may be torn between wanting to do something to ease matters and wanting to stay outside what is happening altogether. This ambivalence can be interpreted by either parent as a lack of individual support. Not surprisingly, there is a greater likelihood that adolescents will run away from home if there is parental violence (Davidson, 1978).

Children who see their father as being clearly in the wrong do not necessarily want to lose all contact with him. Yet such contact can be very difficult for the woman, especially if the children are young and there is likely to be contact between the ex-partners. Contact with male abusive ex-partners is additionally difficult if they are liable to be violent towards the children or generally upset them. Contact is difficult for the children as well, if they realize that their mother is being upset by the visits (Walczak, 1984). Ultimately, the separation is not just an individual process for the woman but can include any children. They also have to work through the process of separation. And here thought has to be given to what is best for the children, not just the mother.

Whether continued contact with the father is likely to be helpful for the children depends on individual cases; it can be helpful, unhelpful, or neither (Hooper, 1994).

Dianne: 'I was annoyed when 'Chelle said she wanted to see her dad, after all she had seen. Then I realized that I couldn't really stop her, so I said it would be OK. It didn't last for long. I asked her a couple of weeks ago if she was going to see him, but she said no, she couldn't be bothered, and was going ice-skating with her pal instead.' However, contact with the father is often an ongoing problem for the woman, especially if the children are used by their father as a weapon against their mother. If there has been any physical or sexual abuse of the children by the male partner there should be no further contact (see Foreman, 1995). It has to be emphasized that many professional helpers tend to take a conciliatory approach (Hester and Pearson, 1993), believing that two parents are better than one, and are in favour of the abuser having access to the children (Ogus et al., 1989). They may insist on joint interviews of abuser and abusee, failing to inform the woman that she has a right to be seen on her own (Victim Support, 1992). Furthermore, men can be supported not just by legal representatives but by organizations such as Families Need Fathers (Harne and Radford, 1994). All of this underlines the continuing danger to both mother and children even after separation from the abuser.

Counselling when children are involved

When counselling parents or mothers in violent relationships, some of the points to be considered include the following:

1. Women, in my experience, are more likely to leave their abusive partner if they are aware of the distress that violence causes to the children, and even more so if they believe the children are at risk from their partner. As a result, counsellors may have to be prepared to consider separation of the couple even if this has not been mentioned. In addition, practical matters may take a high priority, as having to provide for the children can seem an insuperable barrier to leaving.

2. If the family is still all together, many women show reluctance to leave as they believe the children 'need a father'. On the other hand, those outside the family, whether relatives, friends or professional helpers, are likely to advocate the women leaving for the sake of the children. This can lead to situations where women are pressurized to act and may well react by refusing to consider the possibility.

3. A further difficulty can be that if the mother does leave, then she expects the children to be better off and appreciative of the fact. In fact, the children may not want their parents to separate at all, but merely hope the violence will end and that everything will then be perfect. To them, separation may be seen as a form of punishment for things they have done. Counsellors may have to point out that separation is primarily for the abused mother's sake, though the children are likely to benefit and come to appreciate the fact in time.

4. We also have to note that outside helpers are often tied to their job remit, perspectives and beliefs. This makes them more concerned for the children than for the mothers (McWilliams and McKiernan, 1993). In short, women are treated as child-carers rather than simply as women. This merely passes control from their abusive partners to their children, which can be unhelpful. Some helpers might even insist that the family stays together 'for the sake of the children' (Binney et al., 1988).

5. Separation brings further problems as children seldom know in full what is going on between their parents. It is usually best that they do know. It is often assumed by parents either that the children know virtually nothing about what has been happening or that they know everything. Both beliefs make it more likely that the children will not be told, so it is best that counsellors help to prepare abused women for any information-giving.

6. Separated mothers may also need to be helped when their children ask about their father and whether they can see him. Mothers are likely to get lots of advice, often conflicting, and have difficulty coming to any firm decision due to their feelings of guilt. Under the circumstances, it can be useful if mothers are given clear advice, such as that they should have no contact with their ex-partners for a fixed and stated time. At least the children will then know the situation, even if sometimes it is difficult to accept. After the stated period, there might be contact between the children and their father, but this is done under controlled conditions with a third party involved in a supervisory role. This eliminates the need for the woman to see her ex-partner and so diminishes the likelihood of face-to-face arguments or the woman being lured back against her better judgement.

7. Another point is that it is tempting for abused women to criticize their ex-partners. This, whatever the justification, can further upset the children. It is preferable that any reference should be as accurate and factual as possible. This in no way stops women from saying how they feel. But using children against their ex-partners, even if unintentional, is not fair to them and leads to yet more difficulties. The situation can become especially difficult when ex-partners give false accounts, criticize, or try to influence the children. But entering into discussions and arguments is very much what ex-partners want, and being as factual and truthful as possible wins out in the long run.

WORKING ON SELF-IDENTITY

Long-term counselling work

Women who are away from their abusive partners have to come to terms not just with the past abuse but also with themselves and their lives. Whether the process is seen as getting back to their real identity or building up an identity, women have to feel happy and be positive about themselves. This applies to anyone, but is especially relevant to abused women as their self-esteem and self-confidence are likely to have been adversely affected by the violence they have experienced.

What should be understood is that abused women may take a long time to learn to be themselves, and counsellors can help this process. Clients find or rebuild their identity both internally and externally, through how they feel about and see themselves, and also by how others see and feel about them and then how they interpret such reactions. But they start from a given position, from the position that their abusers have placed them in, and as long as they are in an abusive situation they will never be able to be completely themselves. However, work on identity must start from the very beginning as abused women will find it very difficult to leave their abusers until they begin to feel and see themselves as themselves.

The rebuilding of identity can be seen as resting on four main supports: self-awareness, self-esteem, self-confidence and self-direction. These are all increased for abused clients throughout the counselling by the offering of acceptance and respect, through being listened to and allowed to tell their story, and through being allowed to express their feelings and opinions. Nevertheless, it is useful as the counselling progresses to pay particular attention to the aforementioned four concepts.

1. Self-awareness can be divided into awareness of one's own person, mentally and physically, and then being aware of one's awareness of self. These can be covered by clients keeping a diary in which they log what they feel and think (not what they say or do). By going through the diary each week, clients can bring material for counselling, but primarily they can monitor their own selves and so become aware also of that awareness. This secondary stage is important because if one is aware of one's awareness, then one is on the path to greater self-confidence. Sometimes clients find it difficult initially to be self-aware, and this can often be remedied by getting them to stare into a mirror for five minutes and see what takes place and then think about what they were thinking and feeling.

2. Positive self-esteem or feeling good about oneself comes partly from within and is partly the product of the transmitted views of others about oneself. In the case of abused women, the latter is more significant as self-esteem has been lowered by partners and the fact of having been in an abusive situation. Indeed, all the positive input by counsellors can be defeated by a couple of put-downs by male partners. This means self-esteem has to be directly confronted and the topic discussed. There are three separate aspects that may be addressed for the purpose of self-identity.

• Low self-esteem can precede the abusive situation and the cumulative effect is to leave the woman with no belief in herself. There can be retrospective effects as well, where life before the abusive relationship is re-interpreted by battered women to demonstrate their apparent worthlessness. Yet what has happened in the past can be seen either as confirming faults in the abused women or as stepping-stones to personal progress. I stress that no one can change the past, but we can all learn from it. It should be added that counsellors often have to be very positive themselves when working with client self-esteem and thus should self-monitor. It is possible that client low self-esteem and near-depression will affect and even overwhelm counsellors.

Karen: 'I know you are trying to boost me up but I don't learn. I make the same mistakes all the time. That's how I landed up in my position.'

Me: 'Exactly! You make the same mistakes because you have not learned from what has happened to you. This, coming for counselling, is a chance for you to do that. You made the right decision to come, so you must be doing something right.'

Karen: 'But not learning – that proves I'm stupid.'

Me: 'Is a young child who cannot added two and two together stupid, or could it be that the child has yet to learn? And how do we learn? By making mistakes. Remember all those sums as a child, did you always get them right? Of course, not!'

Karen: 'But Grant says I'm stupid. He says I just am.'

Me: 'I was forgetting his degree in stupidology. I reckon he must be able to spot stupid people from a distance. I bet he goes up to people in bus queues and says, "Excuse me, but you are stupid. You just are."'

Karen: 'Noooh!'

Me: 'And if he did, perhaps the person in the bus queue would turn round and say, "What's your problem, pal?"'

Karen: 'Pagger [hit] him.'

Me: 'And the man would be right. It is Grant's problem. He's the one with the problem. You should not take on what belongs to him, take on his problem. The way he calls you stupid is his problem. His problems are his problems and only he can solve them. Your problem is living with someone with problems.'

Karen: 'I suppose that's right.'

Me: 'You agree but do you really feel I was right?'

Karen: 'Yes ... Yes.'

Me: 'So do you feel any better about yourself?'

Karen: 'I suppose I do.'

- In addition to the past, the present also affects self-esteem. One way of helping, which may be politically suspect but I have found effective, is to encourage clients to consider their self-image, and this can be linked with their appearance. Women clients who have agreed to have their hair done or who have bought themselves new clothes do get a lift and feel better. The important counselling aspect is that of building on this temporary advance and discussing possible meanings in the change.

Ruth: 'I've done it, as you can see. Spent my money. New outfit. And I'm blonde!'

Me: 'Wow! You look great. Do you feel great?'

Ruth: 'Yes. For the first time in ages I feel good.'

Me: 'The moment I saw you I wondered, "Who is this woman?" So can you tell me who I am speaking to? I don't recognize the person who first came to see me.'

Ruth: 'That wee mouse has gone. It's the new me.'

Me: 'Sometimes changes on the outside can reflect changes on the inside. Whether it is the new you or the real you, I don't know, but here is a person saying, "This is me!" No longer that submissive person but someone who is proud of herself. That's the message I pick up.'

Ruth: 'That's exactly the message I want to give. I'm me! I'm not somebody's woman. I'm me!'

Me: 'You even walked differently, swinging your hips.'

Ruth: 'You're joking!'

Me: 'Right. You go outside the door and come in again.'

[later]

Ruth: 'You're right. I would never have thought. Is that giving the wrong message?'

Me: '"I am a sexual person." All that says is you are not asexual, you are a complete person.'

Ruth: 'That's right. Years of being a nothing, never looking at another person. You're right, you know. I want to be noticed. No more than that. Well ... we'll see. Perhaps a bit more.'

- Self-esteem rests on people's perceptions of themselves, which is greatly reinforced, or not, by the words and actions of others. Counsellors should see client identity as slowly re-emerging and react accordingly. Clients can go through stages of being nothing (in their eyes), to being abused persons, to being victims, to being survivors, to being themselves. Clients should be treated for the stage they are at, while also slowly introducing them to the next stage, though clients are equally capable at times of appreciating the change in their role and status and acting accordingly. What can be unhelpful is to hurry this process or treat abused clients as persons fully themselves when they do not feel this to be the case.

3. Self-confidence is a positive feeling people feel about themselves and their ability to act and do things in a way satisfactory to them. This feeling is tested through interacting with others. Also important is the ability to deal with the unforeseen, with mistakes, with arguments or with being overruled. There are various ways of helping clients build their self-confidence, and my preference is to concentrate on their planned interactions with others.

- This can be before any action, when the client is losing heart.

  Dianne: 'I can't go back to my mom and ask her to take me back.'

  Me: 'Hold on, let's look at this a bit more. You say you cannot go back to your mum, but what you mean is that you don't want to go back.'

Dianne: 'She wouldn't have me back.'

Me: 'You don't know that for sure. You have made the decision, not your mum, that it is impossible. All I'm saying is that it might be worth a try.'

Dianne: 'You don't know her.'

Me: 'And you are not prepared to give her a chance. She is your mum.'

Dianne: 'You're not going to make me feel guilty. She's an old bat.'

Me: 'I certainly don't want you to go to her from guilt. And I know she can go on a bit, but she has your welfare at heart.'

Dianne: 'She would go berserk ...'

Me: 'If that worries you, then you tell me the worst scenario. What is the worst thing your mum could do if you turned up?'

Dianne: 'I'm not sure.'

Me: 'Well, would she eat the children, for example? Would she batter you? Would she starve you?'

Dianne: 'Of course not.'

Me: 'So what would she do?'

Dianne: 'She would nag on, nip my head about ... about everything.'

Me: 'Everything?'

Dianne: 'OK, OK, so she is going to say "I told you so."'

Me: 'And can you face that?'

Dianne: 'Aye, I suppose I can.'

Me: 'So underneath it all, you are not so helpless.'

Part of the difficulty for abused women as regards self-confidence is simply the fact that they often become used to thinking of others, especially how their partners might react and the welfare of their children, if they have any; that there is no room for themselves. This reinforces the socialized role that many women take up, so is not seen as so unusual. In counselling, one of the tasks can be that of talking through what women clients want for themselves, identifying their wishes and needs, hopes and dreams. This needs counselling help as abused women usually think they have nothing to offer and have no real abilities or skills.

Dianne: 'I know you mean well, but all I know is bringing up bairns. I've never had a proper job and never stayed on at school. The idea of going to college, no. I couldn't do that.'

Me: 'There's other ways of taking an interest in things. What were you telling me a month ago? About chatting to folk about Leith, the docks, and the fishmen in Newhaven and Granton. You were interested in local history.'

Dianne: 'Yes ..., but ... that's not real history.'

Me: 'Yes it is. You'll find there are local history groups around, and possibly an oral history group, people who go around and record what the elderly remember of the old days before they are forgotten. We're talking of ordinary folk doing it, not university researchers.'

Dianne: 'I wouldn't know what to do.'

Me: 'Join your local library, tell them what you're interested in and ask whether there are any local groups. Librarians are always keen to help, so why not let them?'

Dianne: 'Thinking about it, that's an idea. At least it would give me something to talk about. All I know really is the bairns, being a housewife. I would have something, be a bit different. I could go to Old People's Homes and chat to them.'

Me: 'Yes, and you would be good at it. See, you have abilities. What you sometimes lack is a belief in yourself.'

Dianne: 'I know. You're right in what you said. Sometimes you've simply got to do it. I've got to do it.'

- Another aspect is that of ongoing action and self-confidence. Abused clients' self-confidence can be quite fragile, so that any unforeseen incident or difficulty can floor them. Counsellors can help clients to negotiate enforced changes to earlier expectations and plans.

Me: 'So things are a bit difficult at your mum's.'

Dianne: 'I thought I could handle it. It was a mistake.'

Me: 'The children are safe. It's given you a break and time to think.'

Dianne: 'The bairns love it, get spoilt rotten. Get things I could never afford.'

Me: 'It strikes me your parents are happy, the children are happy, but you are not happy. So it is time for you and the children to move on, decide on the next step. After all, you can't stay where you are for ever. In a way it is good that you are discontented as that will spur you to further action.'

Dianne: 'All this changing will upset the bairns.'

Me: 'And them seeing or hearing you being thumped about the house did not upset them? Do you really think you've done the wrong thing?'

Dianne: 'No. You're right. I just thought it would be easy ... I know, I know! Dianne in Wonderland!'

Clients can have different amounts of self-confidence, which can be expressed in different ways. In my experience counsellors should not assume clients' confident behaviour is a sign of internal confidence. Nor should we react negatively to clients who have talked about their plans during counselling yet fail to carry them out. It is all too easy to label clients as uncooperative, as having disordered personalities, as lacking the requisite skills, or as being manipulative, and this further undermines their confidence. Counsellors can have a negative as well as a positive effect.

4. Self-direction is the ability of clients to take control of their lives. This is not to be confused with taking control of others' lives, which is characteristic of their abusive partners. From the counselling point of view, it is helpful to investigate the degree to which clients feel themselves to be in control of themselves, or whether they are controlled by others or by their ongoing situation. Often women clients see themselves as being controlled, and what has to be established is the mental separation from such a perception. Clients can be helped to construct their own space for themselves in their heads, a world where they are not controlled. At this stage the constructed world is no more than a fantasy but it is often a necessary precursor to personal freedom. This freedom is required

to ensure the clients' integrity of self, the freedom of people to be people in their own right.

To ensure personal freedom, clients can look at the way they are controlled, whether through guilt, responsibility, fear, love, anger, anxiety, or other feelings. However, it is not just a matter of abused clients being controlled, as they are also capable of doing the controlling. They can control others such as parents, children, friends, and even their partners at times. Thus clients can come to understand power and control in their lives. This in turn sets the context for conceptual change, as clients can then be brought to understand that each aspect of power contains its opposite. The apparent strength of partners contains weakness, and the weakness of abused clients contains strength. For example, abusive partners may appear to be in control but they are weak in that they have always to maintain that control, they can never allow it to slip. They become prisoners of their own patterns of behaviour. Likewise, abused women have the strength of often having much less to lose, so they are potentially less the prisoner of enforcing behaviour.

It would be naive to think that the aforementioned covers all of the work on self-identity. There are other difficulties to surmount.

- Some clients will take convincing that they should allow themselves space and personal interests, as they see this as self-indulgence. I stress that if these clients were physically injured then treatment is not an indulgence but common sense. Likewise, if clients are injured in mind or spirit, then getting help and looking after themselves is quite normal.

- It can be helpful if clients meet new people who know nothing about the abuse. This helps normalization as clients have the choice of whether or not to disclose their past history.

- An important part of a person's self is his or her sexuality and sexual relationships. One of the myths about battered women is that they 'go off' men and become lesbians. Occasionally, it is indeed a matter of women discovering their true sexuality, but more often, in my experience, battered women are taking time to look around for comfort, companionship and some positive emotional response. Sometimes these may come from other women and include physical contact. Such contact can become sexual.

Moira: 'You look for something, anything. I had a relationship I suppose you would call it with another woman and even sex with her, but I didn't really like it. It wasn't really me.'

The experience need not always be seen in a negative way, even if the woman stays heterosexual.

Paula: 'For a time I turned lesbian, and had an affair with this woman friend. I felt feelings with her that went much further and deeper than with any man. It was a phase and now I prefer men, but I shall never regret that time.'

These examples do not represent the majority of cases, but in general women do need to see themselves as sexual persons, a perspective which some abusers will have tried to eradicate.

- Self-identity depends in part on how clients see themselves and the need to see themselves as they really are. This includes divesting themselves of imposed labels such as 'battered woman' and 'victim'. Though these are useful, helping women to identify with other abused women and breaking through their isolation, these labels diminish in usefulness over time as they lock clients into a certain role. The term 'survivor', which is increasingly used, is a more positive term, but eventually women should be more than mere labels; they should be themselves. This may take a long time as the effects of abuse can last for many years.

11 COUNSELLOR SUPPORT

Introduction

Support is seen nowadays as the necessary accompaniment to counselling, though with little thought given to its reality. There are questions to be asked about its provision.

1. Does it actually happen? Counsellings jobs or jobs involving counselling are advertised as having full support and supervision, but this does not always happen. In particular, there should be a clear remit given as to support and supervision. There is always the danger that in an organization the latter takes precedence.

2. Is support aimed at benefiting the counsellor, the client or the agency? It is essential to be quite sure and realistic about the aims of support. Support for clients can lead merely to case discussions, while support for the agency is likely to lead to managerial supervision. Realism is needed as in-house support can be made largely ineffective as it introduces problems with hierarchies and confidentiality. Counsellors are unlikely to get support from those who also have a supervisory role.

3. Is the support effective? Providing support is not enough; it has to be effective support. Support, poorly done, can worsen the counsellors' situations. Thus there must be regular support evaluation. This requires more than finding out from counsellors whether they feel supported and well able to continue in their work. Counsellors may well be reluctant to admit to high stress, seeing this as failure – a view that might actually be held by the counselling agency to some extent. Thus some form of outside monitoring is required.

4. Is support needed for client work or for working in the agency? Often stress comes from one's colleagues as much as from clients, but this tends not to be addressed. Part of the difficulty might be structural, that the nature of the organization itself is more likely to allow counsellor stress to grow and less likely to deal with it effectively. Organizations which are not power-based, such as counselling cooperatives, could be more appropriate, though this might require a radical change in the agency.

5. Is support being used to maintain the status quo or is it part of the counsellors' ongoing development? Support may allow poor work practices, whether by counsellors or the agency, to continue. Support should not be used to support the insupportable.

6. Questions should be asked as to beliefs about support, especially where it is thought that, for the following reasons, counsellors do not require support.

   (a) They have asked for support or more support.
   (b) There have been no complaints about the lack of support.
   (c) The counsellors seem all right to other non-counsellors.
   (d) Counsellors have been doing this work for years without any support or without further support.
   (e) Counsellors are experienced in this work and so require little support.
   (f) Counsellors say they see current levels of support as being sufficient.
   (g) Counsellors are seen through supervision as not developing.
   (h) In addition, there can be general negative beliefs about support; for example, 'Surgeons have a harder job and they do not receive support', or, 'I did a similar job and never needed support.' Such statements require close examination and discussion.

7. Counselling is supervised and supported, but the same is rarely done for supervision and support. However, the assumption that they are actually helpful is open to as much questioning as counselling.

Perspectives on client work

Before considering counselling, we should recognize that part of the stress experienced comes from personalizing perspectives on the work. It is easy to imagine that there are difficult clients, clients who have behavioural problems and will display such during the counselling. However, clients are merely trying to cope as best they can in difficult situations. The opposite view is that there are no difficult clients as such, only poor counsellors (Altshul, 1977). In fact, this fails to recognize the very real difficulties that counsellors experience with clients who can be highly resistant to being helped, even when it is clearly to their advantage.

Counsellors should bear in mind the possibility of difficulties (Anderson and Stewart, 1983), as only then will they be aware of problems and react accordingly. Rather than placing the blame for difficulties on either the client or the counsellor, it is better to see them as the outcome of the interaction between the two.

Counsellors have to be realistic. In my opinion, counsellors are often poorly prepared for work difficulties. Training and textbooks give an idealized picture or highly selective extracts of counselling. Unfortunately, clients fail to read these books and thus may not act as expected. This leads counsellors to imagine they must be less than competent. In practice, counselling tends to be messier, more intricate, and more prone to errors than is usually portrayed. Counsellors have to work with this reality.

Support and clients

To a large extent, the usefulness of support comes from dealing with what counsellors find most difficult, stressful or taxing. This means they have to be asked from time to time and be given full discretion to answer. As most counsellors are orientated to client work, they expect the required replies to be directed to such work. Thus an indication has to be given of the various possible areas, such as home life, home/work priorities, agency concerns, staff member difficulties, client problems, workloads, self-development or promotion. Client work is merely one area in which support may be required.

Counselling can be stressful and if this stress is not addressed it can lead to burnout, total emotional exhaustion and inability to work. To avoid this situation – and there must be questions about any organization that allows it – all areas of stress must be covered, though not necessarily by the agency, as personal matters that interfere with counselling should be addressed elsewhere. As regards client work, in the role of supervisor, my experience has been that stress is lessened by first analysing what counsellors find to be most difficult. The identified areas include the following.

- Risk of physical harm or death from the abuser

- Risk of physical harm or death to children

- Abused women committing suicide or attempting to do so

- Abused women self-mutilating

- Women returning to their abusive partners

- Possible harm or action taken against relatives, friends, agency staff or the counsellor

The first point to be made is that these are all things that *might* happen, and so part of the difficulty is having to deal with uncertainty.

This calls for a risk assessment, which should be in writing, and with risk goes the possibility of being proved wrong. Risk assessment is not just the chance of an event happening but this being weighed against other outcomes, such as benefits to clients. If no risks are taken by the counsellor then the chance of improvement due to the counsellor is nil. Furthermore, the continuing situation of women being abused clearly has risks, so inaction and risk-free counselling is a non-starter. From this we see that counsellors are always going to make mistakes from time to time, as risks are mis-assessed. What is required is not self-blame but learning from the incident. One mistake is to be regretted but may be expected; a pattern of mistakes is a matter of concern.

Counsellors and stress-induction

Stress is not just a result of the counselling but how it and the counsellor's input is perceived. And the greatest critics can be counsellors themselves, who have unrealistic standards based on certain beliefs, including the following:

- The counsellor has to be successful and solve the presented client problems.

- The counsellor should not make mistakes but should work correctly.

- Clients should appreciate what counsellors do for them.

- Without the counsellor's help, disaster will result.

A more realistic perspective is that success depends more on clients than counsellors, it is about taking judged risks, and sometimes there will be misjudgements. The need for appreciation is nothing more than a sign of stress, and counsellors' sense of omnipotence a sign of their dependency on work. But perhaps the most insidious belief is:

- The welfare of the client is paramount.

In fact, the welfare of the client is merely one aspect of counselling situations. The role of others close to the client or clients, the counsellor, and society in general all have their place, and these are not totally separate but involved with clients. In cases of child abuse, very young children will not be counselled, yet they are at the centre of relevant work. Partner violence is about the welfare of women so abused, even when their partners are being counselled individually.

Sessional work and support

Some of the stress of counselling comes from sessional work itself, and this can be divided into the following.

1. The counsellors' hopes and expectations of counselling and of counselling particular cases may be unrealistic. There has to be acceptance that some fusions of particular client and counsellor will work better than others, and that there are some clients for whom only a limited amount can be done through counselling.

2. Counsellors also have to deal with the hopes and expectations of others, whether they be of clients or the counselling agency. These are not always made overt and may conflict with each other or those of the counsellor. Equally, clients can have unrealistic expectations of counselling and counsellors, and can prove difficult when these expectations are dashed.

3. Clients come to counselling for a variety of reasons, and in abuse cases there are likely to be many reasons, greater or lesser. One of the difficulties is to sort out these reasons, of which some clients may hardly be aware. Counsellors may assume clients are agreed to one or two stated aims, but the picture can be more complicated. What seems to be clients being difficult can be no more than their pursuit of unstated objectives.

4. Counsellors have to accept the limitations of counselling and the fact that it is often only one part of a variety of helping resources. A client who wants accommodation is helped most by getting a house or flat – not by counselling. Counselling abused women has to be linked with practical resource agencies, and this can provide its own frustrations.

5. Counselling has to be related to an approximate time-scale and what the counsellor and client see as a satisfactory outcome. Work with abused women can last a long time, and this has to be accepted. For instance, one client after years of being battered eventually saw that her best option was to leave her husband and get a divorce. However, it was two years before she finally put this plan into action. After many years of a certain way of life, clients may need some time before they can totally change it. What may be seen as resistance or difficulties may be no more than clients taking their time.

6. The ongoing counselling difficulties can be of two sorts. There are the difficulties of applying counselling theory and practice to individual cases, and this can be greatly helped by supervision.

However, there are also the feelings that arise in counsellors during the session. Some of these are described below:

(a) Having to deal with the unexpected. This can lead to anxiety. As a practical measure, counsellors should not feel it necessary to respond immediately. My get-out is to say, "I would like to think about that a bit", and so defer action. Counsellors should see that much of the pressure seemingly put on them by clients actually comes from themselves, which in turn might have originated from other people.

(b) Having to deal with aggression between clients in couples counselling or aggression directed towards the counsellor can be difficult to take, even when we understand the reasons for it. The feelings counsellors have are meant to be taken to support groups or support people and then discharged there, but this is frequently insufficient. By this time the feelings may largely have been internalized and not effectively discharged; moreover, the help is largely cognitive so the feelings are more explained than taken away. What is often needed is for counsellors to be more assertive during the session, to let clients know when they feel invaded or oppressed. This not only helps counsellors but provides a useful model for clients and helps them to appreciate the importance of boundaries.

(c) Counsellors can feel frustrated or irritated with clients. There are problems in that some counsellors think that such feelings are best repressed or kept hidden from others, as it is unprofessional to be openly negative about clients. On the other hand, some clients cause frustration by not taking responsibility for their actions or failing to carry out their agreed plans. It is natural to have feelings about clients and the point is to discharge such feelings as soon as appropriate. It is always surprising that counsellors have feelings about clients and yet rarely share them, thus limiting progress and not allowing clients to see themselves as others see them.

7. Difficulties are often located in the clients' behaviour, but we should remember that the counsellor can be equally challenging at times.

(a) Counsellors can expect clients to pose difficulties, as having mentally labelled them, they are then more likely to see client behaviour as problematic.

(b) Counsellors can project their own ill-feeling onto clients, and consequently see them in a bad light.

(c) If under stress, counsellors can have an unrealistic adverse view of clients.

(d) Dealing with issues such as anger, violence, bad relationships and mortality can set off countertransference problems in counsellors, who have to deal with their own unresolved feelings. There can then be problems in differentiating between what belongs to clients and what belongs to themselves, as counsellors.

8. There can be further difficulties for some counsellors if they are wedded to a given theoretical perspective and approach. Jeffrey Kottler noted that Freud complained of oppressive feelings arising from trying to persuade female patients to abandon their wish for a penis (Kottler, 1992:60). Apart from wondering who had the problem, we see that Freud's frustration was a product of his theorizing and the psychoanalyic situation. In fairness, I have concerns about theory – not its acceptance by clients, but simply whether it is correct.

9. Finally, it should be realized that counselling can produce little positive feedback, and this can be particularly the case with complex cases. Although it is often said counsellors should expect no thanks, yet we would be less than human if we did not benefit from some appreciation.

Summary

Support is sometimes seen as talking through counselling cases or receiving positive messages. In fact, it is as complex as counselling itself and requires considerable analysis and openness of mind. Counsellors are human themselves, can use counselling for their own affective needs (Kovacs, 1976), can dislike clients or over-identify with them (Watkins, 1985). Just as clients need counsellors, counsellors need their own support people. Failure to employ such help reflects a desire for a belief in control, which is precisely what characterizes abusive men.

12 CONCLUSION

Counselling women in violent relationships raises difficult questions regarding both practice and theory. Counsellors often have their own favourite theories, approaches and methods but seem less inclined to marry them to the needs of specific clients. This may not be so important with some clients, but where counsellors are working with clients at risk of physical injury, suicide or death, then getting matters right is of prime concern. Thus there can be no acceptance of counselling as given. Everything is open to question.

1. The initial question for counsellors is that concerning their own attitudes and their relationship to violence. If counsellors have a non-violent attitude in relation to male partnership behaviour then this attitude should logically extend to child abuse, to abuse of the elderly, to any form of violence. This should not be confined to the counselling session but should permeate life. Helpful attitudes are not states of mind we can simply switch on when about to start counselling – they should be part of us.

2. Another aspect is the need for counsellors to be able to identify relationship violence. Too often the question is asked as to the effectiveness of counselling, then no regard is given to those that are passed by. This is not unconnected with the question as to whether counsellors want to recognize or deal with partnership violence. Such violence is one of the most common social problems, yet comparatively little help, and less counselling assistance, is given.

3. We have seen that decisions have to be made as to whether counselling should be with individuals or with couples. A further question is whether counselling is appropriate or whether there should be recourse to other measures, such as a referral on for practical help or to a self-help group. In particular, attention has to be given to counsellors and agencies taking up polar positions – either referring on all cases involving violence or taking on such cases under the assumption that counselling is all that is required.

4. Help for those who are physically abused by their partners requires different inputs from different agencies. The other agencies could be seen as completely separate from counselling, but in practice the situation may be more complex. Clients can pick up different messages from the various persons or agencies involved, to their confusion. However, closer cooperation of agencies can also affect the agencies concerned as there can be anxiety about power imbalance between agencies, and a wish to assert their own identity, but there can also be a coming together with the exchange of ideas. Ultimately, the result can filter down to the counsellors and affect the counselling itself.

5. As we have seen, the role of theory is important and needs to be consistent with what are taken as the relevant human values. We are used to the medical paradigm and decide that theory is to be applied if it is correct and effective. What needs to be included when involved in personal helping is the criterion of values, which is much more apparent in feminist helping. However, the application of values does mean that at times the form of counselling has to be modified.

6. The next point may seem redundant, but I believe it is of paramount importance to really listen to what clients say and what might be behind what they are trying to say. The latter is crucial at times with abused clients who may only dare to hint at situations. Listening is seldom a simple operation, but subject to both listener interpretation and empathy. Counsellors should never accept what they think they have heard, and never reject it either.

7. Another aspect of counselling that has to be considered is that of information-giving. Information is not neutral but a source of power that to some extent can strengthen the postion of women clients. This means that information needs to be correct. Giving information can be poorly regarded by male partners, whatever its nature, so abusers must understand the concept of power-based relationships and that help is given to even up that power imbalance.

8. One aspect of counselling that often puzzles me is the fact that counsellors can experience difficulties in the working relationship but seldom seem to share them with the clients concerned. It is essential that this is done, especially when counselling for relationship problems, as there are likely to be difficulties in the working relationship through power imbalance, which increases the chance of dependency, hostility and unrealistic expectations.

9. For those accustomed to person-centred counselling of individual clients, they might find that the work with violence-affected clients requires them to take on a much more active role. This extends not only to boundary maintenance but equally to other aspects of counselling.

10. One question that deserves further thought is that of when counselling with clients should be ended. Initially this might be linked to the aims and objectives of the counselling, but these are dependent on the wishes and self-perceived needs of clients. What may happen is that help is given to steer the client through crises but little attention is given at subsequent times when help and support are also sorely needed. The whole topic of continuance, for example, tends to be overlooked.

11. With a background of counselling intravenous drug workers, my inclination is to suspend belief at times about some of the accounts given to me by clients. Some counsellors may like to view a lack of truthfulness as the operation of defence mechanisms, bringing the unconscious into play. What is harder for some workers to accept is that clients may deliberately lie to them – quite consciously mislead, fabricate or lie. By pathologizing such dishonesty, counsellors are able to see the behaviour as residing purely in clients and so not involving them. My view is that clients do lie and are quite conscious of their deceptions. This can appear to mean such client behaviour is directed at the counsellor. However, this is not to be taken personally as it is actually directed at the role of counsellors, which includes their influence and power. Thus deception may be a way of coping, but we also have to see it as a possible reaction in the face of counsellor power. It also has to be remembered that counsellors are often less than truthful, succumbing to the sin of omission.

12. Counsellors have to take on board the possibility of a degree of defensiveness from both male and female clients. Women may minimize what has happened and make excuses for their partner. Men can also deny or minimize what has taken place. The difficulty comes not with client deception but with client self-deception.

13. Support and supervision are required for all forms of counselling. This is certainly the case when counselling women in violent relationships, which can be very stressful at times, especially when working with couples.

The conclusions reached about counselling women in violent relation-ships are a product, in part, of personal experience. My clients come from the lower social classes and many have had numerous problems apart from that of violence. I would not therefore claim that the approach in this book is necessarily applicable to all women in violent relationships. Whether it is applicable to any I leave to the judgement of the reader.

BIBLIOGRAPHY

Place of publication is London, unless stated otherwise.

Aguirre, B. (1986) Why do they return? Abused wives in shelters. *Social Work* 30, p. 330.

Allan, G. (1989) *Friendship: developing a sociological perspective.* Harvester Wheatsheaf.

Allen, J. and Haccoun, D. (1976) Sex differences in emotionality: a multidimensional approach. *Human Relations* Vol. 29, p. 711.

Allgood, S. and Crane, D. (1991) Predicting marital therapy dropouts. *Journal of Marital and Family Therapy* Vol. 17, p. 73.

Altman, I. and Taylor, D. (1973) *Social penetration: the development of interpersonal relationships.* New York: Holt, Rinehart and Winston.

Altshul, J. (1977) The so-called boring patient. *American Journal of Psychotherapy* Vol. 31, p. 533.

American Humane Society (1978) *National analysis of official child neglect and abuse reporting.* Denver, CO: American Humane Society.

American Psychiatric Association (1987) *Diagnostic and statistical manual of mental disorders.* Washington, DC: American Psychiatric Association.

Amir, M. (1971) *Patterns of forcible rape.* Chicago, IL: University of Chicago.

Anderson, C. and Stewart, S. (1983) *Mastering resistance: a practical guide to family therapy.* New York: Guilford Press.

Andrews, S. (1987) Violence in normal families. Paper presented at the Marriage Research Centre Conference on Family Violence. London, April 1987.

Archer, D. and Akert, R. (1977) Words and everything else: verbal and non-verbal cues in social interpretation. *Journal of Personality and Social Psychology* Vol. 35, p. 443.

Archer, D. and Gartner, R. (1984) *Violence and crime in cross-national perspective.* Newhaven: Yale University Press.

Argyle, M. and Henderson, M. (1985) The rules of relationships, in S. Duck and D. Perlman (eds) *Understanding personal relationships: an interdisciplinary approach.* Sage.

Askew, S. (1989) Aggressive behaviour in boys: to what extent is it institutionalized? in D. Tattum and D. Lane (eds) *Bullying in schools.* Stoke-on-Trent: Trentham Books, p. 57.

Atkinson, B. and Heath, A. (1990) Further thoughts on Second-Order family therapy – this time it's personal. *Family Process* Vol. 29, p. 145.

Bagarozzi, D. and Rauen, P. (1981) Pre-marital counseling: appraisal and status. American *Journal of Family Therapy* Vol. 9(3), p. 13.

Baken, S. (1979) Victimisation rate, safety and fear of crime. *Social Problems* Vol. 26, p. 343.

Ball, M. (1977) Issues of violence in family casework. *Social Casework* Vol. 58, p. 3.

Ban, P. and Lewis, M. (1974) Mothers and fathers, girls and boys: attachment behaviour in the one year old. *Merrill Palmer Quarterly* Vol. 20, p. 195.

Baron, L. and Straus, M. (1988) Cultural and economic sources of homicide in the United States. *The Sociological Quarterly* Vol. 29, p. 371.

Baron, R. (1979) Aggression, empathy, and race: effects of victim's pain cues, victim's race and level of instigation on physical aggression. *Journal of Applied Social Psychology* Vol. 9, p. 103.

Bateson, G. (1972) Conscious purpose versus nature, in G. Bateson (ed.) *Steps to an ecology of mind.* New York: Ballantine.

Bauer, A. (1996) What do infants recall of their lives? *American Psychologist* Vol. 51, p. 29.

Bavelas, J. (1983) *Situations that lead to disqualification.* Human Communication Research Vol. 9, p. 130.

Beck, A. (1988) *Love is never enough.* New York: Harper and Row.

Becker, T., Samet, J., Wiggins, C. and Key, C. (1990) Violent death in the West: suicide and homicides in New Mexico, 1958–87. *Suicide and Life-threatening Behavior* Vol. 20, p. 328.

Bell, R. (1981) Friendships of women and of men. *Psychology of Women Quarterly* Vol. 5, p. 402.

Berg, J. (1987) Responsiveness and self-disclosure, in V. Derlega and J. Berg (eds) *Self-disclosure: theory, research and therapy.* New York: Plenum, p. 101.

Berger, P. and Kellner, H. (1964) The social construction of marriage. *Diogenes* Vol. 46, p. 1.

Berk, R., Berk, S., Loseke, D. and Rauma, D. (1983) Mutual combat and other family violence myths, in D. Finkelhor, R. Gelles, G. Hotaling and M. Strauss (eds) *The dark side of families: current family violence research.* Beverly Hills, CA: Sage, p. 197.

Berkowitz, L. (1978) Is criminal violence normative behavior? *Journal of Research in Crime and Delinquency* Vol. 15, p. 148.

Berkowitz, L. (1982) Rule-following behaviour, in P. Marsh and A. Campbell, *Aggression and violence*, Oxford: Blackwell, p. 91.

Bersherov, D. (1978) Testimony before the Committee on Science and Technology (DISPAC Subcommittee) US House of Representatives, 14 February.

Bersoni, C. and Chen, H. (1988) Sociological perspectives in family violence, in V. Van Hasselt, R. Morrison, A. Bellack and M. Hensen (eds) *Handbook of family violence*. New York: Plenum.

Binney, V., Harkell, G. and Nixon J. (1981) *Leaving violent men*. Leeds: Women's Aid Federation.

Binney, V., Harkell, G. and Nixon, J. (1985) Refuges and housing for battered women, in J Pahl (ed.) *Private violence and public policy*. Routledge and Kegan Paul.

Bion, W. (1970) *Attention and interpretation*. Tavistock Publications.

Birns, B., Cascardi, M. and Meyer, S. (1994) Sex-role socialization: developmental influences on wife abuse. *American Journal of Orthopsychiatry* Vol. 64(1), p. 50.

Blier, M. and Blier-Wilson, L. (1989) Gender differences in self-rated emotional expressiveness. *Sex Roles* Vol. 21, p. 287.

Bograd, M. (1984) Family system approaches to wife battering: a feminist critique. *American Journal of Orthopsychiatry* Vol. 54, p. 558.

Bok, S. (1982) *Secrets: on the ethics of concealment and revelation*. New York: Pantheon.

Bologna, M., Waterman, C. and Dawson, L. (1987) Violence in gay male and lesbian relationships: implications for practitioners and policymakers. Paper presented at the Third National Conference for Family Violence Researchers. July, Durham: NH.

Bonaparte, M. (1963) *Female sexuality*. New York: Grove Press.

Borkowski, M., Murch, M. and Walker, V. (1983) *Marital violence: the community response*. Tavistock.

Borrill, J., Rosen, B. and Summerfield, A. (1987) The influence of alcohol on judgement of facial expressions of emotions. *British Journal of Medical Psychiatry* Vol. 60, p. 71.

Bourland, M. (1990) Elder abuse: from definition to prevention. *Postgraduate Medicine* Vol. 87, p. 139.

Bowder, B. (1979) The wives who ask for it: an interview with Gayford, McKeith and Pizzey. *Community Care* 1 March.

Bowker, L. (1983) *Beating wife-beating*. Lexington, MA: Lexington.

Bowker, L., Barbittel, M. and McFerrow, J. (1988) On the relationship between wife beating and child abuse, in K. Yllo and M. Bograd (eds) *Feminist perspectives on wife abuse*. Beverly Hills, CA: Sage.

Bradshaw, J. and Millar, J. (1991) *Lone parent families in the UK*. Department of Social Security, Research Report No. 6. HMSO.

Brandon, S. (1976) Physical violence in the family: an overview, in M. Borland (ed.) *Violence in the family*. Manchester: Manchester University Press.

Brannen, J. and Collard, J. (1982) *Marriages in trouble: the process of seeking help*. Tavistock.

Brayfield, A. (1962) Performance is the thing. *Journal of Counseling Psychology* Vol. 9, p. 3.

Brehm, S. (1985) *Intimate relationships*. New York: McGraw-Hill.

Brodie, B. and Shore, P. (1957) A concept for a role of serotonin and norepinephrine as chemical mediators in the brain. *Annals of the New York Academy of Science* Vol. 66, p. 631.

Brown, J. (1964) *Freud and the post-Freudians*. Penguin.

Brown, L. (1994) *Subversive dialogues*. New York: Basic Books.

Browne, A. (1987) *When battered women kill*. New York: Free Press.

Browning, J. and Dutton, D. (1986) Assessment of wife assault with the Conflict Tactics Scale. Using couple data to quantify the differential reporting effect. *Journal of Marriage and the Family* Vol. 48, p. 375.

Brownmiller, S. (1975) *Against our will: men, women, and rape*. New York: Bantam.

Bryan, M. (1984) A question of housing. *Journal of Social Welfare* July, p. 195.

Buchan, I. and Edwards, S. (1991) *Adult cautioning for domestic violence*. Home Office Science and Technology Group and Police Requirements Support Unit, Crown Copyright.

Bull, J. (1991) *Housing consequences of relationship breakdown*. University of York, SPRU.

Burstow, B. (1992) *Radical feminist therapy*. Sage.

Burt, M. (1982) Justifying personal violence: a comparison of rapists and the general public. Paper presented at the Third International Study Institute of Victimology. Bellagio, Italy.

Cahill, A. (1981) Aggression revisited: the value of anger in therapy and other close relationships, in S. Feinstein and J. Looney (eds) *Adolescent psychiatry: developmental and clinical studies*. Chicago, IL: University of Chicago Press.

Campbell, A. (1982) Female aggression, in P. Marsh and A. Campbell, *Aggression and violence*. Oxford: Blackwell, p. 137.

Campbell, J. (1985) Beating of wives: a cross-cultural perspective. *Victimology* Vol. 10, p. 174.

Cantwell, P. and Holmes, S. (1994) Social construction: a paradigm shift for systemic therapy and training. *Australian and New Zealand Journal of Family Therapy* Vol. 15, p. 17.

Caplan, P. (1987) *The myth of women's masochism*. New York: Signet.

Carkhuff, R. and Berenson, B. (1967) *Beyond counseling and therapy.* New York: Holt, Rinehart and Winston.

Carlson, B. (1977) Battered women and their assailants. *Social Work* Vol. 22, p. 455.

Carmen, E., Rieker, P. and Mills, T. (1984) Victims of violence and psychiatric illness. *American Journal of Psychiatry* Vol. 141, p. 378.

Cate, R., Henton, J., Koval, J., Christopher, F. and Lloyd, S. (1982) Premarital abuse: a social psychological perspective. *Journal of Family Issues* Vol. 3, p. 79.

Check, J. and Malamuth, N. (1983) Sex role stereotyping and reactions to stranger versus acquaintance rape. *Journal of Personality and Social Psychology* Vol. 45, p. 344.

Chelune, G., Rosenfeld, L. and Waring, E. (1985) Spouse disclosure patterns in distressed and non-distressed couples. *American Journal of Family Therapy* Vol. 13, p. 24.

Children's Safety Network (1991) *A data book of child and adolescent injury.* Washington DC: National Center for Education in Maternal and Child Health.

Chodorow, N. (1978) *The reproduction of motherhood: psychoanalysis and the sociology of gender.* Berkeley, CA: University of California Press.

Chovil, N. (1991) Social determinants of facial displays. *Journal of Nonverbal Behavior* Vol. 15, p. 141.

Christopoulos, C., Cohen, D., Shaw, D., Joyce, S., Sullivan-Hanson, J., Kraft, S. and Emery, R. (1987) Children of abused women. 1 Adjustment at time of shelter residence. *Journal of Marriage and the Family* Vol. 49, p. 611.

Clarke, K., Craig, G. and Glendinning, C. (1993) *Children come first? The Child Support Act and lone parent families.* Manchester: Barnados, the Children's Society, NCH, NSPCC and SCF.

Cocozza, J. and Steadman, H. (1977) Prediction in psychiatry: an example of misplaced confidence in experts. *Journal of Personality and Social Psychology* Vol. 35, p. 265.

Coleman, E.D. and Straus, M. (1980) Marital power and violence in a nationally representative sample of American couples. *Violence and Victims* Vol. 1, p. 141.

Comstock, G. and Paik, H. (1994) The effects of television violence on anti-social behavior: a meta-analysis. *Communication Research* Vol. 21(4), p. 516.

Cook, M. (1977) The social skill model and interpersonal attraction, in S. Duck (ed) *Theory and practice in interpersonal attraction.* Academic Press, p. 319.

Crockenberg, S. (1985) Toddlers' reactions to maternal anger. *Merrill-Palmer Quarterly* Vol. 3, p. 361.

Currie, D. (1990) Battered women and the State: from the failure of theory to the theory of failure. *Journal of Human Justice* Vol. 1, No. 2.

Davidson, T. (1978) *Conjugal crime: understanding and changing the wife-beating pattern.* New York: Hawthorn.

Davis, L. (1987) Battered women: the transformation of a social problem. *Social Work* Vol. 32 July/August, p. 306.

Davis, L. and Carlson, B. (1987) Observation of spouse abuse: what happens to the children. *Journal of Interpersonal Violence* Vol. 2, p. 278.

Davis, M. (1973) *Intimate relations.* New York: Free Press.

Deal, J. and Wampler, K. (1986) Dating violence: the primacy of previous experience. *Journal of Social and Personal Relationships* Vol. 3, p. 457.

Dell, P. (1989) Violence and the systemic view: the problem of power. *Family Process* Vol. 28, p. 1.

Deschner, J. (1984) *The hitting habit: anger control for battering couples.* New York: Free Press.

Deutch, H. (1944) *The psychology of women.* New York: Grune and Stratton.

Dixson, A. (1980) Androgens and aggressive behaviour in primates: a review. *Aggressive Behavior* Vol. 6, p. 37.

Dobash, R.E. and Dobash, R.P. (1970) *Violence against wives.* New York: Free Press.

Dobash, R.E. and Dobash, R.P. (1977) Wives: the 'appropriate' victims of marital violence. *Victimology* Vol. 2, p. 426.

Dobash, R.E. and Dobash, R.P. (1979) *Violence against wives: a case against patriarchy.* Open Books.

Dobash, R.E. and Dobash, R.P. (1984) The nature and antecedents of violent events. *British Journal of Criminology* Vol. 24(3), p. 269.

Dobash, R.E., Dobash, R.P. and Cavanagh, C. (1985) The contact between battered women and social and medical agencies, in J. Pahl (ed.) *Private violence and public policy: the needs of battered women and the response of the public service.* Routledge.

Dobash, R.E., Dobash, R.P., Wilson, M. and Daly, M. (1992) The myth of sexual symmetry in marital violence. *Social Problems* Vol. 39, p. 71.

Dowd, E. and Seibel, C. (1990) A cognitive theory of resistance and reactance: implications for treatment. *Journal of Mental Health Counseling* Vol. 1/2(4), p. 458.

Drake, R. (1984) Lateral assymmetry of personal optimism. *Journal of Research in Personality* Vol. 18, p. 497.

Duck, S. (1982) A topography of relationship disagreement and dissolution, in S. Duck (ed.) *Personal relationships 4: Dissolving personal relationships.* New York: Academic Press.

Duck, S. and Miell, D. (1986) Charting the development of personal relationships, in R. Gilmour and S. Duck (eds) *The emerging field of personal relationships.* Hillsdale, New Jersey: Lawrence Erlbaum.

Durlak, J. (1979) Comparative effectiveness of para-professional and professional helpers. *Psychological Bulletin* Vol. 86, p. 80.

Dutton, D. (1986) The outcome of court-mandated treatment for wife assault: a quasi-experimental evaluation. *Violence and Victims* Vol. 1(3), p. 61.

Dutton, D. and Browning, J. (1987) Power struggles and intimacy anxieties as causative factors of wife assault, in G. Russell (ed.) *Violence in intimate relationships.* New York: PMA Publishing, p. 163.

Dutton, D. and Painter, S. (1980) *Male domestic violence and its effect upon the victim.* Ottawa: Health and Welfare Canada.

Dutton, D. and Painter, S. (1981) The development of emotional attachments in battered women and other relationships of intermittent abuse. *Victimology* Vol. 6, p. 139.

Dutton, D. and Strachan, C. (1987) Motivational needs for power and spouse-specific assertiveness in assaultive and non-assaultive men. *Violence and Victims* Vol. 2, p. 145.

Dutton, M. (1992) Understanding women's response to domestic violence: a redefinition of traumatic bonding theory. *Violence and Victims* 105(8), p. 139.

Eagly, A. (1978) Sex differences in influenceability. *Psychological Bulletin* Vol. 85, p. 86.

Ehrlich, H. and Lipsey, C. (1969) Affective style as a variable in person perception. *Journal of Personality* Vol. 37, p. 522.

Elbow, M. (1977) Theoretical considerations of violent marriages (personality characteristics of wife abusers). *Social Casework* Vol. 58, p. 515.

Ellis, A., Sichel, J., Yeager, R., DiMattia, J. and DiGiuseppe, R., (1989) *Rational-emotive couples therapy.* Oxford: Pergamon.

Ellis, D., Grasmick, H. and Gilman, B. (1974) Violence in prison: a sociological analysis. *American Journal of Sociology* Vol. 80, p. 16.

Epstein, N. (1986) Cognitive marital therapy; multilevel assessment and intervention. *Journal of Rational-Emotive Therapy* Vol. 4, p. 68.

Epstein, N. and Eidelson, R. (1981) Unrealistic beliefs of clinical couples: their relationship to expectations, goals and satisfaction. *American Journal of Family Therapy* Vol. 9, p. 13.

Epstein, W. (1995) *The illusion of psychotherapy*. New Brunswick, NJ: Transaction Press.

Estrich, S. (1987) *Real rape: how the legal system victimises women who say no*. Cambridge, MA: Harvard University Press.

Fagot, B. (1978) The influence of sex of child on parental reactions to toddler children. *Child Development* Vol. 49, p. 459.

Farmer, L. (1996) The obsession with definition: the nature of crime and critical legal theory. *Social and Legal Studies* Vol. 5, p. 57.

Feifel, H. and Eells, J. (1963) Patients and therapists assess the same psychotherapy. *Journal of Consulting Psychology* Vol. 27, p. 310.

Feild, H. (1978) Attitudes toward rape: a comparative analysis of police, rapists, crisis counsellors and citizens. *Journal of Personality and Social Psychology* Vol. 36, p. 156.

Feild, H. and Barnett, N. (1978) Forcible rape. *Journal of Criminal Law and Criminology* Vol. 68, p. 146.

Ferraro, K. and Johnson, J. (1982) How women experience battering: the process of victimization. *Social Problems* Vol. 30(3), p. 325.

Field, M. and Field, F. (1973) Marital violence and the criminal process: neither justice nor peace. *Social Service Review* Vol. 47, No. 2, p. 221.

Fincham, F., Beach, S. and Baucom, D. (1987) Attributional processes in distressed and non-distressed couples: 4 self–partner attribution differences. *Journal of Personality and Social Psychology* Vol. 52, p. 739.

Fleming, J. (1979) *Stopping wife abuse: a guide to the emotional psychological and legal implications for the abused woman and those helping her*. Garden City, NY: Anchor.

Foreman, J. (1995) *Is there a correlation between child sexual abuse and domestic violence?* London Road, Glasgow: Women's Support Project.

Forgas, J. (1982) Episode cognition: internal representations of interaction routines, in L. Berkowitz (ed.) *Advances in experimental social psychology*. San Diego, CA: Academic Press.

Forgas, J. and Dobosz, B. (1980) Dimensions of romantic involvement: towards a taxonomy of heterosexual relationships. *Social Psychology Quarterly* Vol. 43, p. 290.

Framo, J. (1965) Rationale and technique of intensive family therapy, in I. Boszormeny-Nagy and J. Framo (eds) *Intensive family therapy: theoretical and practical aspects*. New York: Harper and Row, p. 143.

Freeman, J. (1972) The tyranny of structurelessness. *Berkeley Journal of Sociology* Vol. 17, p. 151.

Freud, S. (1956) The economic problem of masochism, in E. Jones (ed.) *Sigmund Freud, collected papers*. Hogarth Press and the Institute of Psycho-analysis, Vol. 2, p. 255.

Frieze, I. (1983) Investigating the causes and consequences of marital rape. *Signs* Vol. 8(3), p. 532.

Frude, N. (1991) *Understanding family problems – a psychological approach*. New York: Wiley.

Gaelick, C., Bodenhausen, G. and Wyer, R. (1985) Emotional communication in close relationships. *Journal of Personality and Social Psychology* Vol. 49, p. 1246.

Galenson, E. (1986) Some thoughts about infant psychopathology and aggressive development. *International Review of Psychoanalysis* Vol. 13, p. 349.

Ganley, A. (1981) Court mandated therapy for men who batter: three-day workshop for mental health professionals: participants' manual. Washington DC: Center for Women's Studies.

Gaquin, D. (1977) Spouse abuse: data from the National Crime Survey. *Victimology* Vol. 2, p. 634.

Gayford, J. (1975) Wife battering: a preliminary survey of 100 cases. *British Medical Journal* January, p. 194.

Gelles, R. (1974) *The violent home*. Newbury Park, CA: Sage.

Gelles, R. (1988) Violence and pregnancy: are pregnant women at greater risk of abuse. *Journal of Marriage and the Family* Vol. 50, p. 841.

Gelles, R. and Cornell, C. (1985) *Intimate violence in families*. Beverley Hills, CA: Sage.

Gifford, Z. (1990) *The golden thread: Asian experiences of post-Raj Britain*. Grafton Books.

Giles-Sim, J. (1983) *Wife batterers: a systems theory approach*. New York: Guilford Press.

Ginsburg, H. and Miller, S. (1981) Altruism in children. *Ethology and Sociobiology* Vol. 2, p. 75.

Goffman, E. (1968) *The presentation of self in everyday life*. Penguin.

Golann, S. (1988) On second-order family therapy. *Family Process* Vol. 27, p. 51.

Goldberg, S. and Lewis, M. (1969) Play behavior in the year old infant: early sex differences. *Child Development* Vol. 40, p. 21.

Goldner, V. (1993) Power and hierarchy: let's talk about it. *Family Process* Vol. 32, p. 157.

Goldner, V., Penn, P., Sheinbeg, M. and Walker, G. (1990) Love and violence: gender paradoxes in volatile attachments. *Family Process* Vol. 29, p. 343.

Gondolf, E. (1985) *Men who batter: an integrated approach for stopping wife abuse*. Holmes Beach, CA: Learning Publications.

Gondolf, E. (with Fisher, E.) (1988) *Battered women as survivors*. Lexington, MA: Lexington.

Goodenough, E. (1931) *Anger in young children*. Minneapolis: University of Minnesota Press.

Goodstein, R. and Page, A. (1981) Battered wife syndrome: overview of dynamics and treatment. *American Journal of Psychiatry* Vol. 138, p. 1036.

Goolishian, H. and Anderson, H. (1992) Strategy and interventions versus non-intervention: a matter of theory. *Journal of Marital and Family Therapy* Vol. 18, p. 5.

Gottfredson, M. (1984) *Victims of crime: the dimensions of risk*. HMSO.

Gottman, J. (1976) *A couple's guide to communication*. Champaign, IL: Illinois Research Press.

Gottman, J. (1979) *Marital interaction – experimental investigations*. New York: Academic Press.

Gottman, J. and Krokoff, L. (1989) Marital interaction and marital satisfaction: a longitudinal view. *Journal of Consulting and Clinical Psychology* Vol. 57, p. 47.

Gottsegan, G. and Gottsegan, M. (1979) Countertransference – the professional identity defense. *Psychotherapy: theory, research, and practice* Vol. 16, p. 3.

Greenbaum, S. (1982) *Set straight on bullies*. Malibu, CA: Natural School Safety Center.

Greenberg, L. and Johnson, S. (1988) *Emotionally focused therapy for couples*. New York: Guilford Press.

Greenspan, M. (1983) *A new approach to women and therapy*. New York: McGraw-Hill.

Griffin, S. (1971) Rape: the all-American crime. *Ramparts* 10, p. 26.

Grossman, W. (1991) Pain, aggression, fantasy, and concepts of sado-masochism. *Psychoanalytic Quarterly* Vol. 60, p. 22.

Gurman, A. and Kniskern, D. (1977) Enriching research on marital enrichment programs. *Journal of Marriage and Family Counseling* Vol. 3, p. 3.

Hafner, R. (1977) The husbands of agoraphobic women and their influence on treatment outcome. *British Journal of Psychiatry* Vol. 131, p. 287.

Hague, G. and Malos, E. (1993) *Domestic violence, action for change*. London: New Clarion Press.

Haley, J. (1967) Toward a theory of pathological systems, in G. Zuk and I. Boszormenyi-Nagy (eds) *Family therapy and disturbed families*. Palo Alto, CA: Science and Behavior Books, p. 11.

Haley, J. (1976) *Problem-solving therapy: new strategies for effective family therapy*. San Francisco, CA: Jossey-Bass.

Hall, E., Howard, J. and Boezio, S. (1986) Tolerance of rape: a sexist or antisocial attitude? *Psychology of Women Quarterly* Vol. 10, p. 101.

Halmos, P. (1978) *The faith of the counsellors*. Constable.

Halson, J. (1991) Young women, sexual harassment and heterosexuality, in P. Abbott and C. Wallace (eds) *Gender power, and sexuality*. Macmillan.

Halweg, K., Schindler, L., Revensdorf, D. and Brengelmann, C. (1984) The Munich Marital Therapy Study, in K. Halweg and N. Jacobson (eds) *Marital interaction*. New York: Guilford Press.

Hamberger, L. and Hastings, J. (1989) Counseling male spouse abusers: characteristics of treatment completers and dropouts. *Violence and Victims* Vol. 1, p. 275.

Hanmer, J., Radford, S. and Stanko, E. (eds) (1989) *Women policy and male violence: International perspectives*. Routledge.

Hanmer, J. and Saunders, S. (1983) Blowing the cover of the protective male: a community study of violence to women, in E. Gamarnikow, D. Morgan, J. Purvis and D. Taylorson (eds) *The public and the private*. Heinemann, p. 28.

Hansen, M., Harway, M. and Cervantes, N. (1991) Therapists' perceptions of severity in cases of family violence. *Violence and Victims* Vol. 4, p. 275.

Harne, L. and Radford, J. (1994) Reinstating patriarchy: the politics of the family and the new legislation, in A. Mullender and R. Morley (eds), *Children living with domestic violence: putting abuse of women on the child care agenda*. Whiting and Birch.

Harris, P. and Gross, D. (1988) Children's understanding of real and apparent emotion, in J. Astington, P. Harris and D. Olson (eds) *Developing theories of mind*. New York: Cambridge University Press.

Hart, B. (1988) *Safety for women monitoring batterers' programs*. Harrisburg, PA: Pennsylvania Coalition against Domestic Violence.

Hartup, W. (1974) Aggression in childhood: developmental perspectives. *American Psychologist* Vol. 29, p. 336.

Harvey, J., Weber, A., Galvin, K., Huszti, H. and Garnick, N. (1986) Attribution and the termination of close relationships: a special focus on the account, in R. Gilmour and S. Duck (eds) *The emerging field of personal relationships*. Hillsdale, NJ: Lawrence Erlbaum.

Hattie, J., Sharpley, C. and Rogers, H. (1984) Comparative effectiveness of professional and para-professional helpers. *Psychological Bulletin* Vol. 95, p. 534.

Hauser, R. (1994) Krafft-Ebing's psychological understanding of sexual behaviour, in R. Porter and M. Teich (eds), *Sexual knowledge, sexual science*. Cambridge: Cambridge University Press.

Hausman, A., Spivak, H. and Prothrow-Stith, D. (1994) Adolescents' knowledge and attitudes about experience with violence. *Journal of Adolescent Health* Vol. 15, p. 400.

Hazan, C. and Shaver, P. (1987) Romantic love conceptualised as an attachment process. *Journal of Personality and Social Psychology* Vol. 52, p. 511.

Hearn, J. (1994) Men's violence to women, in B. Featherstone, B. Fawcett and C. Toft (eds) *Violence, gender, and social work*. Bradford: University of Bradford, Department of Applied Social Studies.

Heineman Pieper, M. (1989) The heuristic paradigm: a unifying and comprehensive approach to social work research. *Smith College Studies in Social Work* Vol. 60(1), p. 8.

Herzeberger, S., Potts, D. and Dillon, M. (1981) Abusive and nonabusive parental treatment from the child's perspective. *Journal of Consulting and Clinical Psychology* Vol. 49, p. 81.

Hess, U., Banse, R. and Kappas, A. (1991) *Journal of Personality and Social Psychology* Vol. 69, p. 280.

Hester, M. and Pearson, C. (1993) Domestic violence, mediation and child contact arrangements: issues from current research. *Family Mediation* Vol. 3(2), p. 3.

Hoff, L. (1990) *Battered women as survivors*. Routledge.

Hoffman, L. (1977) Change in family roles: socialization and sex differences. *American Psychologist* Vol. 32, p. 644.

Hoffman, L. (1985) *Beyond power and control: toward a second-order family systems therapy*. New York: Grune and Stratton.

Hold-Cavell, B. (1985) Showing-off and aggression in young children. *Aggressive Behavior* Vol. 11, p. 333.

Holtgraves, T. (1990) The language of self-disclosure, in H. Giles and W. Robinson (eds), *Handbook of language and social psychology*. Chichester: John Wiley, p. 191.

Holtzworth-Munroe, A., Waltz, J., Jacobson, N., Monaco, V., Fehrenbach, P. and Gottman, J. (1992) Recruiting non-violent men as control subjects for research on marital violence: How easily can it be done? *Violence and Victims* Vol. 7, p. 79.

Home Office (1990) *British Crime Survey*. Home Office Research Study 117. HMSO.

Home Office (1990) Circular 60. HMSO.

Home Office (1995) *Policing domestic violence in the 1990s*. Home Office Research Study 139. HMSO.

Hooper, C. (1994) Do families need fathers? The impact of divorce on children, in A. Mullender and B. Morley (eds) *Children living with domestic violence*. Whiting and Birch.

Hornung, C., McCullough, B., Sugimoto, T. (1981) Status relationships in marriage: risk factors in spouse abuse. *Journal of Marriage and the Family* Vol. 43, p. 675.

Houseknecht, S. and Spanier, G. (1980) Marital disruption and higher education among women in the United States. *Sociological Quarterly* Vol. 21, p. 375.

Huber, J. and Spitze, G. (1980) Considering divorce: an expansion of Becker's theory of marital instability. *American Journal of Sociology* Vol. 86, p. 75.

Hughes, H. (1982) Brief interventions with children in a battered women's shelter: a model preventative program. *Family Relations* Vol. 31, p. 495.

Hull, D. and Schroeder, H. (1979) Some interpersonal effects of assertion, non-assertion, and aggression. *Journal of Behaviour Therapy and Experimental Psychiatry* Vol. 10, p. 10.

Humphreys, A. and Smith, P. (1984) Rough-and-tumble in pre-school and playground, in P. Smith (ed.) *Play in animals and humans.* Oxford: Blackwell.

Humphreys, A. and Smith, P. (1987) Rough-and-tumble, friendship and dominance in school children: evidence for continuity and change with age. *Child Development* Vol. 58, p. 201.

Huston, T., McHale, S. and Crouter, A. (1986) When the honeymoon's over: changes in the marriage relationship over the first year, in R. Gilmour and S. Duck (eds), *The energy science of personal relationships.* Hillsdale, NJ: Lawrence Erlbaum, p. 109.

Ickes, W., Stinson, L., Bissonnette, V. and Garcia, S. (1990) Naturalistic social cognition: empathic accuracy in sex dyads. *Journal of Personality and Social Psychology* Vol. 59, p. 730.

Imam, U. (1994) Asian children and domestic violence, in A. Mullender and R. Morley (eds) *Children living with domestic violence: putting men's abuse of women on the child care agenda.* Whiting and Birch.

Infante, D. (1987) Aggressiveness, in J. McCroskey and J. Daly (eds) *Personality and interpersonal communication.* Newbury Park, CA: Sage, p. 157.

Jacobs, L., Walster, E. and Berscheid, E. (1971) Self-esteem and attraction. *Journal of Personality and Social Psychology* Vol. 17, p. 84.

Jacobson, N. (1993) Domestic violence: what the couples look like. Paper presented at the annual convention of the American Association for Marriage and Family Therapy, Anaheim, CA, October.

Jacobson, N., Gottman, J., Waltz, J., Rushe, R., Babcock, J. and Holtzworth-Munroe, A. (1994) Affect, verbal content, and psychophysiolgy in the arguments of couples with a violent husband. *Journal of Consulting and Clinical Psychology* Vol. 62, p. 982.

Jacobson, N., McDonald, D., Follete, W. and Berley, R. (1985) Attributional processes in distressed and non-distressed married couples. *Cognitive Therapy and Research* Vol. 9, p. 35.

Jaffe, P., Wolfe, D., Telford, A. and Austin, G. (1986) The input of police charges in incidents of wife abuse. *Journal of Family Violence* Vol. 1(1), p. 37.

Jeavons, C. and Taylor, S. (1985) The control of alcohol-related aggression: redirecting the inebriate's attention to socially appropriate conduct. *Aggressive Behavior* Vol. 11, p. 93.

Jenkins, A. (1990) *Invitations to responsibility*. Adelaide: Dulwich Centre Publications.

Johnson, M. (1982) Social and cognitive features of the dissolution of commitment to relationships, in S. Duck (ed.) *Personal relationships: 4 Dissolving personal relationships*. Academic Press.

Johnson, M. and Leslie, L. (1982) Couple involvement and network structure: a test of the dyadic withdrawal hypothesis. *Social Psychology Quarterly* Vol. 45, p. 34.

Johnston, J. (1992) *High-conflict and violent divorcing families. Report on Project*. Corte Madera, CA: Center for the Family in Transition.

Kadushin, H. and Martin, J. (1981) *Child abuse: an interactional abuse*. New York: Columbia University Press.

Kantor, G. and Straus, M. (1987) The drunken bum theory of wife beating. *Social Problems* Vol. 34, p. 213.

Keeney, B. (1979) Ecosystemic epistemology: an alternative paradigm for diagnosis. *Family Process* Vol. 18, p. 117.

Kelly, E., Regan, L. and Barton, S. (1991) *An exploratory study of sexual abuse in a sample of 16–21 year olds*. Polytechnic of North London, Child Abuse Studies Unit.

Kelly, L. (1989) The professionalization of rape. *Rights of Women Bulletin* Spring, p. 8.

Kelly, L. and Radford, J. (1987) The problem of men, in P. Scranton (ed.) *Law, order and the authoritarian state*. Milton Keynes: Open University Press.

Kelvin, P. (1977) Predictability power and vulnerability in interpersonal attraction, in S. Duck (ed.) *Theory and practice in interpersonal attraction*. New York: Academic Press, p. 353.

Kempe, R. and Kempe, C. (1978) *Child abuse*. Fontana.

Kingston, P. and Penhale, B. (1995) *Family violence and the caring professional*. Macmillan.

Kirkwood, C. (1993) *Leaving abusive partners*. Sage.

Kitson, G. and Langlie, J. (1984) Couples who file for divorce but change their minds. *American Journal of Orthopsychiatry* Vol. 54, p. 469.

Klech, G. and Sayles, S. (1990) Rape and resistance. *Social Problems* Vol. 37, p. 149.

Kobak, R. and Hazan, C. (1991) Attachment in marriage: effects of security and accuracy of working models. *Journal of Personality and Social Psychology* Vol. 60, p. 861.

Koss, M. (1990) The women's mental health agenda: violence against women. *American Psychologist* Vol. 45, p. 374.

Koss, M. and Harvey, M. (1991) *The rape victim: clinical and community interventions*. Newbury Park, CA: Sage.

Koss, M. and Oros, C. (1982) Sexual experience survey: a research instrument investigating sexual aggression and victimization. *Journal of Consulting and Clinical Psychology* Vol. 50, p. 455.

Kottler, J. (1992) *Compassionate therapy*. San Francisco, CA: Jossey-Bass.

Kovacs, A. (1976) The emotional hazards of teaching psychotherapy. *Psychotherapy: theory, research and practice*. Vol. 13(4), p. 321.

Koval, J., Ponzetti, J. and Cate, R. (1982) Programmatic intervention for men involved in conjugal violence. *Family Therapy* Vol. 9, p. 147.

Kratchowill, T. (1978) *Single subject research*. New York: Academic Press.

L'Abate, L. and McHenry, S. (1983) *Handbook of marital interventions*. New York: Grune and Stratton.

Lagerspetz, K., Bjorkqvist, K. and Peltonen, T. (1988) Is indirect aggression typical of females? Sex differences in aggressiveness in 11–12 year old children. *Aggressive Behavior* Vol. 14, p. 403.

Lambert, M., Bergin, A. and Collins, J. (1977) Therapist-induced deterioration in psychotherapy, in A. Gurman and A. Razin (eds), *Effective psychotherapy: a handbook of research*. New York: Pergamon.

Lambert, M., Shapiro, D. and Bergin, A. (1986) The effectiveness of psychotherapy, in S. Garfield and A. Bergin (eds) *Handbook of psychotherapy and behavior change*. New York: John Wiley, p. 157.

Lazarus, A. (1985) *Marital myths*. San Luis Obispo, CA: Impact.

Lederer, W. and Jackson, D. (1968) *The mirages of marriage*. New York: W.W. Norton.

LeGrand, C. (1973) Rape and rape laws: sexism in society and law. *California Law Review* Vol. 63, p. 919.

Leonard, K. and Jacob, T. (1988) Alcohol, alcoholism and family violence, in V. Van Hasselt, L. Morrison, A. Bellack and M. Hersen (eds) *Handbook of family violence*. New York: Plenum.

Lerman, L. (1986) Prosecution of wife beaters: institutional obstacles and innovations, in M. Lystad (ed.) *Violence in the home: interdisciplinary perspectives*. New York: Brunner/Mazel, p. 250.

Lever, J. (1978) Sex differences in the complexity of children's play and games. *American Sociological Review* Vol. 43, p. 471.

Liebowitz, M. (1983) *The chemistry of love*. Boston, MA: Little Brown.

Lloyd, C. (1991) The offence: changes in pattern and nature of sex offences. *Criminal Behaviour and Mental Health* Vol. 1, p. 115.

Lobel, K. (ed.) (1986) *Naming the violence: speaking out about lesbian battering*. Seattle, WA: Seal.

Lockley, P. (1996) *Working with drug family support groups*. Free Association Books.

London Rape Crisis Centre (1982) *Annual Report*. London Rape Crisis Centre.

Loseke, D. and Cahill, S. (1984) The social construction of deviance: experts on battered women. *Social Problems* Vol. 31, p. 296.

Luborsky, L.B., Singer, B. and Luborsky, L. (1975) Comparative studies of psychotherapies: Is it true that everybody has won and all must have prizes? *Archives of General Psychiatry* Vol. 32, p. 995.

MacAndrew, C. and Edgerton, R. (1969) *Drunken comportment: a social explanation*. Chicago, IL: Aldine.

Maccoby, E. (1990) Gender and relationships: a developmental account. *American Psychologist* Vol. 45, p. 513.

McDonald, G. (1980) Family power: the assessment of a decade of theory and research. *Journal of Marriage and the Family* Vol. 42, p. 841.

McFarlane, C. and Ross, M. (1987) The relation between current impressions and memories of self and dating partners. *Personality and Social Psychology Bulletin* Vol. 13, p. 228.

McGillivary, A. (1987) Battered women: definition, models and prosecutorial policy. *Canadian Journal of Family Law* Vol. 6, p. 1.

MacKinnon, C. (1987) *Feminism unmodified: discourses on life and law*. Cambridge, MA: Harvard University Press.

McLeod, L. (1980) *Wife battering in Canada: the vicious circle*. Hull, Quebec: Canadian Government Publishing Centre.

McNeil, M. (1987) Flashing: its effect on women, in J. Hanmer and M. Maynard, *Women, violence, and social control*. Macmillan.

McWilliams, M. and McKiernan, J. (1993) *Bringing it out in the open: domestic violence in Northern Ireland*. Belfast: HMSO.

Makepeace, J. (1981) Courtship violence among college students. *Family Relations* Vol. 30(1), p. 97.

Malamuth, N. (1983) Factors associated with rape as predictors of

234   COUNSELLING WOMEN IN VIOLENT RELATIONSHIPS

laboratory aggression against women. *Journal of Personality and Social Psychology* Vol. 45, p. 432.

Malamuth, N. and Briere, J. (1986) Sexual violence in the media: indirect effects on aggression against women. *Journal of Social Issues* Vol. 42(3), p. 75.

Maluccio, A. (1979) *Learning from clients*. New York: Free Press.

Maluccio, A. and Marlow, W. (1974) The case for the contract. *Social Work* Vol. 19, p. 28.

Mama, A. (1989) *The hidden struggle: statutary and voluntary sector response to violence against black women in the home*. London: The London Race and Housing Research Group.

Marangoni, C., Garcia, S., Ickes, W. and Teng, G. (1995) Empathic accuracy in a clinically relevant setting. *Journal of Personality and Social Psychology* Vol. 68, p. 854.

Marsden, D. (1978) Sociological perspectives on family violence, in J. Martin (ed.) *Violence and the family*. Wiley.

Martin, F. (1977) Some implications from the theory and practice of family therapy for individual therapy (and vice versa). *British Journal of Medical Psychology* Vol. 50, p. 53.

Masson, J. (1990) *Against therapy*. Fontana.

Masson, J. (1992) *Final analysis*. Fontana.

Maynard, M. (1985) The response of social workers to domestic violence, in J. Pahl (ed.) *Private violence and public policy: the needs of battered women and the response of the public services*. Routledge and Kegan Paul.

Mazur, A. and Lamb, T. (1980) Testosterone, status and mood in human males. *Hormones and Behavior* Vol. 11, p. 236.

Mehrabian, A. (1972) *Non verbal communication*. Chicago, IL: Aldine Atherton.

Melville, J. (1978) Some violent families, in J. Martin (ed.) *Violence and the family*. Chichester: J Wiley.

Mendler, A. (1992) *How to achieve discipline with dignity in the class-room*. Bloomington, IN: National Educational Service.

Milavsky, J., Kessler, R., Stipp, H. and Reubens, W. (1982) Television and aggression: results of a study panel, in D. Pearl, L. Bouthilet and J. Lazar (eds), *Television and social behavior: ten years of scientific progress and implications for the 80s*. Vol. 2 Technical Reviews. Washington, DC: Government Printing Office, p. 138.

Milgram, S. (1976) *Obedience to authority: an experimental view*. Harper and Row.

Miller, G., Mongeau, P. and Sleight, C. (1986) Fudging with friends and lying to lovers: deceptive communication in interpersonal relationships. *Journal of Social and Personal Relationships* Vol. 3, p. 495.

Miller, L. and Berg, J. (1984) Selectivity and urgency in interpersonal exchange, in V. Derlega (ed.) *Communication, intimacy and close relationships*. Orlando, FL: Academic Press, p. 161.

Millett, K. (1972) *Sexual politics*. Abacus.

Milner, J. and Chilamkurti, C. (1991) Physical child abuse perpetrator characteristics: a review of the literature. *Journal of Interpersonal Violence* Vol. 6, p. 345.

Mitchell, J. (1975) *Psychoanalysis and feminism*. Penguin.

Molme, A. (1989) Punishment power: a balancing process in power-dependence relations. *American Journal of Sociology* Vol. 94, p. 1392.

Mooney, J. (1993) *The hidden figure: domestic violence in North London*. London Borough of Islington.

Morgan, S., Lye, D. and Condran, G. (1988) Sons, daughters, and the risk of marital disruption. *American Journal of Sociology* Vol. 94, p. 110.

Mossman, M. (1986) Feminism and legal method: the difference it makes. *Australian Journal of Law and Society* Vol. 3, p. 30.

Mullender, A. (1996) *Rethinking domestic violence*. Routledge.

Murnen, S. (1988) The sexual behavior sequence of sexually coercive college males. Paper presented at the meeting for the Society for the Scientific Study of Sex, San Francisco.

Murnen, S., Perot, A. and Byrne, D. (1989) Coping with unwanted sexual activity: normative responses, situational determinants, and individual differences. *Journal of Sex Research* Vol. 26, p. 85.

Murphy, C. and O'Leary, K. (1987) Verbal aggression as a predictor of physical aggression in early marriage. Paper presented at the Third National Conference of Family Violence Researchers, Durham, NH.

Mynatt, C. and Allgeier, E. (1990) Risk factors, self-attributions, and adjustment problems among victims of sexual coercion. *Journal of Applied Social Psychology* Vol. 20, p. 130.

Nace, E. (1982) Therapeutic approaches to the alcoholic marriage. *Psychiatric Clinics of North America*. Vol. 5(3), p. 543.

National Association of Citizen's Advice Bureaux (1994) *Child Support: One year on CAB evidence on the first year of the Child Support scheme*. NACAB.

Neidig, P. and Friedman, O. (1984) *Spouse abuse: a treatment program for couples*. Champaign, IL: Research Press.

Newton, D. and Burgoon, J. (1990) Non-verbal conflict behaviors: functions, strategies and tactics, in D. Cahn (ed.) *Intimates in conflict; a communication prespective*. Hillsdale, NY: Lawrence Erlbaum, p. 77.

Nicol, R. (1988) The treatment of child abuse in the home environment, in K. Browne, C. Davies and P. Stratton (eds), *Early prediction and prevention of child abuse*. Chichester: Wiley.

Nietzel, M. and Fisher, S. (1981) Effectiveness of professional and para-professional helpers: a comment on Durlak. *Psychological Bulletin* Vol. 89, p. 555.

Noller, P. (1985) Negative commuications in marriage. *Journal of Social and Personal Relationships* Vol. 2, p. 289.

Noller, P., Feeney, J., Bonnell, D. and Callan, V. (1994) A longitudinal study of conflict in early marriage. *Journal of Social and Personal Relationships* Vol. 11, p. 233.

Noller, P. and Venardos, C. (1986) Communication awareness in married couples. *Journal of Social and Personal Relationships* Vol. 3, p. 31.

Norwood, R. (1985) *Women who love too much*. New York: Pocket Books.

Oakley, A. (1972) *Sex, gender, and society*. M. Temple-Smith.

Ofshe, R. and Watters, E. (1995) *Making monsters*. Andre Deutsch.

Ogus, A., Walker, J. and Lee, M. (1989) *Report of the Conciliation Project Unit, University of Newcastle upon Tyne to the Lord Chancellor on the costs and effectiveness of conciliation in England and Wales*. Newcastle upon Tyne: Newcastle University.

Okun, B. (1986) *Women abuse: facts replacing myths*. Albany, NY: State University of New York Press.

Oldershaw, L., Walters, G. and Hall, D. (1986) Control strategies and noncompliance in abusive mother–child dyads: an observational study. *Child Development* Vol. 57, p. 722.

Oldfield, S. (1983) *The counselling relationship*. Routledge and Kegan Paul.

Oliker, S. (1989) *Best friends and marriage: exchange among women*. Berkeley, CA: University of California Press.

Olweus, D. (1977) Aggression and peer acceptance in adolescent boys: two short-term longitudinal studies of ratings. *Child Development* Vol. 48, p. 1301.

Olweus, D. (1984) Aggressors and their victims: bullying in school, in N. Frude and H. Gait (eds) *Disruptive behavior in schools*. New York: John Wiley, p. 57.

Olweus, D. (1991) Bully/victim problems among schoolchildren: basic facts and effects of a school-based program, in D. Peplar and K. Rubin (eds) *The development and treatment of childhood aggression*. Hillsdale, NJ: Lawrence Erlbaum, p. 411.

Omark, D., Omark, M. and Edelman, M. (1975) Formation of dominance hierarchies in young children, in T. Williams (ed.) *Psychological Anthropology*. The Hague: Mouton.

O'Meara, J. (1994) Cross-sex friendship's opportunity challenge: uncharted terrain for exploration. *Personal Relationship Issues* Vol. 2, p. 4.

Omerod, D. (1994) Sadomasochism. *Journal of Forensic Psychiatry* Vol. 5, p. 123.

Orenstein, S. (1982) The role of mediation in domestic violence cases, in American Bar Association, *Alternative means of family dispute resolution*. Washington, DC: ABA.

Osofosky, J. (1988) Affective exchanges between high risk mothers and infants. *International Journal of Psychoanalysis* Vol. 69, p. 221.

Pagelow, M. (1981) *Woman battering: victims and their experiences*. Beverly Hills, CA: Sage.

Pahl, J. (1978) *A refuge for battered women*. HMSO.

Pahl, J. (1985) *Private violence and public policy*. Routledge and Kegan Paul.

Palmour, R. (1983) Genetic models for the study of aggressive behavior. *Progress in Neuro-psychopharmacology and Biological Psychiatry* Vol. 7, p. 513.

Pan, H., Neidig, D. and O'Leary, K. (1994) Predicting mild and severe husband-to-wife physical aggression. *Journal of Consulting and Clinical Psychology* Vol. 45, p. 475.

Parker, G., Barrett, E. and Hickie, I. (1992) From nurture to network: examining links between perceptions of parenting received and social bonds in adulthood. *American Journal of Psychiatry* Vol. 149, p. 877.

Parloff, M. (1978) *Assessment of psychosocial treatment of mental health disorders: current status and prospects*. Rockville, MD: Clinical Research Branch, National Institute of Mental Health.

Parry, A. (1991) A universe of stories. *Family Process* Vol. 30, p. 37.

Pastore, N. (1949) *The nature–nurture controversy*. New York: Columbia University, King's Crown Press.

Patrick, J. (1973) *A Glasgow gang observed*. Eyre Methuen.

Patterson, M. (1990) in H. Giles and W. Robinson (eds) *Handbook of language and social psychology*. Chichester: John Wiley, p. 101.

Pedder, J. (1991) Courses in psychotherapy: evolution and currect trends. *British Journal of Psychotherapy* Vol. 6, p. 203.

Pellegrini, A. (1988) Elementary school children's rough-and-tumble play and social competence. *Developmental Psychology* Vol. 24, p. 302.

Pence, E. and Paynor, M. (1993) *Education groups for men who batter: the Duluth model.* New York: Springer.

Pennebaker, J. and O'Heeron, R. (1984) Confiding in others and illness rate among spouses and suicide and accidental death victims. *Journal of Abnormal Psychology* Vol. 93, p. 473.

Pernanen, K. (1976) Alcohol and crimes of violence, in B. Kissin and H. Begleiter (eds) *The biology of alcoholism: social aspects of alcoholism.* New York: Plenum.

Perry, D., Kusel, S. and Perry, L. (1988) Victims of peer aggression. *Developmental Psychology* Vol. 24, p. 802.

Persons, J. (1991) Psychotherapy outcome studies do not accurately represent current models of psychotherapy. *American Psychologist* Vol. 46(2), p. 99.

Pillemer, K. and Moore, D. (1989) Abuse of patients in nursing homes: findings from a survey of staff. *The Gerontologist* Vol. 29(3), p. 314.

Pillemer, K. and Suitor, J. (1989) Violence and violent feelings: what causes them among family caregivers? *Journal of Gerontology* Vol. 47(4), p. 165.

Pleck, J., Sonenstein, F. and Ku, L. (1993) Masculinity ideology; its impact on adolescent males' relationships. *Journal of Social Issues* Vol. 49(3), p. 19.

Pocock, D. (1995) Searching for a better story: harnessing modern and postmodern positions in family therapy. *Journal of Family Therapy* Vol. 17, p. 149.

Pressman, B. (1989) Wife-abused couples: the need for comprehensive theoretical perspectives and integrated treatment models. *Journal of Feminist Family Therapy* Vol. 1, p. 23.

Prioleau, L., Murdock, M. and Brody, N. (1983) An analysis of psychotherapy versus placebo studies. *Behavioral and Brain Sciences* Vol. 6, p. 275.

Pruitt, D. and Rubin, J. (1986) *Escalation, stalemate, and settlement.* New York: Random House.

Ptacek, J. (1988) Why do men batter their wives?, in K. Yllo and M. Bograd (eds) *Feminist perspectives on wife abuse.* Beverly Hills, CA: Sage.

Purdy, F. and Nickel, N. (1981) Practice principles for working with groups of men who batter. *Social Work with Groups* Vol. 4, p. 111.

Rambo, A., Heath, A. and Chenail, R. (1993) *Practicing therapy.* New York: W.W. Norton.

Reid, J., Taplin, P. and Lorber, R. (1981) An interactional approach to the treatment of abusive families, in R. Stuart (ed.) *Violent behaviour: social learning approaches to prediction, management and treatment.* Routledge and Kegan Paul.

Report for the Select Committee on Violence in Marriage (1975) Vol. 2, Report and Minutes of Evidence and Appendices. HMSO.

Richardson, D. and Campbell, J. (1980) Alcohol and wife abuse: the effect of alcohol on attributions of blame for wife abuse. *Personality and Social Psychology Bulletin* Vol. 6, p. 51.

Rigby, K. and Slee, P. (1991) Bullying among Australian school children: reported behaviour and attitudes towards victims. *Journal of Social Psychology* Vol. 131, p. 615.

Roberts, A. (1987) Psychosocial characteristics of batterers: a study of 234 men charged with domestic violence offences. *Journal of Family Violence* Vol. 2, p. 81.

Roberts, M. (1988) Schoolyard menace. *Psychology Today* Vol. 17, p. 53.

Rodabaugh, B. and Austin, M. (1981) *Sexual assault.* New York: Garland Press.

Rogers, C. (1967) *On becoming a person.* Constable.

Rogers, K. (1994) Wife assault: the findings of a national survey. *Juristat* 14(9), p. 1.

Roland, E. (1980) *Terror i skolen.* Stavanger, Norway: Rogalandsforskning.

Roland, E. (1987) *Kjonnstypisk mobbing.* Stavanger, Norway: Laererhogskole.

Rose, S. and Serafica, F. (1986) Keeping and ending casual, close and best friendships. *Journal of Social and Personal Relationships* Vol. 3, p. 275.

Rosenberg, M. (1984) Intergenerational violence: a critique and implications for witnessing children. Paper presented to the 1992 Annual Convention of the American Psychological Association, Toronto.

Roth, J. (1994) *Understanding and preventing violence.* Washington DC: National Institute of Justice in Brief, Department of Justice.

Rounsville, B. (1978) Theories in marital violence: evidence from a study of battered women. *Victimology* Vol. 3, p. 11.

Rouse, L., Breen, R. and Howell, M. (1987) Abuse in intimate relationships. A comparison of married and dating college students. *Journal of Interpersonal Violence* Vol. 3, p. 414.

Roy, M. (1977) *Battered women.* New York: Van Nostrand.

Rubin, L. (1983) *Intimate strangers: men and women together.* New York: Harper and Row.

Rusbult, C. (1983) A longitudinal test of the investment model: the development (and deterioration) of satisfaction and commitment to heterosexual involvement. *Journal of Personality and Social Psychology* Vol. 45, p. 101.

Russell, D. (1982) *Rape in marriage.* New York: Macmillan.

Sabini, J. and Silver, M. (1982) *Moralities of everyday life.* Oxford: Oxford University Press.

Sabourin, T., Infante, D. and Rudd, J. (1993) Verbal aggression in marriages: a comparison of violent distressed, nonviolent, and nondistressed couples. *Human Communication Research* Vol. 20, p. 245.

Satir, V. (1978) *Conjoint family therapy.* Souvenir Press.

Saunders, D. (1987) Are there different men who batter? An empirical study of possible implications for treatment. Paper presented at the Third Conference of Family Violence research, Durham, NH.

Saunders, D. and Browne, A. (1990) Domestic violence, in R. Ammerman and M. Herson (eds) *Case studies in family violence.* New York: Plenum, p. 379.

Savin-Williams, R. (1987) *Adolescence: an ethological perspective.* New York: Springer-Verlag.

Scanzoni, J. (1972) *Sexual bargaining: power politics in the American marriage.* Eaglewood Cliffs, NJ: Prentice-Hall.

Schaap, C., Buunk, B. and Kerkstra, A. (1987) Marital conflict resolution, in P. Noller and M. Fitzpatrick (eds) *Perspectives on marital interaction.* Macmillan, p. 203.

Schachter, S. and Singer, J. (1962) Cognitive, social, and physiological determinants of emotional state. *Psychological Review* Vol. 69, p. 379.

Schiavi, R., Theilgaard, A., Owen, D. and White, D. (1984) Six chromosome anomalies, and aggressivity. *Archives of General Psychiatry* Vol. 41, p. 93.

Schindler, F. and Arkowitz, H. (1986) The assessment of mother–child interactions in physically abusive and nonabusive families. *Journal of Family Violence* Vol. 1, p. 217.

Schlesinger, L., Benson, M. and Zornitzer, M. (1982) Classification of violent behaviour for the purposes of treatment planning: a three-pronged approach, in M. Roy (ed.) *The abusive partner: an analysis of domestic battering.* New York: Van Nostrand Reinhold.

Schurger, J. and Reigle, N. (1988) Personality and biographic data that characterise men who abuse their wives. *Journal of Clinical Psychology* Vol. 44, p. 75.

Scutt, J. (1981) Sexism in the Criminal Law, in J. Scutt and S. Mukherjee (eds) *Women and crime.* Australia: George Allen and Unwin.

Sedlak, A. (1988) Prevention of wife abuse, in V. Hasselt, R. Morrison, A. Bellack and M. Hersen (eds) *Handbook of family violence.* New York: Plenum.

Segel-Evans, K. (1994) Treatment issues for men who batter. Paper presented at the Mid-Western Convention of the American Psychological Association, Scottsdale, Arizona.

Sengstock, M. (1991) Sex and gender implications in cases of elder abuse. *Journal of Women and Aging* Vol. 3(2), p. 25.

Shainess, N. (1984) *Sweet suffering: women as victims.* New York: Pocket Books.

Shainess, N. (1986) Psychological aspects of wife-beating, in M. Roy (ed.) *Battered women: a psychological study of domestic violence.* New York: Van Nostrand Reinhold.

Shapiro, D.A. and Shapiro, D. (1982) Meta-analysis of comparative therapy outcome studies: a replication and refinement. *Psychological Bulletin* Vol. 93(3), p. 581.

Shapiro, J., Baumeister, R. and Kessler, J. (1991) A three-component model of children's teasing. *Journal of Social and Clinical Psychology* Vol. 10, p. 459.

Shepard, M. (1987) Interventions with men who batter: an evaluation of a domestic abuse program. Paper at the Third National Conference for Family Violence researchers, Durham NH.

Sherman, L. and Berk, R. (1984) *The Minneapolis domestic violence experiment.* Washington, DC: Police Foundation Report 1, p. 1.

Sherwood, J. and Nataupsky, M. (1968) Predicting the conclusions of Negro–White intelligence research from biographical characteristics of the investigator. *Journal of Personality and Social Psychology* Vol. 8, p. 53.

Shields, S. (1975) Functionalism, Darwinism and the psychology of women: a study of a social myth. *American Psychologist* Vol. 30, p. 739.

Shotland, R. and Goodstein, L. (1983) Just because she doesn't want to doesn't mean it's rape: an experimentally based causal model of the perception of rape in a dating situation. *Social Psychology Quarterly* No. 46, p. 230.

Shupe, A., Stacey, W. and Hazelwood, L. (1987) *Violent men, violent couples. The dynamics of domestic violence.* Lexington, MA: Lexington Books.

Shwed, J. and Straus, M. (1979) The military environment and child abuse. Mimeogragh. Durham, NH: Family research laboratory, University of New Hampshire.

Sierra, P., Carnaccini, D. and Delbert, R. (1991) An approach to the analysis of wife abuse. Family therapy in different cultural contexts: Third World Family Therapy Congress (Abstracts). Jyvaskyla, Finland: University of Jyvaskyla.

Sillars, A., Pike, G., Jones, T. and Murphy, M. (1984) Communication and understanding in marriage. *Human Communication Research* Vol. 10, p. 317.

Silverman, W. (1991) Person's description of psychotherapy outcome studies does not accurately represent psychotherapy outcome studies. *American Psychologist,* December, p. 1351.

Simpson, J., Ickes, W. and Blackstone, T. (1995) When the head protects the heart: empathic accuracy in dating relationships. *Journal of Personality and Social Psychology* Vol. 69, p. 629.

Sluckin, A. (1981) *Growing up on the playground.* Boston, MA: Routledge, and Kegan Paul.

Smith, D. (1986) Police response to interpersonal violence: defining the parameters of legal control. *Social Forces* Vol. 65, p. 767.

Smith, J. and Grunebaum, H. (1976) The therapeutic alliance in marital therapy, in H. Grunebaum and J. Christ (eds) *Contemporary marriage: structure, dynamics and therapy.* Boston, MA: Little, Brown.

Smith, P. (1989) The silent nightmare: bullying and victimisation in school peer groups. Paper presented at the British Psychological Society, London.

Snell, J., Rosenwald, R. and Robey, A. (1964) The wife-beater's wife – a study of family interaction. *Archives of General Psychiatry* Vol. 11, p. 107.

Sonkin, D., Martin, D. and Walker, I. (1985) *The male batterer: a treatment appraisal.* New York: Springer.

Sprecher, S. and Metts, S. (1989) Development of the 'Romantic Beliefs Scale' and examination of the effects of gender and gender-role orientation. *Journal of Social and Personal Relationships* Vol. 6, p. 387.

Stanko, E. (1985) *Intimate intrusions: women's experience of male violence.* Routledge and Kegan Paul.

Star, B., Clark, C., Goetz, K. and OMalia, L. (1981) Psychological aspects of wife battering, in S. Howell and M. Bayes, (eds) *Women and mental health.* New York: Basic Books, p. 426.

Stark, E. (1984) The battering syndrome: social knowledge, social therapy and the abuse of women. Doctoral dissertation, Binghamton, State University of New York.

Stark, E. and Flitcraft, A. (1996) *Women at risk.* Sage.

Statistics Canada (1993) *Violence against women.* Ottawa, ON.

Steadman, H. and Morrissey, J. (1982) Predicting violent behavior: a note on a cross-validation study. *Social Forces* Vol. 61, p. 475.

Steinmetz, S. (1977) *The cycle of violence: assertive, aggressive and abusive family interaction.* New York: Praeger.

Sternberg, R. (1986) A triangular theory of love. *Psychological Review* Vol. 93, p. 119.

Stolk, Y. and Perlesz, A. (1990) Do better trainees make worse family therapists? A follow-up study and client families. *Family Process* Vol. 29, p. 45.

Straus, M. (1980) A sociological perspective in cases of family violence, in M. Green (ed.) *Violence in the family*. Boulder, CO: Westview, p. 7.

Straus, M. and Gelles, R. (1990) Societal change and change in family violence from 1975 to 1985 as revealed in two national surveys, in M. Straus and R. Gelles (eds) *Physical violence in American families*, New Brunswick, NJ: Transaction, p. 113.

Strayer, F. and Trudel, M. (1984) Developmental changes in the nature and function of social dominance among young children. *Ethology and Sociobiology* Vol. 5, p. 279.

Stroebe, W. and Stroebe, M. (1987) *Bereavement and health: the psychological and physical consequences of partner loss*. Cambridge: Cambridge University Press.

Strube, M. (1988) The decision to leave an abusive relationship: empirical evidence and theoretical issues. *Psychological Bulletin* 104, p. 236.

Strube, M. and Barbour, L. (1983) The decision to leave an abusive relationship: economic dependence and psychological commitment. *Journal of Marriage and the family* Vol. 45, p. 785.

Strube, M. and Barbour, L. (1984) Factors related to the decision to leave an abusive relationship. *Journal of Marriage and the Family* Vol. 46, p. 42.

Strube, M. and Hartmann, D. (1982) A critical appraisal of meta-analysis. *British Journal of Clinical Psychology*. Vol. 21, p. 129.

Stulberg, F. (1989) Spouse abuse: an ecosystem approach. *Contemporary Family Therapy* Vol. 11, p. 45.

Tannen, D. (1990) Gender differences in topical coherence: creating involvement in best friends talk. *Discourse Processes* Vol. 13, p. 73.

Tannen, D. (1991) *That's not what I meant!* New York: Simon and Schuster.

Tatara, T. (1990) Elder abuse in the United States, an issue paper. Washington, DC: National Aging Resource Center for Elderly Abuse.

Taylor, S. and Gammon, C. (1975) Effects of type and dose of alcohol on human physical aggression. *Journal of Personality and Social Psychology* Vol. 32, p. 169.

Tedeschi, J., Schlenker, B. and Bonoma, B. (1973) *Conflict, power and games*. Chicago, IL: Aldine.

Tennov, D. (1979) *Love and limerence: the experience of being in love*. New York: Stein and Day.

Tomm, K. (1987) Interventive interviewing: Part 1: Strategizing as a fourth guideline for the therapist. *Family Process* Vol. 26, p. 3.

Trickett, P. and Kuczynski, L. (1986) Children's misbehaviors and parental discipline strategies in abusive and nonabusive families. *Developmental Psychology* Vol. 22, p. 115.

Unruh, D. (1983) Death and personal history: strategies of identity preservation. *Social Problems* Vol. 30, p. 345.

US Merit Systems Protection Board, (1988) *Sexual harassment in the Federal Government: an update*. Washington DC: US Government Printing Office.

van der Kolk, B. (1987) *Psychological trauma*. Washington DC: American Psychiatric Press.

van Praag, H. (1991) Serotonin dysfunction and aggression control. *Psychological Medicine* Vol. 21, p. 15.

Victim Support (1992) Domestic violence: report of a national inter-agency working party on domestic violence convened by Victim Support. Victim Support.

Vogler, C. and Pahl, J. (1994) Money power and inequality in marriage. *Sociological Review* Vol. 42, p. 263.

Vuchinich, S., Emery, R. and Cassidy, J. (1988) Family members as third parties in dyadic family conflict: strategies, alliances, and outcomes. *Child Development* Vol. 59, p. 1293.

Walczak, Y. with Burns, S. (1984) *Divorce: the child's point of view*. Harper and Row.

Walker, L. (1978\79) Battered women and learned helplessness. *Victimology* Vol. 2, p. 525.

Walker, L. (1979) *The battered woman*. New York: Harper and Row.

Walker, L. (1985) Psychological impact of the criminalization of domestic violence on victims. *Victimology* Vol. 10, p. 281.

Walker, L. (1986) Battered women's shelters and work with battered lesbians, in K. Lobel (ed.), *Naming the violence*. Seattle, WA: Seal, p. 73.

Walker, N. (1970) *Crime and punishment in Britain*. Edinburgh: Edinburgh University Press.

Walster, E., Berscheid, E. and Walster, G. (1973) New directions in equity research. *Journal of Personality and Social Psychology* Vol. 24, p. 151.

Ward, C. (1995) *Attitudes to rape*. Sage.

Ward, D., Jackson, M. and Ward, R. (1969) Crimes of violence by women, in D. Mulvihill (ed.) *Crimes of violence*. Washington, DC: US Government Printing Office.

Waring, E., Tillmann, M., Frelick, L., Russell, T. and Weisz, G. (1980) Concepts of intimacy in the general population. *Journal of Nervous and Mental Disease* Vol. 168, p. 1471.

Watkins, C. (1985) Countertransference: its impact on the counseling situation. *Journal of Counseling and Development* Vol. 63, p. 356.

Watzlawick, P., Beavin, J. and Jackson, D. (1967) *Pragmatics of human communication.* New York: Norton.

Weinberg, S., Williams, C. and Moser, C. (1985) The social constituents of sadomasochism. *Social Problems* Vol. 31, p. 379.

Weis, K. and Borges, S. (1973) Victimology and rape: the case of the legitimate victim. *Issues in Criminology* Vol. 8, p. 71.

Weisfeld, G. and Linkey, H. (1985) Dominance displays as indicators of a social success motive, in J. Davidio and S. Ellyson (eds), *Power, dominance and non-verbal behavior.* New York: Springer-Verlag.

Weisfeld, G., Muczenski, D., Weisfeld, C. and Omark, D. (1987) Stability of boys' social success among peers over an eleven year period, in J. Meachan (ed.) *Interpersonal relations: family peers, and friends.* New York: Karger.

Wells, R. and Dezen, A. (1978) The results of family therapy revisited: the nonbehavioral methods. *Family Process* Vol. 17, p. 251.

Welpton, D. (1973) Confrontation in the therapeutic process, in G. Adler and P. Meyerson (eds) *Confrontation psychotherapy.* New York: Science House.

West, J. (1995) Understanding how the dynamics of ideology influence violence between intimates, in S. Duck and J. Wood (eds) *Confronting relationship challenges.* Sage, p. 129.

Wexler, D. (1974) A cognitive theory of experiencing self-actualization and therapeutic process, in D. Wexler and L. Rice (eds) *Innovations in client-centred therapy.* New York: John Wiley.

Whalen, M. (1992) Counseling as a subversive activity: counseling models in battered women's and anti-rape programs. Ann Arbor, MI: UMI Dissertation Services.

Widom, C. and Maxfield, M. (1984) Sex roles and the victimization of women: evidence from the British Crime Survey. Paper presented at the annual meeting of the American Society of Criminology.

Wiederman, M. and Allgeier, E. (1993) Gender differences in sexual jealousy: adaptionist or social learning explanation? *Ethology and Sociobiology* Vol. 14, p. 115.

Willbach, D. (1989) Ethics and family therapy: the case management of family violence. *Journal of Marital and Family Therapy* Vol. 15(1), p. 3.

Wolfe, D. (1987) *Child abuse: implications for child development and psychopathology.* Beverly Hills, CA: Sage.

Wolfe, D., Jaffe, P., Wilson, S. and Zak, I. (1985) Children of battered women: the relation of child behavior to family violence and maternal stress. *Journal of Consulting and Clinical Psychology* Vol. 53, p. 657.

Wood, G. and Middleman, R. (1990) Re-casting the die: a small group approach to giving batterers a chance to change: Paper at the 10th Annual Symposium on Social Work with Groups, Miami, Florida.

Woolf, Lord Justice and Tumim, Jussturbances. (1990) *Report of an inquiry.* Cmmd 1456. HMSO.

Wright, M. (1991) *Justice for victims and offenders.* Milton Keynes: Open University Press.

Yllo, K. (1984) The status of women, marital equality and violence against wives. *Journal of Comparative Family Studies* Vol. 14, p. 67.

Yllo, K. and Straus, M. (1981) Interpersonal violence among married and divorced persons. *Family Relations* Vol. 30, p. 339.

Zilbergeld, B. (1983) *The shrinking of America: myths of psychological change.* Boston, MA: Little Brown.

INDEX

Compiled by Sue Carlton

adolescents, and parental violence 195

agencies *see* helping agencies

aggression
in children 10, 14, 193
differential expression of 11–12
genetically-based 36
types of 10
and violence 11–12, 13, 15
see also domestic violence; verbal abuse/aggression; violence

Aguirre, B. 166

Akert, R. 117

alcohol use 139–46
by women victims 143–4
counselling 144–6
effects of 140
as excuse 141–2
help in stopping 142–3
and judgement 141, 143
role of pub 140
seen as illness 144
and violence 22, 32, 140, 141, 142, 144

Allen, J. 14

Allgeier, E. 9, 25

Allgood, S. 85

Altman, I. 189

Altshul, J. 208

American Humane Society 49

Amir, M. 40

Anderson, C. 208

Anderson, H. 42

Andrews, S. 147

anger 107, 112–13, 136, 138
management courses 137
see also aggression

Archer, D. 48, 117

arguments, tape-recording 118

Argyle, M. 188

Arkowitz, H. 49

Askew, S. 14

Atkinson, B. 41

Austin, M. 4

Bagarozzi, D. 43

Baken, S. 9

Ball, M. 37

Ban, P. 12

Barbour, L. 168

Barnett, N. 4

Baron, L. 48, 112

Bateson, G. 41

'battered woman syndrome' 38

Bauer, A. 192

Bavela, J. 189

Beck, A. 187

Becker, T. 111

behaviour
normal/abnormal 36–7, 40, 45
rationalization/minimization 31–2, 63, 81, 84, 132, 135, 151

Bell, R. 34

Berenson, B. 106

Berg, J. 189

Berger, P. 161

Berk, R. 33

Berkowitz, L. 10, 11

Bersherov, D. 49
Bersoni, C. 41
Binney, V. 11, 50, 166, 192, 197
biological theories 36–7
Bion, W. 41
Blier, M. 14
Blier-Wilson, L. 14
Bograd, M. 44
Bok, S. 161
Bologna, M. 49
Bonaparte, M. 39
Borges, S. 40
Borkowski, M. 20, 34
Borrill, J. 141
Bourland, M. 19
Bowder, B. 40
Bowker, L. 147, 192
Bradshaw, J. 11
Brandon, S. 49
Brannen, J. 161
Brayfield, A. 98
Brehm, S. 188
Briere, J. 15
Brown, L. 39
Browne, A. 172
Browning, J. 134, 136
Brownmiller, S. 5
Bryan, M. 166
Buchan, I. 34
Bull, J. 35
bullying 13–14
  in prisons 11
  in schools 10, 11
Burgoon, J. 117
Burt, M. 4

Cahill, A. 107
Cahill, S. 160
Campbell, J. 37, 143
Canada, no-drop policy 34
Caplan, P. 40
Carkhuff, R. 106
Carlson, B. 20, 193

Carmen, E. 153
case formulation approaches 43
Cate, R. 19
cessation of violence, predicting 133
Check, J. 4
Chelune, G. 189
Chen, H. 41
Chilamkurti, C. 136
child abuse 32, 48–9, 196
  by women 11
  infant homicide 48
Child Support Agency 35
children
  and accurate information 197
  and aggression 10, 14, 193
  contact with father 35, 195–6
  discipline 49
  and domestic violence 32, 192–7
  drawn into conflict 193
  effect on relationship 159
  from previous marriage 28
  and guilt 193, 195
  loyalty 195
  as reason for staying with abusive
    partner 50, 51, 164, 196
  and separation 168, 194, 195
Children's Safety Network 48
Chodorow, N. 167
Chovil, N. 100
Christopoulos, C. 192
circular questioning 57
Citizens Advice Bureaux 11
Clark, K. 35
client, dependency 70, 215
client-centred approach (feminist) 46
clients
  agendas 83–4
  compromise 92
  expectations 77, 89–93, 96, 211,
    215
  feelings from the past 62–3
  goal-setting 64–5
  guilt 113, 155

clients *continued*
  honesty 55, 85, 94, 131, 134–5,
    216
  interpretation of counsellors
    remarks 59
  labels 61–2
  male 84, 88, 93, 134
  need to understand own
    behaviour 28, 31, 59–61,
    134–5, 137–8
  needs 152–3
  positive regard 54–5
  roles 130
  seen as victims 54–5
  self-deception 216
Cocozza, J. 133
Coleman, E.D. 46
Collard, J. 161
communication 117–24
  affective 118, 121
  breakdown of verbal 118
  cognitive 121
  forms of 122–3
  miscommunication 118–20
  non-verbal 117, 122, 123
  positive reinforcement 123–4
  and power 122–3
Comstock, G. 15
consciousness-raising 47, 114–16
  information given 115
contra-helping 170
Conway, M. 190
Cook, M. 163
Cornell, C. 37, 163
counselling
  affirmation 57
  after separation 181–2
  aims 76–7, 98
  assessing risks for women 32,
    108–11
  boundaries 70, 124, 126–7, 130
  cognitive restructuring 68
  contracts 67–8

covert messages 59–61
delabelling 61–2
difficult clients 208–9, 211
effectiveness 43–5, 132, 133, 170
ending 216
and ethnic minorities 171
expectations of 63, 96, 215
goal-setting 63–5
individuals 32, 44, 77, 82, 129–54
intervention 66–7, 71, 74
limitations 74
male collusion 135, 137
methodologies 43–4
parents in abusive relationships
    196–7
power struggle 126–8
risk assessment 210
role of man 82–3
rules 65–7, 78–81, 96, 124
self-identity 198–206
suicidal feelings 153–4
tape-recording sessions 96
ventilation 68–9, 102–6, 120
see also couples; helping agencies;
    treatment programmes
counselling relationship 19, 23, 32,
    59, 70, 129
  client control 23–4, 81–2, 93, 97,
    131
  client jealousy 25
counsellors
  abuse by theory 43, 47, 170
  asking questions 57–61, 74, 97
  attitude to love 184–5, 191
  check points 69–70
  and confrontation 93–4
  control 92–3
  core values 54–5
  counter-oppression 124
  dealing with aggression/conflict 21,
    53, 68, 93, 103–5, 212
  directiveness 70, 91–3
  expressing own beliefs 70–1, 73

counsellors *continued*
    frustration/irritation 212
    gender of 53–4
    honesty 57, 215, 216
    identifying violence in relation-
        ship 2, 43, 45, 69, 72–4, 107–8,
        214
    and the Law 80–1, 92, 108
    listening 55, 215
    long-term objectives 64, 70, 211
    looking for signals 23, 94, 100
    making alliances 88–9, 130
    and moral interpretation 17
    neutrality 32, 41, 70–1
    and outside agencies 35, 45, 73,
        75–6, 214–15
    overall plan 99–100
    own attitudes to violence 52, 214
    paraprofessionals 44
    and personal agendas 17–18, 72
    positive regard 54–5
    and power imbalance 41–2, 52–3,
        54, 55, 56, 65, 70, 94
    and reality 41–2, 85–7, 106, 209,
        210, 211
    response to threats 81–2
    role of 29, 53, 76–7, 87–8, 106,
        111
    seeing whole picture 18–19, 51,
        72
    self-analysis 52–3, 72
    self-disclosure 96
    skills 55–9
    and stress 207, 208, 209, 210–13,
        216
    support and supervision 207–13
    systems approach 44
    talking 55–6
    and theories 45–6, 170, 213, 214,
        215
    training 5, 43–4
    transference/countertransference
        130, 213

    trust 54, 127
    understanding behaviour 17, 29,
        31–2, 41–2, 138
couples, working with 56, 59–61,
    72–98
    advantages/disadvantages 29, 44,
        77–8, 79, 82, 85
    clients conflicting needs 89, 90
    discussing violence 109–10
    drop out rate 85
    ending sessions 97–8
    identifying abuse 107–8
    introductory stage 94–6
    learning 97–8
    power struggle 126
    reality 85–7, 121
    reinforcing individuality 96–7
    reluctance to admit violence 89–90
    rules 65–6
    structure of sessions 85, 87
    ventilation 68
    see also individual counselling
Crane, D. 85
Crockenberg, S. 195
Crown Prosecution Service 34

Davidson, T. 195
Davis, L. 38, 193
Davis, M. 161
Deal, J., 19
deconstructionism 42
defence mechanisms 63, 216
denial 31, 63, 111, 134–5, 136
Deschner, J. 137
Deutsch, H. 39
Dezen, A. 43
Dixson, A. 37
Dobash, R.E. and R.P. 6, 6, 20, 38,
    192
Domestic Abuse Intervention Project
    (Duluth) 11
domestic violence
    and alcohol use 22, 32

domestic violence *continued*
  critical stages 19–20
  definitions of 2–3, 6–7, 8, 15–16
  effects on children 192–7
  foretelling 21–3
  and male control 8, 22–7, 106,
    124, 136, 137, 148
  men as victims 6, 19
  in new relationship 178–9
  pathologizing 45
  pattern/cycle 8, 38, 80, 108
  predicting cessation 133
  reactions to 111–14
  retaliation 111–13
  severity of force 7, 33
  social blindness to 1–2, 9
  stopping 23, 131–9
  theories of 36–44
  variation in 19–21
  see also verbal abuse/aggression;
    violence
dominance hierarchies *see* male
  domination/control
Dowd, E. 70
Drake, R. 21
drinking *see* alcohol use
DSM 40
Dubosz, B. 184
Duck, S. 156
Duluth Domestic Abuse Intervention Project 78
Duluth rule 78, 79
Durlak, J. 44
Dutton, D. 14, 133, 134, 136, 170,
  172
Dutton, M. 40

Eagly, A. 165
Edgerton, R. 142
Edwards, S. 34
Eidelson, R. 19
Elbow, M. 37
elder abuse 11, 19, 48

Ellis, A. 182
empathy 17, 54, 100–1
empowerment 46, 47, 56–7, 215
Epstein, N. 19, 43, 187
Erhlich, H. 178
exclusion from help 77–8, 79

Families Need Fathers 196
family therapy 41, 43
fathers
  absence of 37
  visiting rights 35
feelings 100–7
  and behaviour 106–7
  and counselling sessions 102–6
  empathy 100–1
  expression of 102, 138, 165
  identification of 101–2
  love 184–91
  ventilation in sessions 68–9,
    102–6, 120
feminism/feminists
  complaints about police procedure
    33
  definitions of violence 8, 10, 11
  empowerment 46, 47
  helping abused women 46–7, 135,
    215
  marriage and family 41
  perceptions of violence 9–10
  women's rights 47
Ferraro, K. 38
Field, H. 4
Field, M. and F. 33
fight-or-flight response 37
Fincham, F. 19
Fisher, S. 44
flashing 9
Fleming, J. 47
Flitcraft, A. 153, 170
Forgas, J. 184
Framo, J. 184
Freeman, J. 47

Freud, S. 39, 40, 213
Friedman, O. 47
Frieze, I. 3
Frude, 185

Gaelick, C. 100
Galenson, E. 37
Gammon, C. 140
gang violence 48
Ganley, A. 132, 135
Gaquin, D. 6
Gartner, R. 48
Gayford, J. 49
Gelles, R. 6–7, 20, 37, 141, 163
gender interactions, and violence
    13–14
gender socialization 12, 13–15, 38,
    46, 138
Gifford, Z. 164
Giles-Sim, J. 44, 111
Ginsberg, H. 13
Goffman, E. 161
Golann, S. 41
Goldberg, S. 12
Goldner, V. 44
Gondolf, E. 170, 38, 138
Goodenough, E. 12
Goodstein, L. 113
Goodstein, R. 2
Goolishian, H. 42
Gottfredson, M. 9
Gottman, J. 53, 117
Gottsegan, G. and M. 70
Greenbaum, S. 14
Greenberg, L. 107, 189
Greenspan, M. 46
Griffin, Susan 3
Gross, D. 12, 13
Grossman, W. 40
group therapy 47
Gurman, A. 43

Haccoun, D. 14

Hafner, R. 44
Hague, G. 35
Haley, J. 91–2, 122, 44
Hall, E. 4
Halmos, P. 45
Halweg, K. 117
Hamberger, L. 132
Hanmer, J. 2, 172
Hansen, M. 2
harassment/intimidation 11
Harne, L. 196
Harris, P. 12, 13
Hart, B. 135
Hartmann, D. 43
Hartup, W. 12
Harvey, J. 4, 156
Hastings, J. 132
Hattie, J. 44
Hauser, R. 39
Hausman, A. 48
Hazan, C. 185, 186
Hearn, J. 138
Heath, A. 41
Heineman Pieper, M. 43
helping agencies
    cooperation between 215
    different perspectives 75–6
    suspicion of 78
Henderson, M. 188
Herzeberger, S. 49, 185
Hess, U. 100
Hester, M. 196
heuristic paradigm 43
Hoff, L. 166
Hoffman, L. 12, 41
Hold-Cavell, B. 13
Holtgraves, T. 189
Holtzworth-Munroe A. 2
Hooper, C. 195
Hornung, C. 46
Houseknecht, S. 136
Housing Authorities 35
Huber, J. 165

Hughes, H. 195
Hull, D. 165
Humphreys, A. 12
Huston, T. 189

Ickes, W. 100
Imam, U. 171
indirect aggression 10
individual counselling 32, 44, 77,
    82, 129–54
    advantages/disadvantages
    129–31
    goal-setting 131
    working with men 132–9
    see also couples
International Classification of
    Diseases 40

Jacob, T. 139
Jacobs, L. 188
Jacobson, N. 14, 19, 133
Jaffe, P. 33, 193
jealousy 25–9, 49
Jeavons, C. 140
Jenkins, A. 133
Johnson, J. 38
Johnson, M. 161
Johnson, S. 107, 189
Johnston, J. 35
judicial system 34–5
    see also law/legislation; police

Kadushin, H. 49
Kantor, G. 140
Keeney, B. 44
Kellner, H. 161
Kelly, E. 9
Kelly, L. 10, 11, 47
Kelvin, P. 189
Kempe, R. and C. 48
Kirkwood, C. 164, 166
Kitson, G. 165
Klech, G. 113

Kniskern, D. 43
Koss, M. 2, 4
Kottler, Jeffrey, 213
Kovacs, A. 213
Koval, J. 132
Krafft-Ebing, 39
Kratchowill, T. 43
Krokoff, L. 53
Kuczynski, L. 49

L'Abate, L. 117
labels, positive/negative implications
    62
Lagerspetz, K. 10
Lamb, T. 37
Lambert, M. 43, 44
Langley, J. 165
law/legislation
    anti-discriminatory measures 46
    changes needed 46, 48
    and rape 3, 4, 5
    and violence 2–3, 9
    see also judicial system; police
Lazarus, A. 187
learned helplessness 38
LeGrand, C. 40
Leonard, K. 139
Lerman, L. 34
lesbian relationships, violence in 7,
    11, 49
Lesch-Nyhn's disease 36
Lever, J. 12
Lewis, M. 12
Lewis, S. 208
Liebowitz, M. 185
Linkey, H. 12
Lipsey, C. 178
Lloyd, C. 4
Lobel, K. 11
Lobel, Kerry 49
Lockley, P. 47
London Rape Crisis Centre 4
Loseke, D. 160

love 184–91
    addiction to 38–9
    affective analysis 186
    attachment 185–6
    cognitive distortions 186–7
    and communication 188
    and jealousy 28
    myths 187
    passion 185, 186, 187
    passionate attachment 184–5
    and self-disclosure 188–9
    uncertainty in feelings 28,
        187–8
    and violence 190–1
    see also feelings
Luborsky, L.B. 43
Lystad, M. 6

MacAndrew, C. 142
Maccoby, E. 14
McDonald, G. 136
McFarlane, C. 190
McGillivary, A. 34
McHenry, S. 117
McKiernan, J. 197
McLeod, L. 6, 192
McWilliams, M. 197
Makepeace, J. 14
Malamuth, N. 4, 15
male domination/control
    dominance hierarchies 12–13
    and partner violence 8, 22–7,
        106, 124, 136, 137, 148
    and women's self-esteem 146
Malos, E. 35
Maluccio, A. 67, 107
Mama, A. 11
Marangoni, C. 100
Marlow, W. 67
marriage 158–9
    and patriarchal society 41
    and violence 19–20, 136
Marsden, 165

Martin, F. 44
Martin, J. 49
masochism, female 39–40, 50, 51
Masson, J. 45
Maxfield, M. 9, 47
Maynard, M. 2, 35
Mazur, A. 37
media, and male violence 15
mediation 134
Mehrabian, A. 117
Melville, J. 193
men
    accepting responsibility 133–4
    attitude to counselling 83, 87
    battering groups 44
    change in life-style/friends 138–9
    conflict management 138
    drugs 133
    expressing emotions 165
    need for respect in counselling 88
    neutralization techniques 136
    patriarchal role 25, 26
    psychiatry 133
    reasonableness in sessions 84,
        93, 134
    seeking help 132–3
    and separation 176
    sex socialization 138
    sexist attitudes 137
    unpredictable behaviour 148
Mendler, A. 14
Metts, S. 185
Middleman, R. 137
Miell, D. 156
Milavsky, J. 15
Milgram, S. 133
Millar, J. 11
Miller, G. 188
Miller, L. 189
Miller, S. 13
Millett, K. 39
Milner, J. 136
Mitchell, J. 39

Mooney, J. 11
Moore, D. 148
Morgan, S. 12
Morrissey, J. 133
Mossman, M. 8
mother-child bonding 37
mothers, psychopathology of 37
Murnen, S. 9
Murphy, C. 138
Mynatt, C. 9

NACAB 35
Nace, E. 142
Nataupsky, M. 43
Neidig, P. 47
neurotransmitters 37
Newton, D. 117
Nickle, N. 135
Nicol, R. 138
Nietzel, M. 44
no-drop policy, Canada 34
Noller, P. 53, 117
non-verbal expressions, interpreting
    100, 117
normal/abnormal behaviour 36–7,
    40, 45
Norwood, R. 38–9

Oakley, A. 12
Ofshe, R. 45
Ogus, A. 196
O'Heeron, R. 157
Okun, B. 38
Oldershaw, L 49
Oldfield, S. 85
O'Leary, K. 138
Oliker, S. 14
Olweus, D. 11, 13–14
Omark, D. 13
O'Meara, J. 167
oppression 124–5
Orenstein, S. 134
Ormerod, D. 39

Oros, C. 4
Osofsky, J. 37

Page, A. 2
Pagelow, M. 160
Pahl, J. 20, 38, 136
Paik, H. 15
Painter, S. 136, 170
Palmour, R. 36
Pan, H. 6–7
Parker, G. 186
Parliamentary Select Committee on
    Violence in Marriage 18, 19, 33
Parloff, M. 43
Parry, A. 42
Pastore, N. 43
patriarchy 8, 39, 46, 48, 51
Patrick, J. 15
Patterson, M. 189
Paynor, M. 136
Pearson, C. 196
Pedder, J. 45
Pellegrini, A. 12
Pence, E. 136
Pennebaker, J. 157
Perlesz, A. 43
Pernanen, K. 141
Perry, D. 13
personality trait theories 37–8
Persons, J. 43
Pillemer, K. 48, 148
Pleck, J. 14
Pocock, D. 42
police
    arrest rates 33–4
    attitudes 34
    Breach of the Peace 34
    intervention 18, 19
    procedure 33
    understanding situation 33
    see also judicial system; law/
        legislation
positive regard 54–5

positive reinforcement 56–7, 97,
123–4, 138
possessiveness 25, 26–9, 49, 172
and male identity 29
see also jealousy; male domina-
tion/control
post-modernists 42, 43
post-traumatic stress 180
pregnancy, and increase in violence
20, 136, 159
Pressman, B. 44
Prioleau, L. 43
Pruitt, D. 193
psychological theories 37
Ptacek, J. 132
Purdy, F. 135

R v. Miller 2
racial violence, by white women 11
Radford, J. 11, 196
Rambo, A. 107
rape
characteristics 4
definitions of 3, 5
and legitimized violence 48
myths 4
perceptions 5
resistance 113
victim-precipitated 40
and violence 4, 5
within marriage 3
see also sexual violence
rationalization/minimization 31–2,
63, 81, 84, 132, 135, 151
Rauen, P. 43
Reid, J. 49
Reigle, N. 139
relationships
affective aspect 165
changing 157–60
and children 159
communication 117, 123–4
conflict 138

critical stages 19–20
emotional needs 162
ending 155–6, 161–2, 171
expectations 19, 157–8
new 177–82
parental 157
power imbalance 46, 49–50, 52,
54, 61, 126, 136, 215
trust 110, 124, 178, 181–2, 188
retaliation 111–13, 114, 147
Richardson, D. 143
Rigby, K. 13
Roberts, A. 139
Roberts, M. 14
Rodabaugh, B. 4
Rogers, Carl 97, 106
Rogers, H. 44
Rogers, K. 11
Roland, E. 13
Rose, S. 155
Rosenberg, 192
Ross, M. 190
Roth, J. 9, 48
Rounsaville, B. 136
Rouse, L. 6
Roy, M. 160
Rubin, D. 193
Rubin, L. 167
Rusbult, C. 163
Russell, D. 3

Sabini, J. 133, 163
sadism, male 40
sado-masochism, consensual 40
Satir, V. 121, 147
Saunders, D. 133, 172
Saunders, S. 172
Savin-Williams, R. 12, 13
Sayles, S. 113
Schaap, C. 14
Schachter, S. 187
Scherger, J. 139
Schiavi, R. 37

Schindler, F. 49
Schlesinger, L. 40
Schroeder, H. 165
Scutt, J. 8
Sedlak, A. 143
Segel-Evans, K. 132
Seibel, C. 70
self-actualization 97
self-awareness 198
self-confidence 181, 198, 201–4
self-control 32, 124, 136
    and alcohol use 142
'self-defeating personality disorder'
    40
self-direction 198, 204–6
self-esteem
    counselling 148–52, 198,
        199–201
    and decision-making 148, 181
    and leaving partner 170, 173
    low 38, 46, 56, 57, 147, 199
    self-harm 153
    undue self-criticism 148–9
    unmet needs 152
    and verbal abuse 146, 148
self-identity 198–206
self-punishment 39
Seligman, M. 38
Sengstock, M. 48
separation 155–76
    accommodation 166
    adjustment to 182
    and children 168, 174–5, 194,
        195, 196
    continuation of violence after
        177
    counselling around 182–4
    financial constraints 165
    grief 156–7, 182
    isolation 167
    lawyers 174
    looking to the future 183
    new relationships after 177

preparation for 172, 173–4, 174–5
as process 161–2, 171–4, 175
risks 175
secrecy 173–4
temporary 139
threats 172
Serafica, F. 155
serotonin 37
sex hormones 37
sex-roles see gender socialization
sexual harassment 9
sexual stereotyping 11, 14, 15
sexual violence 3–5, 11, 22
    feminine perception 8, 9–10
    research into 4
Shainess, N. 39
Shapiro, D.A. and D. 43
Shapiro, J. 13
Sharpley, C. 44
Shaver, P. 185, 186
Shepard, M. 133
Sherman, L. 33
Sherwood, J. 43
Shields, S. 43
Shotland, R. 113
Shupe, A. 6
Shwed, J. 48
Sierra, P. 7
silence 123
Sillars, A. 100
Silver, M. 133, 163
Silverman, W. 43
Singer, J. 187
single subject designs 43
Sluckin, A. 13
Smith, M. 43
Smith, P. 12, 13
Snell, J. 39
social helping, as industry 45
social work 35
society
    male domination 8
    see also patriarchy

Sonkin, D. 135
Spanier, G. 136
Spitze, G. 165
split personality 19
Sprecher, S. 185
Stanko, E. 8, 111
Star, B. 38
Stark, E. 143, 153, 170
State v. *Stevens* 3
Steadman, H. 133
Steinmetz, S. 136
Sternberg, R. 185
Stockholm Syndrome 40
Stolk, Y. 43
Strachan, C. 14, 136
Straus, M. 6–7, 11, 46, 48, 136, 140
Strayer, F. 12
strength differential 7–8
Stroebe, W. and M. 157
Strube, M. 43, 168, 170
Stulberg, F. 47
subcultural rules of behaviour 30–1
suicide 153–4
Suitor, J. 48

'talking sticks' 122
Tannen, D. 14
tape-recording arguments 118
Tatara, T. 48
Taylor, D. 189
Taylor, S. 140
Tedeschi, J. 172
Tennov, D. 185
testosterone 37
theories 36–46
  biological 36–7
  medical model 45–6
  personality trait 37–8
  psychological 37
  second-order 41–2
Tomm, K. 41
treatment programmes
  behaviourist 137

and gender of workers 135
Trickett, P. 49
Trudel, M. 12
Tumim, Lord 11

United States, partner abuse 2
Unruh, D. 161
US Merit Systems Protection Board
  9

van der Kolk, B. 133
van Praag, H. 37
Vaughan v. *HM Advocate* 3
Vaughan v. *Vaughan* 3
Venardos, C. 117
verbal abuse/aggression 8, 10, 21,
  110, 117
  reactions to 113
  towards counsellor 93
  and woman's self-esteem 146,
  148
Victim Support 196
victim-centred approach 38–9
violence
  and alcohol 139–46
  by women 11
  circular causality 41
  continuum of 9, 10
  definitions of 2–3, 6–7, 8–9,
  10–11
  as family characteristic 29–30
  gang 48
  and gender 6, 10, 11
  and gender interactions 13–14
  and group life 15
  as learned behaviour 15
  legitimized 48
  psychiatrizing 40
  racial 11
  threats 8, 10, 15, 172
  triggers/patterns of 108–9
  see also aggression; domestic
  violence

Vogler, C. 136
Vuchinich, S. 192

Walczak, Y. 195
Walker, L. 38, 7, 22, 47, 110
Walker, N. 2
Walster, E. 110
Wampler, K. 19
Ward, D. 8
Waring, E. 189
Watkins, C. 213
Watters, E. 45
weapons 6, 112, 113
Weinberg, S. 39, 40
Weis, K. 40
Weisfeld, G. 12, 13
Wells, R. 43
Welpton, D. 107
West, J. 168
Wexler, D. 97
Widom, C. 9, 48
Wiederman, M. 25
Willbach, D. 41
witnesses, lack of 34–5
Wittgenstein, L.J.J. 122
Wolfe, D. 182.193
women
    adjusting to changed partner 139
    and alcohol use 143–4
    ambivalence 169, 170–1, 176
    as assailants 48
    as cause of violence 38–40, 46,
        136
    'doing the right thing' 24–5, 148
    effects of past relationships
        178–82, 183–4
    fear of assault 9–10
    female masochism 39–40, 50,
        51
    guilt 112, 113, 155
    help in leaving a partner 46–7,
        164–5, 173, 176
    helping agencies 35

homicide 8
increased attachment to abuser 40
leaving violent relationships 160–1,
    162–70
new relationships 177
oppression 46
passivity 38
pathologized 50, 170
and personality trait theories 37–40
physical imbalance 112
ploys in counselling 127–8
and psychiatry 40
re-interpreting abuse 26
and reconciliation 165
reluctance to talk about violence 44,
    73
retracting charges 33, 34
returning to abusive partners 50,
    149, 168, 175, 184–5
rights 47, 60
risks of counselling 44, 52
same-sex friends 166–7
sensing imminent attacks 109–10
staying with violent partner 21–2,
    24, 38, 39, 50, 160, 162–70
stress 110–11
strings of abusive relationships 50–1
support groups 44
as survivors 182
tranquillizers 112
trauma 63, 180
violence against men 6–8, 19
wife/mother role 167
Women's Aid hostels/refuges 46, 75,
    166, 173
women's organizations, and treatment
    programmes 135
Wood, G. 137
Woolf, Lord Justice 11
Wright, M. 9, 134, 177

XYY chromosome 36–7
Yllo, K. 41, 136